MOSES
AND
AKHENATEN

MOSES
AND
AKHENATEN

The Secret History of Egypt
at the Time of the Exodus

AHMED OSMAN

Bear & Company
Rochester, Vermont

Bear & Company
One Park Street
Rochester, Vermont 05767
www.InnerTraditions.com

Bear & Company is a division of Inner Traditions International

Library of Congress Cataloging-in-Publication Data
Osman, Ahmed, 1934–
   Moses and Akhenaten : the secret history of Egypt at the time of the
Exodus / Ahmed Osman.
       p. cm.
   Originally published: London : Grafton Books, 1990.
   Includes bibliographical references and index.
   ISBN 1-59143-004-6
       1. Akhenaten, King of Egypt. 2. Moses (Biblical leader) 3. Egypt—
History—Eighteenth dynasty, ca 1570–1320 B.C. 4. Exodus, The. I. Title.

DT87.4 O86 2002
932'.014—dc21

                                                                2002033264

Printed and bound in the United States at Lake Book Manufacturing, Inc.

10 9 8 7 6 5 4 3 2

CONTENTS

APPENDICES

ACKNOWLEDGMENTS

A NUMBER of people have given their help and support to the preparation of this book. I should like to thank in particular Dr Eric Uphill, Honorary Research Fellow in Egyptology at University College, London, for reading the manuscript and for his valuable advice and suggestions; the French archaeologist Professor Jean Yoyotte for discussing the time of the Exodus and the location of Zarw; the French archaeologist Professor Alain-Pierre Zivie for giving details of his recent discoveries, as yet unpublished, in the tomb of Aper-El at Sakkara; Professor Younes A. Ekbatrik, the Egyptian Cultural Counsellor in London, for arranging a discussion about the fortified city recently found at Tell el-Heboua, East Kantarah, and its possible identification with Pi-Ramses; my friend Gerald O'Farrel for his support; Cairo Museum and its director, Mohammed Mohsen, for providing, and allowing the use of, many of the photographs to be found in this volume, and, finally, H. J. Weaver for his assistance in editing the material and making it less complex than it might otherwise have been.

Map of Egypt during the time of the Empire, 16th – 12th centuries BC

Mediterranean Sea

Dead Sea

MOAB

Alexandria

Gaza

Zarw (*Pi-Ramses*)

Qantir
Tell el Dab'a

EDOM

Heliopolis

Gizeh
Sakkara
Memphis

SINAI

Sarabit el Khdem

Fayyum

Mount Sinai

Akhetaten
(*Tell el Amarna*)

Akhmin

Abydos

Thebes

Red Sea

Silsileh

Elephantine
1st CATARACT
Aswan
Philae

PRESENT BOUNDARY BETWEEN
SUDAN AND EGYPT

River Nile

2nd CATARACT

Semna
Seidinga
Soleb

KUSH
(NUBIA)

3rd CATARACT

4th CATARACT

SOUTHERN BOUNDARY
OF THE NEW KINGDOM

The Ways of Horus, the ancient road (mentioned in the Bible) between Egypt and Palestine in northern Sinai

Mediterranean Sea

GAZA
Dêr-el-Beleh
Khân Yûnus
Rafa
Shêkh Zuwêd

MODERN FRONTIER

El 'Arîsh
Bîr Mesûdîyeh
Abu Hawîdât
Abu Mazruh
Umm el-Ushush
El-Khûinât
Bîr el-Mazâr

Boghaz
El-Zaranîk
El-Flusîyeh

Sabkhat Bardawîl

El Kels

LAKE SERBONIS

Bîr el-'Abd
Kasr Ghêt

Pelusiac Mouth
Tell el-Hêr, The Migdol of Menmatre?
Mahemdîyeh

Katiyeh (Katia)
Bir en-Nuss
Avaris
Zarwe-Sile (Pi-Ramses)

PORT SAID

Tell Fârameh
PELUSIUM
Shihor
Tell Habwe
Tell Abu Sêfeh
El-Beda

LAKE BALLÂH
LAKE MENZALEH
Suez Canal
DAPHNAE

Theku
Tell el-Maskhûteh
Ismailîyeh
LAKE TIMSAH

Classical names .... PELUSIUM
Egyptian or Arabic names ... Theku
Roads and tracks _____

**Map indicating the artificial borders of the location hitherto accepted for Pi Ramses/Avaris.
As can be seen, there are no archaeological connections between the different ancient sites**

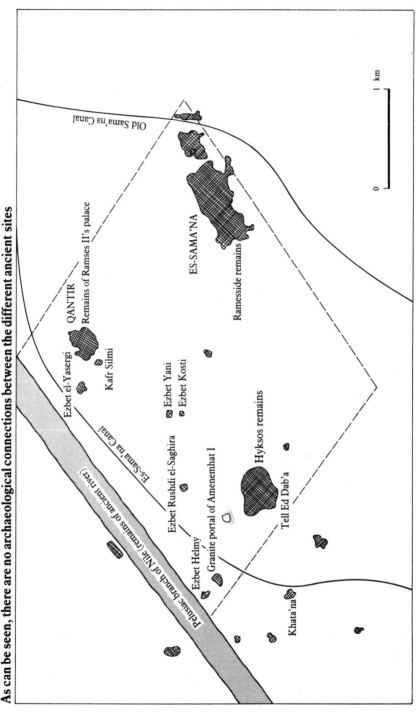

PREFACE

I CAME to London from Cairo a quarter of a century ago, intending to devote most of my time to trying to establish links between the Bible and what we know, from a variety of sources, of Egyptian history. The choice of London was dictated by the far superior research facilities to be found there.

Initially, while earning a living by teaching Arabic, I embarked on a course of intensive study. I enrolled in the Egypt Exploration Society and spent six years familiarizing myself with the ancient history of my country and mastering hieroglyphics. I also learned Hebrew and studied the Bible.

However, when I tried to put this knowledge to use I found myself facing the same problem that had baffled scholars for more than a century – establishing a starting point by identifying a major biblical figure as a major figure in Egyptian history. Who was Joseph, the Patriarch who brought the tribe of Israel down to Egypt from Canaan? Who was the unnamed Pharaoh who appointed him as a senior minister, the virtual ruler of the country in the king's name? Who was Moses? If, as I believed, the Old Testament was fundamentally a historical work, the characters who appear in its stories had to match characters in Egyptian history.

It was another fifteen years before I stumbled upon the vital clue (in what seems in retrospect a moment of inspiration) embedded in a biblical text so familiar that I found it hard to believe that its significance had not struck me years earlier. The passage in question occurs in the Book of Genesis. The brothers of the Patriarch Joseph, we are told, had sold him into slavery in Egypt where, as a result of interpreting Pharaoh's dream about the seven good years that would be followed by seven lean years, he was appointed the king's senior minister. The brothers later paid two visits to Egypt at times of famine in Canaan. On the second occasion, Joseph revealed his identity to them, but told them reassuringly that they should not blame themselves for having sold him into slavery because it was not they who had sent him 'hither, but God; and he hath made me a father to Pharaoh' (Gen. 45:8).

A father to Pharaoh! I thought at once – and, as I have said, could not understand why I had not made the connection before – of Yuya, minister to two rulers of the Eighteenth Dynasty. Although Yuya was not apparently of royal blood, his tomb had been found in the Valley of the Kings in 1905. Little attention was devoted to him because he was considered comparatively unimportant. Yet Yuya is the *only* person in whose tomb the title *it ntr n nb tawi* – holy father of the Lord of the Two Lands, Pharaoh's formal title – has been found. It occurs once on one of his *ushabti* (royal funeral statuette No. 51028 in the Cairo Museum catalogue) and more than twenty times on his funerary papyrus.

Could Joseph and Yuya be the same person? The case for this being so is argued in my first book, *Stranger in the Valley of the Kings*. Once this link was established, all manner of things began to fall into place:

• It became possible to create matching chronologies from Abraham to Moses on the one hand, and from Tuthmosis III, the sixth ruler of the Eighteenth Dynasty, to Seti I, the second ruler of the Nineteenth Dynasty, on the other.

It also became clear that:

• Of the three periods of time given in the Old Testament – four generations, 400 years and 430 years – for the Israelite Sojourn in Egypt, four generations is correct, a view which Jewish scholars have arrived at by another reckoning;

• As it is known that the Israelites were in Egypt at the end of the Eighteenth Dynasty and beginning of the Nineteenth, the Descent must have taken place more than two centuries later than most scholars believed, which explains why their efforts to match biblical figures with Egyptian figures has been so protracted; they focused their quest on the wrong era;

• The four Amarna kings – Akhenaten, Semenkhkare, Tutan-khamun and Aye – who ruled during a tumultuous period of

Egyptian history when an attempt was made to replace the country's multitude of ancient gods with a monotheistic God, were all descendants of Joseph the Patriarch;

• The Exodus was preceded by the ending of Amarna rule by Horemheb, the last king of the Eighteenth Dynasty.

This book is an attempt to take further the story told in *Stranger in the Valley of the Kings* by demonstrating that Moses is to be regarded as the Pharaoh Akhenaten.

INTRODUCTION

IN August 1799, while French troops were repairing fortifications to the north of Rasheed – on the left bank of the Nile, thirty miles east of Alexandria – an officer engaged in demolishing an ancient wall struck a black stone with his pick. The stone, thought to have formed part of a temple in earlier times, proved to bear three inscriptions. At the top were fourteen lines of hieroglyphs; in the centre thirty-two lines of demotic, the simplified form of Ancient Egyptian writing; and, at the bottom, fifty-four lines of Greek. The Greek text was translated and published, but the real importance of the Rosetta Stone, as it was called from the European name of the place where it was found, did not emerge until 1818. Then Thomas Young (1773–1829), a British physician, scientist and philologist, succeeded in deciphering the name of Ptolemy in the hieroglyphic section and in assigning the correct phonetic value to most of the hieroglyphs. Although the British scholar took the first steps, the final decoding of the stone was done three years later by a brilliant young French philologist, François Champollion (1790–1832).

With his new-found knowledge Champollion was able to translate some Egyptian texts that had until that time been a complete mystery to historians. Among them were the cartouches of the king-list on the walls of the Osiris temple at Abydos in Upper Egypt. The list, which included the names of the kings of the Eighteenth Dynasty, made no mention of Akhenaten or the other three Amarna kings – Semenkhkare, Tutankhamun and Aye – who followed him. In the circumstances it is not surprising that when, in the middle of the last century, archaeologists came across the strangely-drawn figure of Akhenaten in the ruins of Tell el-Amarna in Middle Egypt they were not sure initially what to make of him.

Some thought that, like Queen Hatshepsut, this newly-discovered Pharaoh was a woman who disguised herself as a king. Further cause for conjecture arose from the fact that Akhenaten had ascended to the throne as Amenhotep IV and later changed his name. Were they dealing with one Pharaoh or two?

By the early years of this century, when the city of Amarna had been excavated and more was known about Akhenaten and his family, he became a focus of interest for Egyptologists of the period, who saw him as a visionary humanitarian as well as the first monotheist. Akhenaten was revealed as a revolutionary king, who abolished the Ancient Egyptian religious system, with its many deities represented by fetish or animal shapes. He replaced the old gods with a sole God, the Aten, who had no image or form, a universal God not just for Egypt, but also for Kush (Nubia) in the south and Syria in the north, a God for the whole world.

He was a poet who wrote the hymn to Aten that has a striking resemblance to Psalm 104 of the Bible. He instructed his artists to express freely what they felt and saw, resulting in a new and simple realistic art that was different in many respects from the traditional form of Egyptian artistic expression. We were allowed to see the king as a human being with his wife and daughters, eating, drinking and making offerings to the Aten. Nor was he like the military prototype of Pharaohs of the Eighteenth Dynasty. Although the kings and princes of Western Asia tried hard to involve him in recurrent wars, he refused to become a party to their disputes. It is no wonder that the early Egyptologists of this century saw in him an expression of their own modern ideas.

'The most remarkable of all the Pharaohs and the first individual in human history' are the words that James Henry Breasted, the American scholar, chose to describe him.[1] It is a theme he returned to and developed in a later book: 'It is important to notice ... that Akhenaten was a prophet ... Like Jesus, who, on the one hand drew his lessons from the lilies of the field, the fowls of the air or the clouds of the sky, and, on the other hand, from the human society about him in stories like the Prodigal Son, the Good Samaritan or the woman who lost her piece of money, so this revolutionary Egyptian prophet drew his teachings from a contemplation both of nature and of human life ...'[2]

The same theme finds an echo in the work of Arthur Weigall, the

British Egyptologist: '... at the name of Akhenaten there emerges from the darkness a figure more clear than that of any other Pharaoh, and with it there comes the singing of the birds, the voices of the children and the scent of many flowers. For once we may look right into the mind of a King of Egypt and may see something of its workings, and all that is there observed is worthy of admiration. Akhenaten has been called "the first individual in human history"; but if he is thus the first historical figure whose personality is known to us, he is also the first of all human founders of religious doctrines. Akhenaten may be ranked in degree of time, and, in view of the new ground broken by him, perhaps in degree of genius, as the world's first idealist.'[3]

For the Reverend James Baikie, another British Egyptologist, he was '... an idealist dreamer, who actually believed that men were meant to live in truth and speak the truth.'[4]

Not all scholars, however, took such an enthusiastic and flattering view of the first of the Amarna kings. Some, like the British philologist Alan H. Gardiner, wrote of him that 'the standing colossi from his peristyle court at Karnak have a look of fanatical determination, such as his subsequent history confirmed only too fatally':[5] John Pendlebury, who was involved in much of the early exploration at Amarna, came to the conclusion: 'His [Akhenaten's] main preoccupation was with religion. He and [Queen] Nefertiti became devotees of the Aten. Today we should call them religious maniacs.'[6]

The controversial nature of Akhenaten's character and teachings eventually engaged the interest of Sigmund Freud, the Jewish father of psychoanalysis, who introduced a new element into the debate as Europe began its lurch towards war in the middle of the 1930s. In July 1934 Freud wrote the draft of what would later become the first part of his book *Moses and Monotheism*. This introductory section was published initially in the German magazine *Imago* in 1937 under the headline 'Moses an Egyptian'.

Freud demonstrated in this article that the name of the Jewish leader was not derived from Hebrew, as had been thought up to that time, but had as its source an Egyptian word, *mos*, meaning a child. He showed also that the story of the birth of Moses is a replica of other ancient myths about the birth of some of the great heroes of history. Freud pointed out, however, that the myth of Moses' birth and exposure stands apart from those of other heroes and varies from them on one essential point. In order to hide the fact that Moses was Egyptian, the myth of his birth has been reversed to make him born to humble parents and succoured by the high-status family: 'It is very different in the case of Moses. Here the first family – usually so distinguished – is modest enough. He is a child of Jewish Levites. But the second family – the humble one in which as a rule heroes are brought up – is replaced by the royal house of Egypt. This divergence from the usual type has struck many research workers as strange.'

Later in 1937 *Imago* published a further article by Freud under the title 'If Moses was an Egyptian'. This dealt with the question of why the Jewish law-giver, if actually Egyptian, should have passed on to his followers a monotheistic belief rather than the classical Ancient Egyptian plethora of gods and images. At the same time, Freud found great similarity between the new religion that Akhenaten had tried to impose on his country and the religious teaching attributed to Moses. For example, he wrote: 'The Jewish creed says: "*Schema Yisrael Adonai Elohenu Adonai Echod*".' ('Hear, O Israel, the Lord thy God is one God'.) As the Hebrew letter *d* is a transliteration of the Egyptian letter *t* and *e* becomes *o*, he went on to explain that this sentence from the Jewish creed could be translated: 'Hear, O Israel, our God Aten is the only God.'

A short time after publication of these two articles, Freud was reported to be suffering from cancer. Three months after the Germans invaded Austria, in June 1938, he left Vienna and sought refuge in London where, feeling his end approaching, he decided that he wished to see the two articles, plus a third section, written in Vienna but hitherto unpublished, make their appearance in the form of a book in English. This, he felt, would provide a fitting climax to his distinguished life. His intentions did not meet with the approval of a number of Jewish scholars, however: they felt that some of his views, and, in particular, his claim in the unpublished third section that Moses had been murdered by his own followers in protest against the harshness of his monotheistic beliefs, could only add to the problems of the Jews, already facing a new and harsh Oppression by the Nazis. Professor Abraham S. Yahuda, the American Jewish theologian and philologist, visited Freud at his new home in Hampstead, London, and begged him not to publish his book, but Freud refused to be deterred and *Moses and Monotheism* made its first appearance in March 1939. In his book Freud suggested that one of Akhenaten's high officials, probably called Tuthmose, was an adherent of the Aten religion. After the death of the king, Tuthmose selected the Hebrew tribe, already living at Goshen in the Eastern Delta, to be his chosen people, took them out of Egypt at the time of the Exodus and passed on to them the tenets of Akhenaten's religion.

Freud died at the age of 83, six months after his book was published. The outbreak of the Second World War not only brought all excavations in Egypt to an end, but delayed response to the bombshell that Freud had left behind. This was not too long in being remedied once the world returned to peace. The new contestant to enter the lists was another Jewish psychoanalyst, Immanuel Velikovsky, who had been born and educated in Russia in the early years of this century and had then emigrated to Palestine before settling in the United States. In 1952 he published the first part of his book *Ages in Chaos*, in which he tried to use some evidence of volcanic eruptions in Sinai to date the Jewish Exodus from Egypt at the start of the Eighteenth Dynasty, two centuries before the reign of Akhenaten, in order to place Moses at a distant point in history that *preceded* the Egyptian king. Not only that. In a separate work, *Oedipus and Akhenaten*, he set out to show that Oedipus of this classic Greek myth had an Egyptian historical origin and that Akhenaten was the Oedipus king who married his own mother, Queen Tiye.

The work of Velikovsky may be said to have set the tone in the post-war years for assessments of Akhenaten. Scholars have been on the whole at pains to destroy his flattering early image and to sever any connection between him and the monotheism of Moses. One of the earliest to embark on this crusade was Cyril Aldred, the Scottish Egyptologist. In his book about the first of the Amarna kings, published in 1968, he tried to explain the absence of genitalia in a nude colossus of the king from Karnak by the fact that Akhenaten must have been the victim of a distressing disease:

> All the indications are that such peculiar physical characteristics were the result of a complaint known to physicians and pathologists as Fröhlich's Syndrome. Male patients with this disorder frequently exhibit a corpulence similar to Akhenaten's. The genitalia remain infantile and may be so embedded in fat as not to be visible. Adiposity may vary in degree, but there is a typical feminine distribution of fat in the region of the breasts, abdomen, pubis, thighs and buttocks. The lower limbs, however, are slender and the legs, for instance, resemble plus-fours ... There is warrant for thinking that he suffered from

Fröhlich's Syndrome and wished to have himself represented with all those deformities that distinguished his appearance from the rest of humanity.[7]

However, we do have conclusive evidence that Akhenaten had at least six daughters by Queen Nefertiti. Aldred put forward an ingenious explanation for this apparent contradiction: 'Until recently it was possible to speculate that, though the daughters of Nefertiti are described as begotten of a king, it is by no means certain that such a king was Akhenaten, particularly if Amenhotep III was still alive two years after the youngest had been born. Though it may seem preposterous that Amenhotep III should have undertaken the marital duties of a sterile coregent, in the milieu of divine kingship such an enlargement of his responsibilities is not unthinkable.'

Later in the same book, however, he tells us that Akhenaten was not, after all, impotent. The author contradicts his earlier speculation by suggesting that Akhenaten married his own eldest daughter, Merytaten, and fathered a child by her: 'On the death of Nefertiti, her place was taken by Merytaten ... It would appear that she was the mother of a Princess Merytaten-the-less, from a recently published inscription from Hermopolis [The city across the river from Amarna where Ramses II had used Amarna stones for his building], but it is impossible to say who the father was, though the inference seems to be that it was Akhenaten.'

The author then goes on even to suggest that the king had a homosexual relationship with his brother/coregent/son-in-law, Semenkhkare. Aldred's attempt to destroy the earlier flattering image of Akhenaten took him down a path that a number of other scholars proved only too happy to follow. The most recent was Professor Donald Redford of Toronto University, an eminent scholar of both Old Testament studies and Egyptology, who wrote in his book *Akhenaten, the Heretic King*, published in 1984:

The historical Akhenaten is markedly different from the figure popularists have created for us. Humanist he was not, and certainly no humanitarian romantic. To make of him a tragic 'Christ-like' figure is a sheer falsehood. Nor is he the mentor of Moses: a vast gulf is fixed between the rigid, coercive, rarified monotheism of the Pharaoh and Hebrew henotheism [belief in one God without asserting that he is the only God] which in any case we see through the distorted prism of texts written seven hundred years after Akhenaten's death.

Redford summarizes his distaste for the king in the following words: 'A man deemed ugly by the accepted standards of the day, secluded in the palace in his minority, certainly close to his mother, possibly ignored by his father, outshone by his brother and sisters, unsure of himself, Akhenaten suffered the singular misfortune of acceding to the throne of Egypt and its empire.' And then: 'If the king and his circle inspire me somewhat with contempt, it is apprehension I feel when I contemplate his "religion".'[8]

The post-war attempt to crucify Akhenaten and discredit his religion has been unanimous in the sense that any scholars who may hold less hostile views have maintained a suspicious silence. At the root of the campaign of vilification lies a desire to enhance Moses and his monotheism by discrediting Akhenaten, the Egyptian intruder, and the beliefs he attempted to introduce into his country. Ironically, those scholars who have led this ruthless campaign chose the wrong target. In attacking Akhenaten, they were, in fact, attacking their own hero – for, as Freud came so close to demonstrating, Akhenaten and Moses were one and the same person.

Some of the arguments in support of this statement are of necessity long and complicated, and the ordinary reader may find them difficult to follow and somewhat wearing. Where it seemed appropriate I have therefore tried to summarize such arguments briefly, plus the conclusions to be drawn from them, and, for those who wish more detail, given a fuller account in a series of appendices.

CHRONOLOGY OF THE EIGHTEENTH DYNASTY

	Highest Dated	*Conjectural Dates* BC
Ahmosis	22	1575–1550
Amenhotep I	21	1550–1528
Tuthmosis I	4 or 9	1528–1510
Tuthmosis II	18	1510–1490
Hatshepsut	20 or 22	1490–1468
Tuthmosis III	54	1490–1436
Amenhotep II	23	1436–1413
Tuthmosis IV	8 or 9	1413–1405
Amenhotep III	38 or 39	1405–1367
Amenhotep IV (Akhenaten)	17	1367–1350
Semenkhkare	3	1350–1347
Tutankhamun	9	1347–1339
Aye	4	1339–1335
Horemheb	27 or 28	1335–1308

CHRONOLOGY OF THE NINETEENTH DYNASTY

Ramses I	2	1308–1307
Seti I	14	1307–1291
Ramses II	67	1290–1224
Merenptah	10	1224–1214

Source: Alan H. Gardiner, *Egypt of the Pharaohs* (Clarendon Press, Oxford, 1961)

These dates are given here to be helpful to the reader: the accuracy of some of them, and the question of whether there was a coregency between any of the kings mentioned, will be argued later.

1

BRICKS WITHOUT STRAW

IF MOSES and the king Akhenaten were the same person, certain
other things must follow. It is necessary to demonstrate that they
were born of the same parents in the same place at the same time;
that the monotheistic religion of Moses and the monotheistic
religion of Akhenaten, which he tried to impose upon Egypt, are
similar; that, on falling from power in Year 17 of his reign,
Akhenaten did not meet his end but fled to Sinai, where subsequent
traces of worship of his God, the Aten, are to be found; that a
number of other biblical characters can be identified with characters
in Egyptian history; and, finally, that a chronology can be established for the Sojourn of the Israelites in Egypt which matches the
chronology of the Pharaohs who ruled at the end of the Eighteenth
Dynasty and the beginning of the Nineteenth.

These, as will be seen, are complex matters. The evidence available
is often contradictory and has been interpreted – and often mis-
interpreted – in various ways. The length of the Sojourn, the length
of the reigns of various kings, whether or not Akhenaten had a
coregency with his father, Amenhotep III, the precise location of the
frontier fortified city of Zarw, where I believe Moses/Akhenaten
was born, and various other matters have been the subject of
protracted scholarly debate and disagreement. It will therefore be
necessary not merely to put forward the positive evidence that points
to the truth, but to expose the flaws in a variety of other theories that
have been advanced.

The most detailed, but not the only, source we have for information
about the life of Moses is the Old Testament and, in particular, the
Book of Exodus.

The Book of Exodus begins with a brief repetition of the account in Genesis of the Israelite Descent into Egypt to join the Patriarch Joseph, who, having initially been sold into slavery by his brothers, had risen to the role of the country's vizier after interpreting Pharaoh's dreams about the seven good years that would be followed by seven lean years. As a result of occupying his high position, Joseph was able to obtain permission for his father Jacob (Israel) and the tribe of Israel to come down from Canaan and live in Egypt. In all, we are told, the number of Israelites, including Joseph and his family, who settled in Egypt as a result of this arrangement totalled seventy, sixty-nine of whom are named. The Israelites, who were shepherds, were not allowed to settle in Egypt proper, however, because shepherds had been looked upon as 'an abomination' to Egyptians since the century-long occupation and rule of the Eastern Delta by the pastoralist Hyksos that preceded the foundation of the Eighteenth Dynasty. Instead they were given land at Goshen, in the same area to the east of the Nile Delta, which by biblical tradition was remote from the seat of Pharaoh's power.

The rest of the opening chapter of the Book of Exodus is taken up with a rather muddled summary of the story that is to follow. Almost at the very beginning of the tale, which is clearly set in the Eastern Delta, we are told that the Israelites had 'waxed exceeding mighty; and the land was filled with them' (1:7). As the tribe of Israel consisted of only seventy men, women and children at the time of their arrival in Egypt, this vast increase in numbers suggests that some years must have elapsed in the interval, a view which appears to be confirmed by the next verse, with its reference to the king 'which knew not Joseph' (1:8): until the time of Horemheb, who finally ended the Amarna era, there is no king of whom it can strictly be said that he did not know Joseph – whom I have identified as Yuya[1], vizier to Tuthmosis IV and his successor, Amenhotep III – since all the Amarna kings were descended from Joseph. Next comes an account of the Oppression, whose motive, it is said, is that 'when there falleth out any war, they join also unto our enemies, and fight against us ...'(1:10). The Egyptians set the Israelites to the task of building the treasure cities of Pithom and Raamses and made their lives 'bitter with hard bondage, in morter, and in brick, and in all manner of service in the field' (1:14). Then we encounter a contradiction. When the Israelites continued to multiply, the ruling

Pharaoh ordered that all male children born to them were to be killed. Yet we learn that at the time – just when Moses is about to make his appearance in the story – the Israelites had only two midwives, 'of which the name of the one was Shiphrah, and the name of the other Puah'. (1:15). This argues that the incident must have taken place *early* in the Sojourn when two midwives were sufficient for the needs of the Israelite women, and that, as Pharaoh was able to speak to the midwives in person, he must have been resident at the time in the vicinity of Goshen where the Israelites had settled. The midwives failed to carry out Pharaoh's orders, where-upon he issued a further order that all male children born to the Israelites in Egypt were to be cast into the river.

With the second chapter we come to the story of Moses – his birth, his slaying of an Egyptian which caused him to flee from Egypt, his marriage and his eventual return to lead the Exodus – recounted with a more satisfactory chronology. He was born, we are told, to a man of the house of Levi and a daughter of Levi, whose name is given later as Jochebed. In face of the threat to all newly-born male Israelite children, Jochebed kept her son in hiding for three months. Then, unable to conceal him herself any longer, she hid him among the reeds along the banks of the Nile in a papyrus basket coated with pitch and tar. Pharaoh's daughter saw the basket when she went down to the river to bathe and sent a slave girl to fetch it. When she opened the basket the baby was crying and she felt sorry for him. 'This is one of the Hebrew babies,' she said.

The implication up to this point is that Moses was the first-born in his family. Here, however, we learn that he already had an elder sister, Miriam, who had watched these events from a distance. She now approached and said to Pharaoh's daughter: 'Shall I fetch one of the Hebrew women to nurse the baby for you?' When this suggestion proved acceptable, the sister summoned her mother, who agreed to nurse her own baby in return for payment. Later, when the child grew older, she took him back to Pharaoh's daughter, who adopted him as her son and only now, we learn, gave him the name of Moses, her choice (which will be the subject of analysis later) being explained by the laconic phrase 'because I drew him out of the water'.

This familiar account of the birth of Moses has some curious aspects. It hardly seems logical that a mother, anxious to preserve the life of her three-month-old son, would set him afloat on the Nile in such a frail craft. Then, after the intervention of the princess, we have no further indication that, having been returned to his mother, the child was still in danger of losing his life. Finally, the explanation of his later being reared in the palace because the princess adopted him seems inherently improbable as the customs of the time would not have allowed an unmarried princess to adopt a child.

The Book of Exodus provides no details of the childhood of Moses. We next hear of him when he was grown up. He went out one day to watch his own people at their forced labour, came across an Egyptian beating a Hebrew, slew him and hid his body in the sand. On learning that news of the episode had reached Pharaoh's ears, Moses fled to Midian in Sinai to avoid execution. There, while he was resting by a well, the seven daughters of a priest of Midian arrived on the scene to water their father's flock of sheep. Some shepherds appeared shortly afterwards and tried to drive the daughters away, but Moses came to their rescue. On the girls' return home, Reu'el, their father, asked them: 'Why are you back so early today?'

They told him about the encounter with the shepherds. 'But an Egyptian rescued us,' they explained. 'He even drew water for us and watered the flock.'

'And where is he?' their father asked. 'Invite him to have something to eat.' The invitation proved to be the start of a protracted stay. Moses became a guest in the house of the priest, who gave him one of his daughters, Zipporah, in marriage, and she bore Moses a son, whom he named Gershon.

Back in Egypt, after the passage of many years, a new Pharaoh had come to the throne, but the miseries of the Israelites continued and God heard their cries for help. One day when Moses was out tending the flock of his father-in-law — whose name is given at this point in the narrative as Jethro, not Reu'el — he found himself with the sheep at Mount Horeb (Mount Sinai), the mountain of God, where the Lord appeared to him in a bush that seemed to be burning but was not consumed by the flames. Attracted by this curious phenomenon, Moses approached, whereupon the Lord said to him: 'I am the God of your father, the God of Abraham, the God of Isaac and the God of Jacob.' (3:6) He then went on: 'I am sending you to the Pharaoh to bring my people, the Israelites, out of Egypt.'

Moses expressed doubts about his ability to carry out this task and asked: 'If I go to the Israelites and say the God of their forefathers has sent me to them, and they ask me his name, how shall I answer them?'

The Lord replied: 'I AM, that is who I am. Say that I AM has sent you to them ... You must tell the Israelites that it is Jehovah, the God of their forefathers, the God of Abraham, the God of Isaac, the God of Jacob, who has sent you to them.'

Moses protested that the Israelites would never believe that the Lord had appeared to him. God asked: 'What have you in your hand?'

Moses answered: 'A staff.'

The Lord told him to throw it down on to the ground, whereupon it turned into a snake. The Lord said: 'Put out your hand and seize it by the tail.' Moses did as he was told and the snake was transformed again into a staff.

The Lord then instructed him: 'Put your hand inside the fold of your cloak.' Moses again did as he was told and, when he withdrew his hand, it was white with leprosy. The Lord told him to put his hand inside his cloak a second time and, when he withdrew it, his hand was healthy again. Finally, the Lord told him: 'If they are not convinced by these two signs, fetch some water from the Nile and pour it out on dry ground, and the water will turn to blood.'

Moses continued to protest: 'Lord, I have never been eloquent. I am slow and hesitant of speech. O Lord, please send someone else.' As this was the first time that Moses was to address the Israelites, it would appear that he was not sure he would be able to make them understand him.

The Lord's reply makes it clear that, in addition to the sister we already know of, Moses had a Levite brother who, in a subsequent passage, we are told was three years the elder: 'What about your brother, Aaron? He will do all the speaking. He is already on his way to meet you. You will speak to him and put words in his mouth. He will be your mouthpiece.' God also reassured Moses that his life would not be in any danger if he returned to Egypt because 'all those who wished to kill you are dead'.

Moses 'took his wife and sons' – hitherto we had heard of only one son, Gershon – 'and set them upon an ass, and he returned to the land of Egypt: and Moses took the rod of God in his hand.' (4:20) In the course of the journey he met his brother Aaron. On arriving in

Egypt they appeared together before an assembly of the elders of Israel where Aaron gave an account of everything the Lord had said to Moses. Moses and Aaron then went to Pharaoh – here again there is no indication that they had to travel any distance – and asked permission to undertake a three-day trip into the wilderness to offer a sacrifice to the Lord. Pharaoh refused their request. Instead, he ordered the Israelites' overseers not to provide them with any more straw for brickmaking: they were to gather their own, yet still produce the same number of bricks. 'They are a lazy people,' said the king. 'That is why they are clamouring to go and offer a sacrifice to their God. Take no notice of a pack of lies.'

The Israelites blamed Moses and Aaron for their plight. Moses and Aaron, for their part, renewed their pleas that the Israelites should be set free to worship their Lord, but Pharaoh remained obdurate. God therefore kept his earlier promise that in these circumstances he would stretch out his hand and 'smite the Egyptians'. He inflicted a series of ten plagues – blood, frogs, gnats, maggots, swarms of flies, pestilence, boils, hail, locusts and darkness – upon the country. As a final punishment, God assured Moses: 'It is the Lord's Passover. On that night I shall pass through the land of Egypt and kill every first-born of man and beast.' Before that night – the fourteenth of the month of Abib, which is to be regarded as the first month of the Jewish Year – was over Pharaoh sent again for Moses and Aaron and told them: 'Be off. Leave my people, you and your Israelites. Go and worship the Lord, as you ask.'

The Exodus began, from Rameses to Succoth, the next day, the fifteenth. Six hundred thousand men, plus their dependants, are said to have left the country that had been their home for 430 years. From Succoth the Israelites made their way to Eltham where they camped before setting off on their journey across the wilderness to the Sea of Reeds.

Back in Egypt, Pharaoh had second thoughts about his decision to let his former unwilling slaves depart and mounted an expedition with his chariots and troops to recapture them. They came upon the Israelites on the shores of the Red Sea, apparently trapped between the water and the pursuing Egyptians. Naturally terrified, they protested to Moses: 'Did you bring us to the desert to die because there were no graves in Egypt?' However, Moses used his staff to create a path across the sea bed with a wall of water on either side.

When the Egyptians eventually set out in pursuit, the water flowed back over them and they were drowned to a man. The Israelites were free – and Miriam, the sister of Aaron, 'took up her tambourine, and all the women did the same, dancing to the sound of tambourines, while Miriam sang to them:

> Sing to the Lord, for he has risen up in triumph,
> The horse and his rider he has hurled into the sea.'

From the Red Sea, the Israelites made their way into the desert, where they journeyed for three days without finding water, and when they did eventually locate some it was so bitter that they could not drink it. They grumbled to Moses, asking: 'What are we to drink?' This grumbling, accompanied at times by threats to choose a new leader who would take them back to Egypt, is a recurrent theme in the rest of the Pentateuch, the first five books of the Old Testament.

In the third month after the Exodus, the wandering tribe reached Mount Horeb (Mount Sinai), the mountain of God, where Moses received the Ten Commandments. The Israelites became impatient, however, during his absence of forty days. Aaron collected everyone's gold earrings, cast the metal into a mould and made it into the image of a bull-calf. The next day the Israelites rose early, made offerings at an altar in front of the golden calf and then sat down to eat and drink before giving themselves up to revelry. When he returned and discovered what had happened, Moses was so angry that he threw down the two tablets inscribed with the Lord's teaching, shattering them, and destroyed the golden calf in the fire. Then he asked: 'Come here to me whoever is on the Lord's side.' It was the Levites who rallied to him, and he said to them: 'Each of you take his sword and go through the camp from one end to the other, each killing his brother and friend and neighbour.' The Levites followed his orders and about three thousand of the idolators died that day.

After Moses had returned to the mountain of God, where he obtained two fresh tablets listing the Lord's teachings, he gave the Israelites instructions about the creation of a Tabernacle, the first mobile Jewish temple. The Tabernacle, the Tent of the Presence, was set up, we are told, on the first day of the first month of the second year.

In the middle of the Book of Exodus we are also given details about the family of Moses. It provides us with the name of his second son, Eleazar; the names of the sons of Levi, the grandfather of Moses (Gershon, Kohath and Merari); the names of the sons of Kohath (Amram, Izhar, Hebron and Uzziel), and details of the marriage of Amram: 'Amram married his father's sister, Jochebed, and she bore him Aaron and Moses.'

While the Book of Exodus is the main source, three other books of the Pentateuch – Numbers, Leviticus and Deuteronomy – provide some additional facts about the wanderings of the Israelites between their departure from Egypt and their arrival on the frontiers of the Promised Land, with complaints about the leadership of Moses still a recurrent theme. The Book of Numbers tells us that Moses sent one leader from each of the twelve ancestral tribes to explore the Promised Land of Canaan. On their return they reported: 'The land does flow with milk and honey – here is some of its fruit – but the people who inhabit it are powerful, and their cities are fortified and very large.'

Caleb, one of the twelve in the advance party, argued: 'Let us go up and conquer the country. We are strong enough to do it.' All but one of the others, however, protested: 'We can't attack those people. They are stronger than we are. We felt no bigger than grasshoppers, and that is how we looked to them.' That night all the Israelites turned on Moses and Aaron and said to them: 'Wouldn't it be better for us to return to Egypt?' and among themselves suggested: 'We should choose a new leader and go back to Egypt.'

Caleb and Joshua, the other optimist, told them: 'The land we explored is exceedingly good. If the Lord is pleased with us, he will lead us there. Do not be afraid of the people of the land because the Lord is with us.' The Israelites thereupon threatened to stone them, with the result that as a punishment the Lord condemned the whole generation, apart from the trusting Caleb and Joshua, to spend forty years in the desert instead of entering the Promised Land.

Again, when the Israelites arrived in the Desert of Zin and settled for a time at Kadesh – where Miriam, the prophetess sister of Aaron, died and was buried – there were more complaints about lack of water. The Israelites quarrelled with Moses again, asking: 'Why did you bring us to this desert for us and our livestock to face death? Why did you bring us out of Egypt to this terrible place where nothing will grow – neither corn nor figs, vines nor pomegranates? There is not even any water to drink.'

It is then that Moses used his rod to smite the rock and bring forth water. It was called 'the water of Meribah' – a location in the north-centre of Sinai, south of Canaan – and it was for this action, we learn later, that the Lord punished Moses by not allowing him to cross into the Promised Land.

The Book of Numbers also tells us that the Tabernacle constructed by the Israelites faced to the east, and that from Kadesh they made their way ultimately to a point near the frontier of Edom, in the north-east of Sinai and to the south of the Dead Sea, where Aaron died on the top of Mount Hor. In addition, both the Book of Numbers and the Book of Leviticus contain some references to leprosy. In the Book of Numbers we learn that: 'The Lord spoke to Moses and said: "Command the Israelites to expel from the camp everyone who suffers from a malignant skin disease or a discharge, and everyone ritually unclean from contact with a corpse ..."' We are given an account of an incident when both Aaron and Miriam were critical of Moses for having taken as a second wife a Kushite (Nubian or Ethiopian) woman. The Lord appeared and asked angrily: 'How dare you speak against my servant Moses? He alone of all my household is to be trusted.' Then, when the Lord left, Miriam's skin was seen to be diseased and as white as snow. Leprosy and skin purification also form the subject of three chapters (13–15) on purification and atonement in the preceding book, Leviticus, which also indicates that it was the Israelite custom to pray twice a day, in the morning and the evening.

Moses, after all his struggles, did not reach the Promised Land himself. When the Israelites were camped on the banks of the Jordan, near Jericho and opposite Canaan, he learned, according to the Book of Deuteronomy, that he was to be denied the opportunity to cross the river, no matter how hard he pleaded:

> I pray thee, let me go over, and see the good land that is beyond Jordan, that goodly mountain, and Lebanon. ... the Lord said ... speak no more unto me of this matter ... ... thou shalt not go over this Jordan. (3:25–7)

Later in the Book of Deuteronomy we have an account of the actual death of Moses. The Lord said to him: 'Get thee up into this

mountain Abarim, unto Mount Nebo, which is in the land of Moab'
– the borders between Sinai and eastern Jordan – 'that is over against
Jericho; and behold the land of Canaan, which I give unto the
children of Israel for a possession ... And die in the mount ...
Because ye trespassed against me among the children of Israel at the
waters of Meribah-Kadesh, in the wilderness of Zin ... thou shalt
not go thither unto the land which I give the children of Israel.'
(32:49–52)

After admonishing and blessing his people, Moses left them with
Joshua and climbed the mountain. There, after viewing the
Promised Land, he met his death – and was buried by the Lord in an
unmarked grave in the plains of Moab below.

The last mention of Moses in the Old Testament is as curious as
some aspects of the story of his birth. It occurs in the second Book of
Kings, which gives an account of various rulers, more than five
centuries after the Exodus, some of whom tried to keep to the Lord's
teachings, some of whom did not. Among the former, we are told,
was Hezekiah:

> And he did that which was right in the sight of the Lord, according to
> all that David his father did.
> He removed the high places and brake the images, and cut down the
> groves; and brake in pieces the brazen serpent that Moses had made:
> for unto those days the children of Israel did burn incense to it. (II
> Kings, 18:3–4)

The reference is particularly significant because a staff topped by a
bronze serpent was the symbol of Pharaoh's authority.

2

WAS MOSES A KING?

APART from a rather muddled chronology at the start of the Book of Exodus, the story of Moses it tells is quite straightforward. However, the picture changes when we examine other holy books and the work of Manetho, the third century BC native Egyptian historian, which was subsequently transmitted by the Jewish historian, Flavius Josephus.

While we know from the Old Testament that Moses was brought up in the royal palace, it does not suggest that he ever succeeded to the throne. Yet the story of Moses in the Talmud – the compilation of Hebrew laws and legends, dating from the early centuries AD and regarded as second only to the Old Testament as an authoritative source of the early history of the Jews – contains some details not to be found in the Bible and often parallels Manetho's account of the Exodus, derived from Egyptian folklore. One of the details is that Moses was a king.

According to the Talmud, which agrees that Moses was brought up in Pharaoh's palace, he grew into a handsome lad, dressed royally, was honoured by the people and seemed in all things of royal lineage. However, at about the age of eighteen he was forced to flee from Egypt after, on a visit to Goshen, he came across an Egyptian smiting one of his Israelite brethren and slew him.

The Talmud goes on to relate that, at about this time, there was a rebellion against the King of Ethiopia. The king appointed a magician's son named Bi'lam – one of Pharaoh's advisers, who was considered exceptionally wise but had fled to Ethiopia from his own country, Egypt – to be his representative in his absence and marched at the head of a large army, which vanquished the rebels. Bi'lam betrayed his trust, however, and, usurping the power he was supposed to protect, induced the Ethiopians to appoint him in place of their absent king. He strengthened the walls of the capital, built huge fortresses and dug ditches and pits between the city and the nearby river. On his return the Ethiopian king was astonished to see all these fortifications, which he thought were defences against a possible attack by an enemy. When he found that the gates of the city were actually closed against him, he embarked on a war against the usurper, Bi'lam, that lasted nine years.

One of the soldiers who fought on the side of the king, according to the Talmud story, was Moses, who, after fleeing from Egypt, had made his way not to Midian in Sinai, as the Old Testament says, but to Ethiopia. He became a great favourite with the Ethiopian ruler and his companions with the result that, when the king died, this inner circle appointed Moses as their new king and leader. Moses, who, according to the Talmud, was made king 'in the hundred and fifty-seventh year after Israel went down into Egypt', inspired the army with his courage and the city eventually fell to him. The account goes on: '... Bi'lam escaped and fled back to Egypt, becoming one of the magicians mentioned in the Scriptures. And the Ethiopians placed Moses upon their throne and set the crown of State upon his head, and they gave him the widow of their king for a wife.'

Moses reigned 'in justice and righteousness. But the Queen of Ethiopia, Adonith [Aten-it in Egyptian], who wished her own son by the dead king to rule, said to the people: "Why should this stranger continue to rule over you?" The people, however, would not vex Moses, whom they loved, by such a proposition; but Moses resigned voluntarily the power which they had given him and departed from their land. And the people of Ethiopia made him many rich presents, and dismissed him with great honours.'[1]

So, according to this tradition, which has survived in the Talmud, Moses was elevated to the post of king for some time before eventually seeking the sanctuary of Sinai. Furthermore, where Akhenaten, as we shall see, looked upon himself as the high priest of his God, the Talmud tells us that 'Moses officiated as the high priest. He was also considered the King of Israel during the sojourn in the desert.' Where did the rabbis obtain the facts in the Talmud? They can hardly have invented them and, indeed, had no reason to do so. Like the accounts of the historian Manetho, the Talmudic stories contain many distortions and accretions arising from the fact that they were transmitted orally for a long time before finally being set down in writing. Yet one can sense that behind the myths there must have lain genuine historical events that had been suppressed from the official accounts of both Egypt and Israel, but had survived in the memories of the generations.

The Talmud description of Moses as a ruler is also supported by a verse of the Koran where Moses tells the Israelites after the Exodus that God has made of them kings:

> Remember Moses said
> To his people: 'O my people!
> Call in remembrance the favour
> Of Allah unto you, when He
> Produced prophets among you,
> Made you kings, and gave
> You what he had not given
> To any other among the peoples . . .' (Sura V, 20)

The reference here is not to two kings, but more than two, for Arabic has different plural forms for dual and multiple, and it is difficult to see in the light of later evidence how this can be anything other than a reference to the four Amarna kings.

The Koran also provides a different picture of Moses' departure from the Ethiopian capital. Where the Talmud indicates that it was a friendly farewell, the Koran suggests that it was an escape from a threat to his life:

> And there came a man,
> Running, from the furthest end
> Of the city. He said:
> 'O Moses! the Chiefs
> Are taking counsel together
> About thee to slay thee:
> So get thee away, for I
> Do give thee sincere advice.' (Sura XXVIII, 20)

The Talmud also provides a different reason for the attempt to kill Moses at birth. It was Moses specifically who was to be murdered because he posed a threat to the throne of Egypt. Pharaoh, according to the Talmud, had a dream in which he was sitting on the throne when he saw an old man holding a large pair of scales. The old man placed the elders and princes of Egypt on one side of the scales and a lamb on the other. The lamb proved to be heavier. The king asked his adviser Bi'lam the significance of this strange dream. Bi'lam explained that a great evil would befall the country: 'A son will be born in Israel who will destroy Egypt.'

Reu'el the Midianite, who is described in the Old Testament as the father-in-law of Moses, enters the scene here as another of the king's counsellors, who advised him that he should not oppress the Israelites, but allow them to leave for Canaan. This advice did not find favour with the king, who responded by banishing Reu'el to his own country and accepting an alternative course of action recommended by Bi'lam – that as a precautionary measure all boys born to the Hebrews should be cast into the river.

Prior to this, coinciding with the accounts in the Bible, we are told that Amram had married Jochebed, who bore him a daughter, Miriam, described in the Old Testament as 'a prophetess', followed by a son, Aaron. Now we learn of a prophesy by Miriam that a second son would be born to her parents and this son would ultimately deliver the Israelites from their Egyptian oppressors. When the baby appeared as predicted, Jochebed hid the new-born infant in her home for three months, but a strict search of the Israelites' homes was carried out regularly and various ruses were employed to discover any male children who had been concealed. One was for Egyptian women to bring their own babies into houses in Goshen and make them cry, whereupon any Hebrew babies hidden on the premises would start to cry as well and betray their place of concealment.

The birth of a male child to Jochebed came to light in this way, but she hid the baby in the reeds of the Nile before Pharaoh's officers arrived to take him away. There, as in the Old Testament, he was rescued by a daughter of the king, Bathia – identified in a subsequent passage as the first-born of her mother – who gave him the name of Moses, saying: 'I have drawn him from the water.' Moses 'became even as a son to Bathia ... as a child belonging rightly to the palace of the king'.[2]

When Moses was about three years of age, the story goes on, in the course of a banquet at which his family and princes of the realm were present, Pharaoh took Moses on his lap, whereupon the child stretched out his hand, removed Pharaoh's crown from his head and placed it on his own. The king felt this action had some possibly sinister significance. 'How shall this Hebrew boy be punished?' he asked.

Bi'lam confirmed the king's suspicions. 'Think not, because the child is young, that he did this thing thoughtlessly,' he said. 'Remember, o king, the dream this servant read for thee, the dream of the balances. The spirit of understanding is already implanted in this child, and to himself he takes thy kingdom.'

The judges and wise men, including Jithro (Reu'el), the priest of Midian, assembled and Pharaoh related what had happened and the interpretation Bi'lam had placed upon Moses' action. Jithro, who was anxious to save the child's life, suggested: 'If it be pleasing to the king, let two plates be placed before the child, one containing fire, the other gold. If the child stretches forth his hand to grasp the gold, we shall know him to be an understanding being, and consider that he acted towards thee knowingly, deserving death. But if he grasps the fire, then let his life be spared.' Two bowls were brought, one containing gold, the other fire, and placed before the child, who put out his hand and grasped the fire, which he put into his mouth, burning his tongue and becoming thereafter, as the Bible says, 'heavy of mouth and heavy of tongue'. However, his life was saved.

Manetho, a native Egyptian, was a contemporary of the first two Ptolemies, rulers at the start of the Thirty-second and last Egyptian Dynasty early in the third century BC, and is said to have described himself in a letter to Ptolemy II as 'High Priest and scribe of the sacred shrines of Egypt, born at Sebennytus and dwelling at Heliopolis'.[3] He is one of the early Egyptians who wrote about his country in Greek, assembling tales that he had found in the temple library, made up in part of ancient stories that had initially been transmitted orally before being set down in writing.

Scholars disagree about how many books can actually be attributed to Manetho, but it is accepted that he was the author of *The History of Egypt* (or *Aegyptiaca*) in three volumes. The main difficulty we face in trying to establish the contents of Manetho's original work, however, is the fact that we do not have direct access to it: the fragments available have all come to us via other authors. Quotations from his work have been preserved mainly by the Jewish historian Flavius Josephus (AD 70); the Christian chronographers Sextus Julius Africanus (3rd century AD) and Eusebius (4th century AD); in isolated passages in Plutarch and other Greek and Latin authors, and a later compiler called George the Monk – an 'attendant', also known as Syncellus (AD 800), of Tarasius, Patriarch of Constantinople – who contributed greatly to the transmission.

According to Josephus in his book *Contra Apionem*, Alexandria had become a main centre for the Jews during the time of the Ptolemies. They enjoyed both Alexandrian citizenship and the city's 'finest residential quarter' by the sea. The Alexandrian Jews were naturally interested in Manetho's account of their historic links with Egypt, although they found some aspects of it objectionable. His original work therefore did not survive for long before being tampered with. The efforts of Jewish apologists account for much of the subsequent corruption of Manetho's text and the creation of what is known as 'Pseudo-Manethonian' literature.

Although, as we shall see, Egypt tried to wipe out all trace of the four Amarna kings – Akhenaten, Semenkhkare, Tutankhamun and Aye – by excising their names from king lists and monuments after the fall of the Amarna regime, they are correctly named by Manetho as having ruled between the reigns of Amenhotep III, Akhenaten's father, and Horemheb, who is to be identified as the Pharaoh of the Oppression. In addition, an epitome of Manetho's history had already been made as early as Ptolemaic times in the form of lists of dynasties accompanied by short notes on outstanding kings and important events, including the defeat of the Hyksos invaders, followed by the founding of the Eighteenth Dynasty and the Exodus. These versions of the epitome differ from one another, indicating that some distortion has occurred in the process of transmitting and editing Manetho's *Aegyptiaca* itself. However, a number of points are worth making:

• The list of Syncellus (according to Africanus) places the Exodus, when 'Moses went forth from Egypt', in the reign of Amos (Ahmosis), founder of the Eighteenth Dynasty, who drove out the Hyksos shepherds: this is an error arising from wrongly identifying, as Josephus did, the arrival of the conquering Hyksos as the Descent into Egypt of the Israelites and the subsequent expulsion of the Hyksos by Ahmosis as the Exodus;

• The lists of Syncellus (according to Eusebius) and the version of Eusebius which was found translated into Armenian place the Exodus of the Jews, with Moses at their head, more than two centuries later in the reign of the king who succeeded Orus (Amenhotep III, *c.* 1405–1367) – his son and coregent Amenhotep IV (Akhenaten);

• Syncellus (according to Africanus) also states that it was in the reign of Amos (Ahmosis), the first king of the Eighteenth Dynasty, that Moses led the Exodus;

• Syncellus (according to Eusebius) claims that it was 'about' the reign of a Pharaoh named Achencherres (Amenhotep IV, who later became Akhenaten) – that 'Moses led the Jews in their march out of Egypt';

• The Armenian version of Eusebius similarly lists the reign of Achencheres (Akhenaten) as the time 'when Moses became the leader of the Jews in their Exodus'.

Josephus made an error by identifying the arrival of the conquering Hyksos as the Descent into Egypt of the Israelites and their subsequent expulsion by Ahmosis as the Exodus. What helped him to make the mistake was his desire to show that the Israelites had left Egypt long before Amenhotep III and the religious revolution that began in his reign. Josephus begins by saying that the Jews' ancestors, whom he regarded as the Hyksos, 'entered Egypt in their myriads and subdued the inhabitants'.[4] Later they were driven out of the country, occupied Judaea and founded Jerusalem. At this point he complains that Manetho 'took the liberty of introducing some incredible tales, wishing to represent us [the Israelites] as mixed up with a crowd of Egyptian lepers and others who for various maladies were condemned ... to banishment from the country.' (We should not take the descriptions of the rebels as being literally lepers or suffering from other maladies, the sense here being that they were impure because of their denial of Egyptian gods.) This sequence of events, says Josephus, is linked with a king named Amenophis (Amenhotep III), whom Josephus – believing that the Jews (Hyksos) had left Egypt centuries earlier – describes as 'an imaginary person'. Josephus' account then goes on: 'This king, he [Manetho] states, wishing to be granted ... a vision of the gods, communicated his desire to his namesake, Amenophis, son of Paapis [son of Habu], whose wisdom and knowledge of the future were regarded as marks of divinity. This namesake replied that he would be able to see the gods if he purged the entire country of lepers and other polluted persons, and sent them to work on the stone quarries to the east of the Nile, segregated from the rest of the Egyptians. They included, he adds, some of the learned priests, who were afflicted with leprosy. Then this wise seer Amenophis was seized with a fear that he would draw down the wrath of the gods on himself and the king if the violence done to these men were detected; and he added a prediction that the polluted people would find certain allies who would become masters of Egypt for thirteen years . . .'

The adviser known as son of Habu started his career under Amenhotep III as an Inferior Royal Scribe, was promoted to be a Superior Royal Scribe and finally reached the position of Minister of all Public Works. He was also appointed as Steward of Sitamun, the sister Amenhotep III had married in order to inherit the throne but failed to make his Great Royal Wife (queen). Son of Habu lived to be at least eighty and the last date we have for him is the thirty-fourth year of Amenhotep III. Later he became for the Egyptians a kind of saint whose cult was reported as late as Roman times.

Eventually, after the men in the stone quarries had spent many miserable years, the king heard their pleas for less harsh treatment and gave them the abandoned city of the Hyksos, Avaris. There, having at last a base of their own, they appointed as their leader one of the priests of Heliopolis (On), called Osarseph, and undertook to obey all his orders. By his first law, Osarseph ordained that his followers should not worship the gods of Egypt, nor abstain from the flesh of any of the animals held in special reverence in the country. He also commanded that they should form an exclusive society, mixing only with their own kind. Manetho's account, as interpreted by Josephus, then goes on:

> After laying down these and a multitude of other laws, absolutely opposed to Egyptian custom, he [Osarseph] ordered all hands to repair the city walls and make ready for war with King Amenophis [Amenhotep III]. Then, in concert with other priests and polluted persons like himself, he sent an emissary to the shepherds who had been expelled by Tethmosis [the Asiatic Hyksos, who were expelled by

Ahmosis] in the city of Jerusalem, setting out the position of himself and his outraged companions and inviting them to join in a united expedition against Egypt. He undertook to escort them first to their ancestral home at Auaris [Avaris], to provide abundant supplies for their multitudes, to fight for them when the moment came and, without difficulty, to reduce the country to submission. The shepherds, delighted with the idea, all eagerly set off in a body numbering two hundred thousand men ...

In the face of this threatened invasion, Amenophis (Amenhotep III) 'sent for the sacred animals which are held in most reverence in the temples and instructed the priests in each district to conceal the images of the gods as securely as possible.' However, he did not do battle with the invaders, but retreated to Ethiopia (Kush), 'whose king was under obligation to him and at his service'. This king made Amenophis welcome and provided accommodation and food for him and his followers for the thirteen years of banishment that the son of Habu had predicted. Manetho's account, according to Josephus, then continues:

'Meanwhile, the Solymites [who originated in Jerusalem] came down with the polluted Egyptians and treated the inhabitants in so sacrilegious a manner that the regime of the shepherds seemed like a golden age to those who now beheld the impieties of their present enemies. Not only did they set cities and villages on fire, not only did they pillage the temples and mutilate the images of the gods, but, not content with that, they habitually used the very sanctuaries as kitchens for roasting the venerated sacred animals, forced the priests and prophets to slaughter them and cut their throats, and then turned them out naked ...' Manetho adds that Amenophis subsequently advanced from Ethiopia with a large army and his son, Rampses, at the head of another, and that the two attacked and defeated the shepherds and their polluted allies, killing many of them and pursuing the remainder to the frontiers of Syria.

Modern scholars have tended to accept the view that Manetho did not rely in his account of the Israelites' sojourn in Egypt entirely on Ancient Egyptian historical sources. Gardiner, for instance, says in his book *Egypt of the Pharaohs*: '... the story of Amenhophis (Amenhotep III) and the lepers quoted from him by Josephus ... show that he made use not only of authentic records, but also of popular romances devoid of historical value.' He also makes the point a page earlier: '... Josephus' excerpts from Manetho were introduced to support the latter's belief that the biblical account of the Exodus and the expulsion of the Hyksos under Tethmosis refer to one and the same historical event ... Admittedly the lengthy excerpts in question embody also several popular stories of the most fantastic description, explicitly recognized as such by the Jewish historian.'

This view has been challenged recently, however, by Redford in *Pharaonic King-Lists, Annals and Day Books*. After giving an account of the surviving library of the temple of Sobek in Fayum, which dates from the first century BC to the fourth AD, has been brought to light over the last hundred years and is currently in process of publication, he comments, in discussing some aspects of Manetho's work that is conventionally dismissed as 'Pseudo-Manethonian': 'There is absolutely no justification in ... construing them as interpolations. Nor is it correct to imagine Manetho garnering oral traditions and committing them to writing. He would have had no use for, and probably would have despised, material circulating orally and not found formally represented by the temple scroll. What he found in the temple library in the form of a duly authorized text he incorporated in his history; and, conversely, we may with confidence postulate for the material in his history a written source found in the temple library, and nothing more.' Redford identified the source of Manetho's Osarseph story as the events of the Amarna religious revolution, first remembered orally and later set down in writing.

Although the leader of the contaminated people was given as Osarseph by Manethos, other writers have favoured the name of Moses. In his *History of Egypt* in five books, Apion himself – who lived in the first half of the first century AD, was born in Upper Egypt, studied in Alexandria and taught rhetoric in Rome under Tiberius, Caligula and Claudius – wrote in his third book, as quoted by Josephus: 'Moses, as I have heard from old people [the elders] in Egypt, was a native of Heliopolis who, being pledged to the customs of his country, erected prayer-houses open to the air in various precincts of the city, all facing eastwards, such being the orientation also of Heliopolis. In place of obelisks he set up pillars, topped by human figures, beneath which was a model of a boat; and the shadow cast on this basin by the boat described a circle corresponding to the course of the sun in the heavens.'[5]

Another Alexandrian author named Chaereman (1st century AD philosopher and librarian of Alexandria, who afterwards became the tutor of Nero), also favoured Moses: 'Moses and another sacred scribe Joseph',[6] as did Lysimachus (Alexandrian writer of uncertain date, but later than the 2nd century BC), also quoted by Josephus.[7]

There are a number of conflicts between these various accounts of the life of Moses, which one would expect with stories passed on by word of mouth for centuries before they were finally written down. We are, for instance, given two dates, more than two centuries apart, for the Exodus. Furthermore, while the Talmud tells us that it was Moses who fled to Ethiopia, Manetho claims that it was Amenhotep III, whom I look upon as having been Moses' father. For the moment, however, several points in these two opening chapters are worth emphasizing.

Both at the time of the birth of Moses and when he was seeking permission for the Israelites to leave Egypt, the indications are that the ruling Pharaoh was in residence in the vicinity of Goshen, where the Israelites had been allowed to settle ... Moses, who is described as a native of Heliopolis, where Akhenaten is thought to have spent much of his childhood, protested to the Lord that he would have difficulty in communicating with the Israelites ... the Exodus is linked in three cases with the reign of Akhenaten ... the name of the Egyptian queen who became the wife of Moses is given as Adonith (Aten-it) and is clearly derived from the Aten, the one God whom Akhenaten attempted to force upon the Egyptian people ... Moses remained in Egyptian memory also by the name of Osarseph, a priest of Heliopolis, which links him with vizier Joseph, the Patriarch who brought the tribe of Israel down to Egypt, whom I have identified as Yuya, Akhenaten's maternal grandfather[8] ... Manetho's identification of the reign of Amenhotep III – while the son of Habu was still alive, some time before the king's Year 34 – as the right time for the start of religious rebellion and the Jewish Oppression is not built simply on popular tales of his time, but on old traditions, already set down in writing, that he found in his temple library ... it is clear from the biblical narrations that the Oppression of the Israelites took two separate forms – the threat to the lives of Hebrew male children and the use of the Israelites' forced labour to build the cities of Pithom and Raamses, which, as we shall see, followed a period of religious upheaval ... Moses was not allowed to enter the Promised Land for the alleged offence of striking a rock with his rod to obtain water for his followers.

On the subject of the Israelite occupation of the abandoned Hyksos city of Avaris, Redford has also commented: 'The occupation of a deserted area, set apart (though in the modified form of the story replaced by Avaris) sounds like the hegira to Amarna' – Akhenaten's move from Thebes to his new capital in the face of opposition to his religious ideas by nobles and priests of the State god Amun – 'and the thirteen years of woe wrought by lepers and shepherds can only be the term of Akhenaten's stay in his new city. The figure of Osarseph/Moses is clearly modelled on the historic memory of Akhenaten. He is credited with interdicting the worship of all the gods and, in Apion, of championing a form of worship which used open-air temples oriented east, exactly like the Aten temples of Amarna.'[9]

What are the historical events that inspired these varied, and often contradictory, accounts – and at what precise point in history did they take place?

3

THE ISRAEL STELA

A CHRONOLOGY for the life of Moses clearly depends upon establishing in the first place when the Descent of the Israelites into Egypt took place and how long they remained there before the Exodus. It is generally accepted that they were in the country at the end of the Eighteenth and start of the Nineteenth Dynasties (c.1308 BC), but when they arrived and departed have both been the subject of considerable disagreement. The Old Testament is not very helpful in this matter. It does not give any dates, or the names of any reigning monarch, referring to him only as 'Pharaoh', 'King' or 'Pharaoh, King of Egypt'. Nor does it tell us where the capital city of the Pharaoh in question was situated. It also provides us with some conflicting statements about how long the Sojourn lasted:

> And he said unto Abram, Know of a surety that thy seed shall be a stranger in a land that is not theirs, and shall serve them; and they shall afflict them four hundred years. (Genesis, 15:13)
> But in the fourth generation they shall come hither again ... (Genesis, 15:16)

> Now the sojourning of the children of Israel, who dwelt in Egypt, was four hundred and thirty years.
> And it came to pass at the end of the four hundred and thirty years, even the selfsame day it came to pass, that all the hosts of the Lord went out from the land of Egypt. (Exodus, 12:40–41)

In addition, the Old Testament always provides us with the names of heads of tribes and the names of their descendants who are important to the story that is being related. In the case of the Sojourn we are given the names of four generations – Jacob's (Israel's) third son, Levi, and Levi's son (Kohath), grandson (Amram) and great-grandson (Moses).

If we examine Egyptian sources we find nothing that matches precisely the broad outline of the biblical account of the Descent, Sojourn and Exodus. Yet this lack of precise evidence cannot be taken as a reason to dismiss the account as a complete fabrication or to suppose a mythological origin for these narrations. The Bible gives some inside details of life in Egypt during the Empire (the Eighteenth and Nineteenth Dynasties) that in many cases have to be seen as originating as a result of first-hand knowledge. These details cannot be regarded as a later colouring, as some scholars maintain, for how could a Jewish priest and scribe like Ezra, returning to Jerusalem from the Exile in Babylon in the fifth century BC, be expected to have inside details about life in Egypt during the Empire eight centuries earlier? The only logical explanation is that the biblical accounts of the Descent into Egypt and eventual Exodus have at their core real historical characters and events. It is therefore a matter of seeking clues within the Old Testament that may help us to determine to which period of Egyptian history these events belong.

The historical period we have to examine is a long one, ranging from the seventeeth century BC until the thirteenth. In the seventeenth century BC Lower and Middle Egypt came under the control of the invading Hyksos – Asiatic shepherd rulers, with some Semitic elements among their followers – who set up their capital at Avaris in the Eastern Delta, where they ruled for just over a hundred years. They were eventually defeated in battle and driven from the country by Ahmosis (c.1575–1550), founder of the Eighteenth Dynasty, which would develop into a golden age in the history of Ancient Egypt and lasted until almost the end of the fourteenth century BC. During this period Thebes in Upper Egypt became the capital and chief religious centre of the country, while the king's main residence was at Memphis in Lower Egypt. With the arrival of Ramses I, the first Pharaoh of the Nineteenth Dynasty, Thebes retained its importance, but the king's main residence moved to the old city of Avaris, now rebuilt by the Israelites as Pi-Ramses and named after the Ramses kings of the dynasty. It is also from this period that the whole of the Eastern Delta area named as Goshen in the Bible became known as the Land of Ramses.

The name Ramses (spelled Rameses) is also found in the Pentateuch, but not as the name of a ruling king. In Genesis, 47:11, it is
given as the name of the land where the Israelites were allowed to
settle on their arrival in Egypt. As the Goshen area did not become
known as the Land of Ramses until the Nineteenth Dynasty, and
nobody disputes that the Israelites arrived in Egypt at some time
before this era, it seems that the name Ramses is simply being used
here as an equivalent of Goshen as it became known as 'the Land of
Ramses' at the time of the Exodus. The name Rameses occurs again
in Exodus, 12:37, where it is described as the starting point of the
Exodus. Further pointers to a northern residence at the start of the
Nineteenth Dynasty are provided by the accounts of the way Moses,
having returned to the Eastern Delta to rescue his people, was urged
by the Lord to confront Pharaoh in the morning when he went
down to the banks of the Nile (Exodus, 7:15; 8:20).

It would seem that two reasonable deductions might be made
from these brief summaries of the biblical account of the Sojourn
and what we know of the seat of power in ancient Egypt: firstly, that
as shepherds were looked upon already as 'an abomination' when the
Israelites arrived in Egypt, their appearance on the scene must have
post-dated the Hyksos period, which was the root cause of the
anti-shepherd hostility; and, secondly, the fact that they were settled
in Goshen, remote from the seat of Pharaonic power, suggests that
this seat must at the time have been at Thebes, some 400 miles away
in Upper Egypt, rather than Avaris, the Hyksos capital and capital of
the land of Goshen in the Eastern Delta.

However, with no archaeological evidence to help them, early
Egyptologists were persuaded to believe – correctly, as it happens –
that the Exodus could not be assigned to an earlier time than the
Nineteenth Dynasty. It was when they attempted to decide in which
reign of the Nineteenth Dynasty it took place that they went astray.
Two points misled them: firstly, the figure of 430 years, given in the
Old Testament as the duration of the Sojourn, which they appear to
have accepted literally; and, secondly, the statement by Flavius
Josephus, the Jewish historian of the first century AD, which they also
seem not to have questioned, that the Israelite arrival took place
during the period of Hyksos rule. This view appeared to be justified
by some elaborate mathematical guesswork, for if we add up the
figures in the Bible between the start of the Sojourn and the Exodus,

and compare them with the then accepted Egyptian dates, we arrive at the following totals:

Biblical Figures	Years
Joseph in prison on a false charge of trying to seduce his master's wife (Gen., 41:1)	2
The good years before the famine in Egypt	7
The time when the Israelites came to Egypt after the second year of famine (Gen., 45:6)	2
The length of the Sojourn	430
Total:	441

Egyptian Dates:		Years
The length of the Hyksos rule		108
The length of the Eighteenth Dynasty[1]		240
The reigns of the first four kings of		
the Nineteenth Dynasty: Ramses I		2
	Seti I[2]	14
	Ramses II	67
	Merenptah	10
	Total:	441

The implication of these calculations is that Joseph must have arrived in Egypt as a slave, and been imprisoned, in the very first year of Hyksos rule. Despite the inherent improbability of this having happened, early Egyptologists, working forward from this date, came down firmly in favour of the Exodus under Moses having taken place during the reign of Merenptah, the fourth ruler of the Nineteenth Dynasty. Furthermore, as the Bible indicates that the Pharaoh of the Oppression, during whose reign Moses fled to Sinai, died while Moses was still in exile, it followed that, if Merenptah was the ruling king at the time of the Exodus, his predecessor, Ramses II, must have been king at the time of the Oppression.

These assumptions were shattered in 1896 when the British Egyptologist W. M. Flinders Petrie found a great granite stela in the funerary temple of Merenptah to the west of Thebes. The stela, which had originally belonged to Amenhotep III and bore a text of his, had been later usurped by Merenptah, who recorded on the other side what some scholars believed to be two separate military campaigns – one his victory over Libyan invaders, the other an expedition into Palestine/Syria, matching the biblical account of the pursuit of the Israelites by the Egyptians. The stela, now in the Cairo Museum, has come to be known as the Israel Stela because it includes – in an epilogue to its main story – the first, and only known, mention of Israel in an Egyptian text. As this stela is dated to Year 5 of Merenptah's reign and speaks of Israel as people already resident in Palestine, it upset completely the accepted wisdom of Egyptologists of the time. Not only had the Israelites left Egypt proper by that date, but, after spending a supposed forty years in the wilderness of Sinai, had made their way to Palestine and had been there long enough to develop into a power that posed a threat impelling the ruling Pharaoh to send troops to try to subdue them.

This caused the scholars of the time to adjust their position. Faced with the facts, and lacking any alternative explanation, they decided that at least one of the figures in the biblical account of Exodus, the forty years spent wandering in the wilderness, should not be taken literally. In addition they became ready to disregard the two Pharaohs of the biblical account – one for the Oppression and the other, his successor, for the time of Exodus – and came to the conclusion that Ramses II was the Pharaoh of both events during his long reign of sixty-seven years. This belief has since become widely accepted by the majority of both biblical scholars and Egyptologists, who have come to regard it as unquestionable historical fact. However, the choice of Ramses II as the Pharaoh of the Exodus assumes that the military confrontation between the people of Israel and Egyptian forces in Palestine took place during the first five years of Merenptah, but careful examination of the Israel Stela shows that this cannot have been the case.

In Year 5 of Merenptah's reign, Egypt was invaded by a Libyan leader named Merey, who had gathered to his banner a great army of Libyan tribes as well as five groups of 'peoples of the sea', who are believed to have come from the Greek islands. They attacked the Western Delta. Memphis, Heliopolis and other Lower Egyptian cities were forced to shut their gates against the invaders, citizens were unable to cultivate their land in safety or move from town to town. On this occasion the invaders were not merely looking for plunder, as had been the case with previous Libyan invasions, for they brought their women, children and cattle with them, clearly

intending permanent settlement. On learning of this threat, Merenptah sent an army that met the invaders at a locality in the Western
Delta known as 'The Fields Of Piyer'. After six hours of fierce
fighting, Merey fled, leaving his followers to their fate. The number
of Libyans killed in the fighting is said to have been 6000 with a
further 9000 taken prisoner.

The section of the Israel Stela devoted to these events opens with the
date: 'Year 5, third month of the third season (Spring), day 3'. This is
followed by the titulary and epithets of Merenptah and, after giving a
general picture of Egypt after the Libyan invasion, the defeat of the
enemy is described: 'Their advanced guard abandoned their rear.
Their legs did not stop, except to run. Their archers abandoned their
bows. The heart of their runners was weak from travelling. They
untied their waterskins . . . their packs were loosed and cast aside. The
wretched enemy prince of Rebu [Libya] was fled in the depth of the
night, by himself. No feather was on his head' – a sign of dishonour, as
Libyan warriors used to wear a feather in their head-dress – 'his feet
were unshod. The loaves for his provision were seized; he had no water
. . . to keep him alive. The face of his brother was fierce, to slay him;
among his commanders one fought his companion. Their tents were
burned up, made ashes. All his goods were food for the troops.'[3]

Then come some narrative sections, giving an account of the
defeat of the Libyans and the saving of Memphis, which are
followed by a religious composition in which the gods of Heliopolis
praise Merenptah for saving Memphis and Heliopolis. The last
section depicts the Egyptians joyful after their victory:

> Jubilation has gone forth in the towns of Egypt. They talk about
> victories . . . One walks with unhindered stride on the way, for there is
> no fear at all in the heart of the people. The forts are left to themselves,
> the wells [lie] open, accessible to the messengers. The battlements of
> the wall are calm in the sun until their watchers may awake . . . The
> cattle of the field are left as free to roam without herdsmen, [even]
> crossing the flood of the stream. There is no breaking out of a cry in
> the night: 'Halt! Behold, a comer comes with the speech of strangers!'
> but one goes and comes with singing. There is no cry of people as
> when there is mourning. Towns are settled anew again. He who
> ploughs his harvest will eat it. Re has turned himself [again] to Egypt.
> He [the king] was born as the one destined to [be] her protector, the
> King of Upper and Lower Egypt: Ba-en-Re, Meriamon; the son of
> Re: Merenptah Hotep-hir-Maat.

We have further accounts of the campaign against the Libyans in the war inscriptions of the Cairo and Heliopolis Columns, the Karnak War Inscriptions, the Athribis Stela (also called the Kom el Ahmar Stela), texts in which Merenptah has given accounts of the Libyan war in different parts of Egypt, and the Nubian Stelae, found in Nubia at Amada, Toshka, Wadi es Seboua and Amara West. With the exception of the Nubian Stelae, which describe a second war against the Nubians in Year 6 of Merenptah's reign, the only hostilities mentioned are those against the Libyans twelve months earlier.

What distinguishes the Israel Stela is that, unlike other texts, the account of the campaign against the Libyans is followed by a separate concluding section of twelve lines (three on the original stela), naming some foreign locations and peoples:

> The princes are prostrate, saying 'Mercy!' (The word used
>   here is the Canaanite *shalam*, meaning 'peace').
> Not one raises head among the Nine Bows.
> Desolation is for Tehenu; Hatti is pacified;
> Plundered is the Canaan with every evil;
> Carried off is Ashkelon; seized upon is Gezer;
> Yanoam is made as that which does not exist;
> Israel is laid waste, his seed is not;
> Hurru is become a widow for Egypt!
> All lands together, they are pacified;
> Everyone who was restless, he has been bound
>   by the King of Upper and Lower Egypt: Ba-en-Re
>   Meriamon; the son of Re: Merenptah Hotep-hir-Maat,
>   given life like Re every day.

Various interpretations have been placed upon the Israel Stela. It has been described, because of the poetic nature of its composition, as a hymn of victory. Some scholars have dismissed it as unhistorical and being rather a poetic eulogy of a universally victorious Pharaoh, while others have accepted that it provides a historical account of Merenptah's wars and victories. Although the stela is devoted almost entirely to the war against the invading Libyans, Libya (Tehenu) is also mentioned in the twelve-line epilogue. The other foreign references featured are:

• Hatti, the land of the Hittites in Asia Minor, then extending to include northern Syria;

• Canaan, west and south Palestine, bordering Sinai in the south, the Dead Sea to the east and the Mediterranean to the west;

• Ashkelon, a Canaanite port on the Mediterranean north of Gaza;

• Gezer, a Canaanite city west of Jerusalem:

• Yanoam, an important town of northern Palestine at the southern end of the Sea of Galilee;

• Israel: the sign used here does not indicate a land, but a people; and

• Hurru: although this word is sometimes used to indicate the whole land of Palestine/Syria, it could also mean the land of the biblical Horites, north of Mount Seir at the foot of the Dead Sea.

Merenptah was already an old man of about sixty when he came to the throne. At the time Egypt had enjoyed half a century of peace with Palestine/Syria since Merenptah's father, Ramses II, had concluded a treaty with the Hittites in Year 21 of his reign. No record of any major Egyptian conflict in Asia has been found during the remainder of the reign of Ramses II, and it is hardly to be believed that Merenptah, in the first five years of his reign and at his advanced age, fought these major wars against the Hittites in northern Syria and in Palestine/Syria without leaving any record of it other than the list of names in the epilogue to the Israel Stela.

This does not mean, however, that the epilogue is without historical value. We find no claim on the part of the king that it was *he* who subdued these foreign peoples, no dates or other details of any specific confrontation are to be found, only lasting peace. Yet, as the section implies, this peace had been achieved only through the defeat of Egypt's enemies in Asia. If Merenptah was not the king who confronted and vanquished the Israelites and other peoples in Palestine/Syria, who did? To find the answer we have to go back ninety years before Merenptah's accession to the throne, back to the very beginning of the Nineteenth Dynasty.

4

REBELLION IN SINAI

IF, as is generally accepted, the Israelites were still in Egypt at the end of the Eighteenth and beginning of the Nineteenth Dynasties, and if Egyptian troops set out in pursuit of them after the Exodus, as the Old Testament tells us, we should expect to find some evidence of this campaign in Egyptian records.

When Ramses I, founder of the Nineteenth Dynasty, came to the throne towards the end of the fourteenth century BC, Egyptian influence in Asia had been weakened. The Hittite kingdom of central Asia Minor, which had emerged as a new power under the rule of the energetic King Suppiluliuma, had conquered first the city states of northern Syria, then Mitanni, Egypt's northern ally, thus threatening Egyptian control of central Canaan. Yet, despite this circumstance, the only stela of Ramses I, found at Wadi Halfa in Nubia, makes no mention of any campaign in the north during his short reign. A reference to 'the captivity of his majesty' is taken to imply a possible military confrontation in Nubia.

Ramses I, already a very old man at the time of his accession, did not survive the end of his second year on the throne and was succeeded by his son, Seti I – and it is here, and in the earlier part of the reign of Seti's son and successor, Ramses II, that we find details of campaigns that match both the Exodus story and the Israel Stela.

At some point in Seti's first regnal year, a messenger arrived with the news: 'The Shasu enemies are plotting rebellion. Their tribal leaders are gathered in one place, standing on the foothills of Khor (a general term for Palestine and Syria), and they are engaged in turmoil and uproar. Each of them is killing his fellow. They do not consider the laws of the palace.'

There is evidence that this campaign took place immediately after the death of Ramses I, before the process of his mummification, which took seventy days, had been completed and before Seti I had been crowned as the new Pharaoh: 'The evidence ... suggests that Seti had already returned from his first campaign (against the Shasu) when he visited Thebes in his accession year, there to attend to the burial of his predecessor and to initiate the benefactions in the Amun Temple which have been dated to his first regnal year.'[1] This reinforces the idea that Ramses I could have died while pursuing the Israelites in Sinai. The name 'Shasu' was used by the Egyptians to designate the bedouin tribes of Sinai, nomadic people who spoke a west-Semitic language, and to differentiate between them and the Palestinians, whom they called 'Aamu'. (Later on, in the early centuries AD, the word 'Shasu' became the Coptic word *shos*, meaning shepherd.) The full account of this campaign against the Shasu, here identified as a people by the determinative that can indicate either a people or a land, is found in Seti I's war reliefs which occupy the entire exterior of the northern wall of the great Hypostyle Hall in Amun's temple at Karnak (see Appendix A(i): The Shasu Wars). The extreme point in the king's first war, shown on the bottom row of the eastern side of the wall and dated to his first year, is the capture of the city of Pe-Kanan (Gaza).

The second and middle row of this eastern wall shows a further war of Seti I to the north. Shortly after his coronation, Seti I set out again for western Asia. On this occasion the king marched with his army up the Mediterranean coast until he reached a point in north Palestine on the same level as the southern end of the Sea of Galilee, probably the city of Acco. He then divided his army into three divisions which moved eastward in three different branches to the cities of Yanoam in the north, Beth-Shan in the centre and Hammath in the south. The extreme end of this row shows the princes of Canaan felling the cedars in the Lebanon for the sacred boat of Amun in Thebes where, in his yearly festivals, the god was carried in a celebratory procession indicating the submission of the whole of Canaan and the Phoenician coast to the Pharaoh.

The first row of scenes at the bottom of the western wall of the Karnak temple façade depicts a war against the Hittites, who were at the time in northern Syria, where their strong centre was the city of Kadesh on the Orontes river, but the Hittite power was not broken. Although here again we have no date for the Hittite war, it is accepted that it could not have taken place in Year 1 of Seti I. The second, middle row of this western wall deals with two separate wars Seti I fought against the Libyans. No date is given, but they could have occurred any time after Year 1. The third, and top, row is again lost apart from a scene on the right extremity representing the war with the Hittites at Kadesh.

Ramses II, who followed his father, Seti I, on the throne in the early part of the thirteenth century BC, spent the first decade fighting in Asia. His first campaign began in Year 4 when he swept through Canaan and along the Phoenician coast, probably as far as Simyra, which had been under the control of the kingdom of Amurru, to the east in northern Syria. He then attacked Amurru itself, which had an allegiance with the Hittite king, Muwatallis.

In the spring of the following year Ramses II returned to Syria, this time to conquer Kadesh. After fierce fighting, in which the king himself played a courageous role, he succeeded in defeating the Hittites and capturing the city. His third Asiatic campaign took place in Year 8 of his reign. On this occasion he had first to crush unrest in Galilee before embarking on other campaigns – recovery of the area of Damascus, strengthening his hold upon the Phoenician coast lands and attacking the Amurrite city of Dapur to the north of Kadesh. Two years later, in Year 10, the king engaged in a second attack upon Dapur, which had rebelled: 'Sometime in regnal Year 10, or shortly afterwards, Ramses II appears to have left Egypt; perhaps at this time he conducted the campaigns into Transjordan that are represented at the walls of Luxor since they do not fit into the accounts of his earlier campaigns.'[2]

Ramses II returned to Beth-Shan in Year 18, after which negotiations began between himself and Hattusili III, the new King of the Hittites, that resulted ultimately in a treaty of peace and alliance between them in Year 21. This treaty was later consolidated by a marriage between Ramses II and a Hittite princess in his Year 34 and a second princess a decade later. Details of the treaty, known from both Egyptian and Hittite sources, can be found in Appendix A(ii): The Hattusili Treaty, but the subsequent situation that obtained between the two countries is summed up by Schmidt, an American Egyptologist, in the following terms in his book *Ramses II*: 'With Year 30 and the first Jubilee, a time of peace and tranquility seems to have descended upon Egypt; from that year onward, there is no reference to warfare or strife. Building activity seems to have become Ramses's primary public concern, and, as far as one can tell, the economy of the land prospered.'

Some of the wars conducted by Ramses II were a continuation of the campaigns against the Shasu that had been initiated by his father, Seti I. There are several references to them, although no specific dates are to be found, at Tanis, one of the Ramesside cities in the north-east of the Delta, south of Lake Menzalah:

> Obelisk V, W. Face: ' . . . who made a great slaughter in the land of the Shasu'; Obelisk IX, W. Face: ' . . . who plunders the Shasu-land'; Stela II: ' . . . he has destroyed the inheritance of the Shasu-land and made them [the chiefs] bring their tribute to Egypt for ever and ever'; Stela V: ' . . . who made great slaughter in the land of the Shasu'; Stella [VIII], frag. 3: ' . . . the Shasu, taken off as c[aptives . . .]'; Stela IX, Face B, 3: ' . . . who plundered the Shasu-land'.

We also find at Karnak, south of the Hittite treaty and Ascalon-scene, over a file of prisoners: ' . . . the Shasu whom His Majesty plundered'.[3]

Where did these battles against the Shasu take place? Professor Kenneth A. Kitchen of Liverpool University, citing various Egyptian sources, has concluded that Mount Seir formed part of the Shasu-land and is to be equated with Edom of Genesis (36: 8–9). (See also Appendix A (iii): A Dissenting Voice.) Of a number of other names mentioned he says that Bernard Grdseloff, the Polish Egypt-ologist, has 'aptly compared *Rbn* with the Laban of Deuteronomy, 1:1 (and Libnah of Numbers, 33:20–21) and *Sm't* with the Shimea thites of I Chronicles, 2:55, all in the area of Seir/Edom, the Negeb, or the Araba rift valley between them', and concludes that the evidence 'clearly suggests that Ramses or troops of his raided the Negeb, the uplands of Seir or Edom, and perhaps part of the inter-vening Araba rift valley . . . Thus we have evidence for the activity of Ramses II (or at least of his forces) in both Edom and Moab (to the south and south-east of the Dead Sea).'[4]

Dr Kitchen next proceeds to try to provide possible dates for the military confrontations between Ramses II and the Shasu: 'It is difficult to place these Transjordanian activities within the general pattern of Ramses II's Asiatic wars as at present known, and a summary must suffice. The first campaign would be that of Year 4: the "middle" stele at Nahr el-Kelb, north of Beirut, gives this date clearly. The second campaign – explicitly so-called – is that of Year 5 in Syria that ended in the notorious battle of Kadesh. Then a campaign in Year 8 in Palestine, Syria and Phoenicia is commemorated on the rear face of the pylon of the Ramasseum. Then comes the south stele of Ramses II at Nahr el-Kelb, perhaps dated Year 10, indicating further activity in Phoenicia. At some time in this general period belong the Syrian wars commemorated by the Karnak series of reliefs and related scenes at Luxor, besides other traces. However, the Egyptians had also to deal with matters nearer home, in Palestine. An undated scene at Karnak showing the submission of Ascalon is usually ascribed to Ramses II. And in his Year 18 is dated a stele from Beth-Shan that records virtually no concrete facts, but in itself may indicate activity in that region. This brings us to Year 21 and the Hittite Treaty, after which dated records of warfare cease.

'The foregoing picture may suggest that for his first ten years Ramses's Asiatic activities were concentrated on Syria and the Hittite problem. Perhaps this gave way to a stalemate ending in the treaty of Year 21. In the meantime, in the Years 11–20, unrest had developed in Palestine (Ascalon relief; Beth Shan stele, Job Stone)' – inscribed stones of Ramses found in Syria/Palestine – 'Perhaps one may also place the Edomite and Moabite undertakings within this period.'[5]

It would seem that all military confrontations in Asia came to an end for the Egyptians by Year 21 of Ramses II when the peace treaty was concluded with the Hittites. The wars with the Shasu must, consequently, all have taken place before this date.

We therefore have the situation that, in the first year of Seti I, the Shasu were emerging from Sinai and posing a threat to Canaan, Edom and Moab. Then, at the time of Ramses II, about two decades later, they have left Sinai and are to be found in Edom and Moab. If we compare the sudden appearance of the Shasu bedouin and their movements with the Israelite Exodus from Sinai we find that they followed the very same route. Dr Kitchen, too, was struck by this fact: 'For Old Testament studies, the new information has some bearing on the date of the Hebrew conquest of central Transjordan and their entry into W. Palestine, not to mention the date of the Exodus.'⁶

And so to return to the epilogue of the Israel Stela . . .

The evidence available makes it clear that Merenptah had only peace in Asia during his reign. There is no reference whatever to his having conducted any war in Palestine/Syria. It therefore seems clear that the epilogue to the Israel Stela refers not to his own campaigns, but to the status quo he inherited, the situation created by his grandfather, Seti I, and his father, Ramses II:

• **Tehenu (Libya)**: Here Seti I's wars are meant, as Merenptah's own war with the invading Libyans had been described in the Israel Stela and elsewhere.

• **Hatti**: The land of the Hittites. We saw how both Seti I and Ramses II fought the Hittites in northern Syria until a peace treaty was ultimately agreed. There is no account of any war after that date.

• **Canaan**: The land of western Palestine, which also includes the cities of Ascalon and Gezer. It was Seti I who regained this section in the Nineteenth Dynasty and Ramses II consolidated his victory.

• **Yanoam**: To the south of the Sea of Galilee in north Palestine. It was captured by Seti I in his Year 1.

• **Hurru**: Whether it referred to Palestine/Syria in general or the Horite land to the south of the Dead Sea, both Seti I and Ramses II fought in these areas.

There is one other name in the epilogue – Israel. Yet there is no mention at all of the Shasu, bedouin of Semitic origin, nomads with no fixed city or country, striking north from Sinai and threatening Canaan, Edom and Moab. On the evidence the inescapable conclusions are that Merenptah never fought Israel, but his father and grandfather did, and the terms Israelites and the Shasu are, in this particular case, one and the same people. As Moses and the tribe of Israel united in Sinai with some local Midianite elements, they were first identified as Shasu by Egyptian scribes. Later, when the Israelite identity became clear – and now that they were no longer in Sinai, but had settled in Palestine – the scribe of the Merenptah Stela was able to recognize them as such.

It is the preconceptions of the majority of scholars, Dr Kitchen among them, that have been the basic barrier to acceptance of this historical truth. They have failed to take into consideration the point made by Jean Yoyotte, one of the leading French Egyptologists of our time, that the 'biblical account of the Exodus, which was written much later by Hebrew scribes, contains literary embellishments about miraculous events of the flight'.[7] Thus they have sought evidence of great catastrophes that befell Egypt and expected to find the names of Moses and Joshua in Egyptian texts. More misleading, through misinterpretation of the Israel Stela and their belief that the Sojourn lasted 430 years, they have sought evidence of the Exodus into Sinai in the wrong eras, the reign of Ramses II or of Merenptah.

As long ago as the early 1960s, however, Yoyotte, who had done a great deal of work in the Delta and among the Ramesside remains, became one of the few to see through the 'embellishments' of the biblical account and identify the historical core of the story – that the Shasu wars are the only possible equivalent of the biblical story of the Exodus:

'The persecution of the Jews was undoubtedly part of the Ramesside campaign against the Shasu (bedouin) ... The exact date of the Exodus is disputed. According to the Bible, the Jews toiled in a town called Ramses, and a stele of the time of Merenptah, a son of Ramses II, speaks of the "annihilation" of Israel. From this evidence it has been deduced that their persecutors were Ramses II and Merenptah and that the Exodus took place under the latter in about 1200 BC. But the "Israel Stele", in fact, gives the impression that the Jews had already returned to Palestine by this time. Considering biblical chronology and the results of excavations at Jericho, it seems probable that their sufferings took place at the time of Seti I ...

'The "Israel Stele" is a misleading name for a document consisting of twenty-eight lines, twenty-five of which describe the triumph of the king over Libya. Mention is made of Palestine only in a three-line epilogue in which the famous name Israel appears among others. As far as the Ramesside government was concerned, the Exodus was merely a migration of bedouin labour, the Shasu among others.'[8]

As we said before, there are strong indications that the Exodus did not take place before the Ramesside period of the Nineteenth Dynasty. However, as Seti I campaigned against Israel in north Sinai and south Palestine immediately on succeeding to the throne, the

Israelites must have left Egypt proper during the short reign of his father, Ramses I.

This chronology would make sense in more ways than one in the light of the Book of Exodus. As we shall see, before coming to the throne, Pa-Ramses (later Ramses I) had been appointed by Horemheb as his vizier, Commander of the Troops, Overseer of Foreign Countries, Overseer of the Fortress of Zarw, Master of the Horse. Ramses, himself said to have come from the Eastern Delta, was therefore at that time the most powerful man in Egypt after Horemheb. If the Bible, which never gives the name of the ruling Pharaoh, names the Eastern Delta city built by the harsh labour of the Israelites as Ramses, the name must derive not from Pharaoh but from vizier Ramses, who personally forced them to work. Then, while Moses was still hiding in Sinai, the Lord informed him that the King of Egypt (Horemheb) had died. In this case, the king whom Moses met after his return must have been a new king (Ramses I). Yet this new king could not have ruled for a long time as, after the different punishments inflicted upon him for not allowing the Israelites to depart, that by their nature take one full year as they are seasonal and follow the inundation of the Nile, they leave, he follows them and dies.

The Bible does not state directly that the pursuing Pharaoh died in the waters although this is implied:

> And the waters returned, and covered the chariots, and the horsemen, and all the host of Pharaoh that came into the sea after them; there remained not so much as one of them. (Exodus, 14:28)

The Koran, however, makes it clear that the pursuing Pharaoh, too, was drowned:

> We took the Children
> Of Israel across the sea:
> Pharaoh and his hosts followed them
> In insolence and spite.
> At length, when overwhelmed
> With the flood, he said:
> 'I believe that there is no god
> Except Him Whom the Children
> Of Israel believe in: ...'
>
> (It was said to him) ...

'This day shall We save thee[9]
In thy body, that thou
Mayest be a Sign to those
Who come after thee!
But verily, many among mankind
Are heedless of Our Signs!'(Sura X:90–92)[10]

Ramses I is known to have ruled for less than two years. The biblical account of this part of the Exodus story cannot therefore agree more precisely than it does with what we know of the history of Ancient Egypt at this time. If Ramses I was the Pharaoh of the Exodus, Horemheb was the Pharaoh of the Oppression. But how long had the Israelites been in Egypt when these events took place?

5

SOJOURN – AND THE
MOTHER OF MOSES

CONTRADICTORY accounts in the Old Testament make it difficult
to arrive at the precise date when the Patriarch Joseph and the
Israelites arrived in Egypt. As we saw earlier, we are offered a choice
of three periods for the Sojourn – 430 years, 400 years and four
generations. In *Stranger in the Valley of the Kings* I argued that the
figure of 430 years was wrongly arrived at by the biblical editor in
the following way: firstly, he added up the four generations named
in the Old Testament account of the Descent into Egypt as if each
new generation were born on the very day that his father died,
having lived for more than a century:

Levi	137 years
Kohath	133 years
Amram	137 years
Moses	120 years
Total:	527 years

Then he deducted the years (fifty-seven) that Levi lived before the
Descent – according to the Talmud he lived eighty years after the
Descent and died at the age of 137 – plus the forty years Moses is said
to have lived after the Exodus. This left him with his total of 430
years. This method of computation is obviously unsound, and I have
since been pleased to find that many biblical scholars agree with my
view that the figure of 430 years for the Sojourn is not to be taken
literally – a variety of explanations are put forward – while it is,
surprisingly, the majority of Egyptologists who appear to look upon
it as a sacred figure not to be challenged.

One eminent biblical scholar who has commented on the length of the sojourn is the late Umberto Cassuto, formerly Professor of Biblical Studies at the Hebrew University of Jerusalem, who wrote: '... the numbers given in the Torah are mostly round or symbolic figures, and their purpose is to teach us something by their harmonious character ... these numbers are based on the sexagesimal system, which occupied in the ancient East a place similar to that of the decimal system in our days.

'The chronological unit in this system was a period of sixty years, which the Babylonians called a šuš. One šuš consisted of sixty years and two šuš of a hundred and twenty years – a phrase that is used by Jews to this day. In order to convey that a given thing continued for a very long time, or comprised a large number of units, a round figure signifying a big amount according to the sexagesimal system was employed, for example, 600, 6000, 600,000 or 300, 3000 or 300,000 or 120, 360, 1200, 3600 and so forth. I further demonstrated there that, if it was desired to indicate a still larger amount, these figures were supplemented by seven or a multiple of seven. The number 127, for instance (Genesis, 23:1), was based on this system.'[1] Elsewhere Professor Cassuto makes the point that the figure forty, found frequently in the Bible, is similarly used as a kind of shorthand for a period of time and is not to be taken literally.

He then goes on to try to harmonize the two Israelite traditions – that the Sojourn lasted 430 years (six times sixty, plus seventy) and four generations. He cites as his four generations Levi, Kohath, Amram and Aaron, who is said to have been the brother of Moses, and adds together the years they are given in the Old Testament. This approach is permissible, he argues, because

> a) Each generation endured the burden of exile throughout the times of its exile, and its distress was not diminished by the fact that it was shared by another generation during a certain portion of that period; hence in computing the total length of exile suffered, one is justified to some extent in reckoning the ordeal of each generation in its entirety, b) A similar and parallel system was used in the chronological calculations of the Mesopotamians. In the Sumerian King List, dynasties that were partly coeval, one reigning in one city and the other elsewhere, are recorded consecutively, and are reckoned as if they ruled successively. Consequently, if we add up the years that these dynasties reigned, we shall arrive at a total that is actually the sum of the periods of their kingship, although it will exceed the time that elapsed from the commencement of the first dynasty to the end of the last.

Professor Cassuto then proceeds to make the following calculation:

Levi	137 years
Kohath	133 years
Amram	137 years
Aaron	83 years
Total:	490 years

Here he points out that 'upon deducting from [this total] (in order to allow for the time that Levi and Kohath dwelt in the land of Canaan before they emigrated to Egypt) one unit of time, to wit, sixty years, we obtain exactly a period of 430 years, which is the number recorded in Exodus, 12:40.' The 430 years are thus the total years of the four generations and are not to be taken as representing the period of time that elapsed between the Israelites' arrival in Egypt and their departure.

Only two Hebrew generations, Amram and Moses, were actually born in Egypt – Kohath arrived with his father, Levi (Genesis, 46:11) – and, in working backwards from the reign of Ramses I, the Pharaoh of the Exodus, to try to establish the time of the Descent, calculation depends upon the age young Hebrew boys married at the time and had their first child. It seems reasonable to suggest that the period in which the Descent took place should be sought within the range of some fifty to eighty years earlier than the Exodus.

It may be helpful at this point to show how this chronology accords with that arrived at, through a different approach, in *Stranger in the Valley of the Kings*, which sought to establish that Joseph the Patriarch was the same person as Yuya – vizier, Master of the Horse and Deputy of the King in the Chariotry to both Tuthmosis IV and Amenhotep III – whose mummy, despite the fact that he did not appear to be of royal blood, was found in the Valley of the Kings in the early years of this century.

There I argued that Joseph/Yuya arrived in Egypt as a slave during the reign of Amenhotep II and, after his spell of service in the household of Potiphar, captain of Pharaoh's guard, followed by his imprisonment on a false charge of adultery, was eventually released and appointed vizier by Tuthmosis IV, who was a dreamer like Joseph himself. Once in office he brought the tribe of Israel down from Canaan to join him in Egypt where they settled at Goshen in the Eastern Delta.

According to the Book of Genesis, the total number of Israelites who settled in Egypt was seventy. Yet we are provided with only sixty-nine names – sixty-six who made the Descent, plus Joseph and his two sons, Manasseh (Egyptian, Anen) and Ephraim (Egyptian, Aye). It is a reasonable deduction that the seventieth member of the tribe of Israel was also already in Egypt. I believe that she was a daughter of Joseph, Tiye. Why would her name be omitted? It may be because it is common in the Bible not to mention the names of women unless they are particularly important to the story that is being told. Alternatively, in the lingering bitterness surrounding the Exodus, her name may have been suppressed centuries later by the biblical editor in order to conceal this historical link between the royal house of Egypt and the tribe of Israel which would show that Moses, their greatest leader, was of mixed Egyptian-Israelite origins.

The positions held by Joseph and his wife, who was the king's 'ornament' (khrt nsw), a post which might be said to combine the duties of a modern butler and lady-in-waiting, meant that both had to live in the royal residence. It was thus that the young prince, Amenhotep, grew up with, and fell in love with, Tiye. Then, after his father's early death when the young prince was about twelve, he married his sister, Sitamun, who was most probably an infant, in order to inherit the throne, but soon afterwards also married Tiye and made her, rather than Sitamun, his Great Royal Wife (queen). The evidence that Tiye was about eight at the time of the wedding indicates that Tuthmosis IV must have appointed Joseph to his various positions, including vizier, early in his short eight-year reign.

Tiye, we know, was the mother of Akhenaten – but she must also have been the mother of Moses if he and Akhenaten were the same person.

While the second chapter of the Book of Exodus describes the daughter of Pharaoh as being the royal mother of Moses, the Koran claims that the mother was the queen, Pharaoh's wife. It is strange that, as both holy books must have had the same origin, whether God's inspiration or a literary source, they should not agree in this important matter, particularly when Egyptian custom would not have allowed an unmarried princess to adopt a child. How then has the variation arisen?

There are two sources for the misunderstanding. In the first place, the scribe who wrote down the Book of Exodus was faced with two traditions – that the mother of Moses was an Israelite and that she was *b-t Phar'a*, literally 'the house of Pharaoh'. Unaware, as she had already been omitted from the Joseph story in the Book of Genesis, that Joseph had a daughter named Tiye, who became Pharaoh's wife, he resolved this initial difficulty by creating two mothers, one Hebrew, who gave birth to Moses, and one royal, who adopted him and brought him up as her son. That he chose to identify this adoptive mother as a princess rather than a queen has a philological explanation.

The word for 'daughter' and the word for 'house' were written identically *b-t* in early Hebrew and open to misconstruction by anyone not familiar with Egyptian usage. To an Egyptian the word 'house' was also used – and, indeed, still is – to signify a wife: to a Hebrew it meant either 'house' in the sense of a building or 'household'. Later, both Hebrew and the language of Ancient Egypt, which had no written vowels, began to use some consonants like *y* to indicate long vowels. Thus, for example, we find a slightly different spelling of *b-t Phar'a* in the Book of Genesis account of events when Jacob, the father of Joseph, died. Joseph, who wanted permission to take him back to Canaan for burial, did not speak to the king directly but to *b-y-t Phar'a*, the Hebrew word signifying 'the house of Pharaoh': 'And when the days of his mourning were past, Joseph spake unto the house of Pharaoh, saying, If now I have found grace in your eyes, speak, I pray you, in the ears of Pharaoh . . .' (Genesis, 50:4). 'Pharaoh' itself means literally 'the great house'. Thus *b-y-t Phar'a* signifies the 'house of the great house', which in the Egyptian sense would mean the queen, whom in this case I regard as Joseph's own daughter, Tiye, whose intercession he sought in the matter of his father's burial.

There is an example of similar usage earlier in the Book of Genesis when the brothers who had earlier sold Joseph into slavery made their second trip to Egypt at a time of famine. On this occasion Joseph revealed his true identity and was so moved that he 'wept aloud: and the Egyptians and the house of Pharaoh heard' (Genesis, 45:2). This has been construed as meaning that Joseph's weeping was so loud that it was audible in the royal palace, but I interpret it as meaning that the queen, his daughter, heard the news of his brothers' arrival.

In this second example the word used is again *b-y-t Phar'a*. However, in the Book of Exodus, where we have the story of Pharaoh's daughter going down to bathe, finding the Hebrew child in the rushes and later adopting him, the *y* is absent and we have simply *b-t Phar'a*. My suspicion was that during the ninth century BC, the early stages of written Hebrew when the Old Testament was given permanent form, all three words had been written in this way, referring in each instance to the 'house of Pharaoh', the reigning queen, and the *y* in the two Genesis references had been added later, as written Hebrew developed, because the scribe did not understand the special Egyptian usage of the word 'house'. This, while not easy to establish, proved to be the case.

The Hebrew Masoretic text we have now goes back only to around the tenth century AD and could not throw any light on the matter. Nor could sections of the Old Testament found in the caves of Qumran, near the Dead Sea, some of which belong to the second century BC. Confirmation was eventually provided by the Moabite Stone. This black basalt inscribed stone was left by Mesha, King of Moab, at Dhiban (biblical Dibon, to the east of the Dead Sea) to commemorate his revolt against Israel and his subsequent rebuilding of many important towns (II Kings, 3:4-5). The stone was found by the Revd F. Klein, a German missionary working with the Church Missionary Society, on 19 August 1868 and is now in the Louvre in Paris. The inscription refers to the triumph of 'Mesha, ben Chemosh, King of Moab', whose father reigned over Moab for thirty years. He tells how he (Mesha) threw off the yoke of Israel and honoured his god, Chemosh.[2]

According to the American archaeologist James B. Pritchard, a professor at the University of Pennsylvania: 'The date of the Mesha Stone is fixed roughly by the reference to Mesha, King of Moab, in II Kings, 3:4, after 849 BC. However, since the contents of the stela point to a date toward the end of the king's reign, it seems probable that it should be placed between 840 and 820, perhaps about 830 BC in round numbers.'[3] The text reads: 'I [am] Mesha, son of Chemosh ... King of Moab ... I said to all the people: "Let each of you make a cistern for himself in his house."'

The inscription, written in the Semitic language used for writing at the time by the Jews of Israel, confirms that the word for 'house' was then written simply *b-t*, without the insertion of 'y' and was the same as the word for daughter. This is also true of the way it was written in the Phoenician language.[4]

When 'house' and 'daughter' were written identically there was no cause to differentiate between them. The situation changed when development of the Hebrew language made it possible to alter the spelling slightly to give two different words. The scribes then found themselves in a dilemma, based on their ignorance of the fact the 'house' had the Egyptian meaning 'wife'. It now becomes clear what happened. If the word simply meant 'house' or 'household', it made sense that Joseph approached the house of Pharaoh on the subject of his father's funeral and that his weeping could be heard in the king's house, but it made no sense at all to suggest that the whole of the king's household had come 'down to wash herself at the river' (Exodus, 2:5) or had become the mother to the child. The scribe therefore decided in the Exodus reference to retain the alternative meaning of 'daughter' whereas it, too, should have been changed to 'house', signifying the wife of Pharaoh, his queen.

There is a similar case of semantic confusion, cited by Professor Cassuto, with the source again the Book of Exodus: 'And Moses took his wife and sons, and set them upon an ass, and he returned to the land of Egypt ...' (Exodus, 4:20). Professor Cassuto remarks: 'The plural – sons – is somewhat difficult, for till now only one son (Gershom) had been mentioned (Exodus, 2:22), and below, in Exodus, 4:25, we find "her son", in the singular, as though Moses and Zipporah had just one son. Possibly the ancient spelling here was *b n h*, which could be read as either singular or plural, and the singular was actually intended; when, however, the scribes introduced the present spelling they wrote *ba na w* [his sons] (the Septuagint [the Greek version of the Old Testament], too, has the plural) because they thought the two sons spoken of (later) in Exodus, 18:3-4 were already born.'[5]

The royal mother of Moses was therefore the Queen of Egypt. But which queen? As we saw earlier (Chapter Two), Manetho, the third century BC historian, identified the reign of Amenhotep III and Queen Tiye – while son of Habu was still alive, some time before the king's Year 34 – as the right time for the religious rebellion that led to the persecution of Akhenaten's followers, and Redford has made the point that it is not built simply on popular tales and traditions of Manetho's time, but on old traditions, passed on orally at first, then set down in writing, that he found in his temple library.

If we compare in greater detail the Koran account (Sura XX:38–40 and Sura XXVIII:7–15) with the biblical account (Exodus, 2:1–12) of Moses' birth and eventual flight after the slaying incident, we find the stories are fundamentally the same, yet also contain some interesting differences:

EXODUS	KORAN
A man of the house of Levi marries a daughter of Levi, who bears him a son. She conceals him for three months before hiding him in a rush basket among the reeds by the bank of the Nile.	Moses's mother feeds him for a while. Then, afraid for his life, places him in a chest and throws it into the *water*, which floats it on to the bank.
The child's sister watches from afar. Yet it seems her position was close to Pharaoh's residence as she saw Pharaoh's daughter when she came down to the river to bathe. The princess notices the rush basket in its hiding place and sends her maid to fetch it. On opening the basket, she sees the child, which is crying, and takes pity on it.	The child is picked up by 'Pharaoh's people'. Pharaoh's wife asks them not to kill him.
	Moses' mother becomes worried about his safety and is on the brink of revealing her fears. She asks Moses' sister to follow him and she is able to watch Pharaoh's people without their noticing.
The sister offers to fetch a nurse for the child. The princess accepts, and the sister fetches the child's mother. She is asked by the princess to nurse the child in return for payment.	The child refuses to accept a feeding nurse, but his sister walks in and offers to tell them about a household that would look after the child for them.

The child grows and the nurse-mother returns him to Pharaoh's daughter to be brought up as her son. Pharaoh's daughter names the child Moses.	Moses returns to his real mother.
Moses grows up and, going out to visit his Israelite relatives, comes across an Egyptian smiting a Hebrew and slays him.	Moses grows up. One day he enters the city, unnoticed by its inhabitants, and sees two people – one a believer in his own religion, the other an enemy – and slays the enemy.

The significant differences in these accounts are:

• The Koran story does not give us the names of Moses' parents;

• While the biblical story tells us that the rush basket was left by the river, the Koran refers to 'the water', which could be a lake joined to the river;

• While Pharaoh's daughter (or wife, as we saw before) is said by the Bible to have been the child's rescuer, it was 'Pharaoh's people' according to the Koran;

• The biblical version says that Moses' sister watches events while the child is in its basket, hidden in the reeds outside Pharaoh's palace, but this is not the case in the Koran; there it is only after the child was in the possession of 'Pharaoh's people' that his sister is asked by the mother, who must have been in the vicinity at the time, to follow after him, which she does secretly, indicating that this incident must have taken place in the palace itself;

• Pharaoh's wife, who, according to the Koran, had nothing to do with the child until he had fallen into the hands of 'Pharaoh's people', then intervened to prevent them – probably the guards – from killing him;

• Once the child was in the custody of 'Pharaoh's people', we are told in the Koran that the child's mother became worried about what might happen to him. Why would she be worried unless she was in a position to know what was going on inside the palace?

• The mother, according to the Koran, was about to reveal her hidden fears for the safety of the child. This is the strongest indication so far that the child's mother and Pharaoh's wife were one and the same person. After her intervention to prevent him from being killed, he was taken away from her. She then became so worried that she was about to reveal that she was the mother of the baby, but instead she sent the sister to find out what was happening inside the palace;

• Rather than killing the child, Moses' sister, according to the Koran, succeeded in persuading 'Pharaoh's people' to place him in the care of a family that would look after him. Here there is another crucial point. Where the Bible indicates that the child was later returned to Pharaoh's daughter to be brought up by her, the Koran makes it clear that this event was the actual return of Moses to his real mother;

• The Koran story states that Moses went out of the palace and 'entered the city', thus implying that the palace was not far from the city, and use of the word 'unnoticed' here can only mean that he was neither dressed in princely attire at the time, nor was he attended by guards;

• While the biblical account of the slaying incident describes the two men who were fighting as an Egyptian and a Hebrew, the Koran version of the story makes them a follower of Moses' religion and an enemy, implying that at this stage, even before his flight to Sinai, Moses had a different religion that had followers as well as enemies.

6

THE RIGHTFUL SON AND HEIR

IF we assume for the moment what is as yet far from proved – that Moses and Akhenaten were the same person – it is possible to assemble a brief outline of the historical facts behind the varied, and at times extravagant, accounts of the life of the greatest Jewish hero that we find in the Old Testament and other holy books, and to offer an explanation of why the world should have remembered him by the name of Moses.

Moses, the second son of Amenhotep III and Queen Tiye, was born, I believe, at the frontier fortified city of Zarw, probably in 1394 BC (see also Chapter Eleven). His elder brother, Tuthmosis, had already disappeared mysteriously, and, in view of the threats that were about to be made to the life of Moses, it seems more than likely that the disappearance of Tuthmosis was not the result of natural causes. The reason for the king's hostility to the young princes was the fact that Tiye, their mother, was not the legitimate heiress. She could therefore not be accepted as the consort of the State god Amun.

Furthermore, as she herself was of mixed Egyptian-Israelite blood, her children would not, by Egyptian custom, be regarded as heirs to the throne. If her son acceded to the throne, this would be regarded as forming a new dynasty of non-Egyptian, non-Amunite, part-Israelite kings over Egypt. This is exactly the light in which the Amunite priests and nobles of Egypt, the watchdogs of old traditions, regarded Akhenaten. It was not he who first rejected the position of son of Amun: it was they, the Amunists, who refused to accept him as the legitimate heir to the throne.

Consequently, the king, motivated by the possible threat to the dynasty and confrontation with the priesthood, instructed the midwives to kill Tiye's child in secrecy if it proved to be a boy. The

Talmud story confirms that it was the survival of Moses that Pharaoh wanted to prevent, because, once he knew that Moses had been born and survived, his attempt to kill all the male Israelite children at birth was abandoned: 'After Moses was placed in the Nile, they [Pharaoh's astrologers] told Pharaoh that the redeemer had already been cast into the water, whereupon Pharaoh rescinded his decree that the male children should be put to death. Not only were all the future children saved, but even the . . . children [who had already been] cast into the Nile with Moses.'[1]

Zarw was largely surrounded by lakes and a branch of the Nile. On learning – perhaps from the midwives – that her son's life was in danger, Tiye sent Moses by water to the safe-keeping of her Israelite relations at nearby Goshen. Yet the biblical story makes it clear that the king was still afraid of Moses. Why should the mighty Pharaoh fear Moses if he was simply a child of the despised Asiatic shepherds? In those circumstances, how could he have posed a threat to the Dynasty?

Moses spent most of his youth in the Eastern Delta where he absorbed the traditional Israelite beliefs in a God without an image. It was not until he was a grown boy that he was finally allowed to take up residence at Thebes, the capital city in Upper Egypt and the principal centre of worship of the State god, Amun. By this time the health of his father had begun to deteriorate and Tiye's power had increased correspondingly. In order to ensure her son's ultimate inheritance of the throne, she therefore arranged for him to marry his half-sister Nefertiti – the daughter of Amenhotep III by *his* sister, Sitamun, the legitimate heiress – and to be appointed his father's coregent, with special emphasis on Nefertiti's role in order to placate the priests and nobles.

Moses, whose religious ideas were already well developed, offended the Amunite priesthood from the start of the coregency by building temples to his monotheistic God, the Aten, at Karnak and Luxor. In a climate becoming increasingly hostile, Tiye eventually persuaded him to leave Thebes and found a new capital for himself at Tell el-Amarna, some 200 miles to the north, roughly halfway between Thebes and the Eastern Delta. Moses named his new city Akhetaten – the city of the horizon of the Aten – in honour of his new God.

It was during this period that the old king became concerned about the growing power of the Israelites and sought advice about how to deal with them. But this cannot be simply because they had grown in number and might side with his enemies: the growth in their numbers would simply have provided him with more slaves to work for him and made him stronger in the face of foreign aggressors. What we are dealing with is a religious revolution. The vast increase in the numbers of the Israelites by this time was not simply a matter of their birth rate: the declaration by Moses that the Aten, his God, was the only true God, had attracted many Egyptian adherents who, as a result of their conversion to the new religion, became regarded as Israelites. Other evidence suggests that the Israelites had also achieved political importance and high position in the land, with, according to Manetho, priests and learned people in their ranks. At the same time, those of Moses' followers who did not follow him to Amarna were, according to Manetho, set to harsh work in the stone quarries.

At Amarna the monotheistic ideas of Moses underwent further development and, when he became sole ruler on the death of his father, Amenhotep III, after the end of his Year 38 – Year 12 of Moses – he shut down the temples of the ancient gods of Egypt, cut off all financial support for them and sent the priests home. These actions caused so much bitter resentment that, in his Year 15, Moses was forced to install his brother, Semenkhkare, as his coregent at Thebes. This action served only to delay the eventual showdown. In his Year 17 Moses was warned by his uncle, Aye, the second son of the Patriarch Joseph (Yuya), of a plot against his life, and he abdicated and fled to Sinai, taking with him his pharaonic symbol of authority, the staff topped by a bronze serpent. Semenkhkare did not long survive the departure of Moses – perhaps only a few days – and was replaced on the throne by Moses' son, the boy king Tutankhamun, who restored the old gods, but attempted a compromise by allowing the Aten to be worshipped alongside them. Tutankhamun ruled for at least nine, and perhaps ten, years and was succeeded by Aye, his great-uncle, who ruled for four years before the army leader, Horemheb, brought the era of Amarna rule to an end.

The bitterness which divided the country at the time is indicated by the actions of Horemheb and the Ramesside kings who followed him. The names of the Amarna kings were excised from king lists and monuments in a studied campaign to try to remove all trace of them from Egypt's memory, and it was forbidden even to mention in conversation the name of Akhenaten. In addition, the Israelites were put to the harsh work of building the treasure cities of Pithom and Raamses.

On the death of Horemheb, there was no legitimate Eighteenth Dynasty heir. Ramses, Horemheb's elderly vizier, took power as Ramses I, the first ruler of the Nineteenth Dynasty. On hearing of Horemheb's death, Moses returned from Sinai to challenge Ramses' right to the throne. With him he brought his sceptre of authority, the bronze serpent. The wise men of Egypt were assembled to decide between the rival claimants to the throne, but, while they chose Moses as the rightful heir, Ramses controlled the army, which was to prove the decisive factor in the power struggle. For a short time, however, Moses did succeed in establishing his followers as a community in Zarw, which for the Israelites may be likened to the Paris Commune briefly established in the French capital in 1871. Then, having failed in his attempt to restore his former position as ruler, Moses eventually persuaded Ramses I to allow him and the Israelites to leave the country.

How long was the Oppression? If the chronology in the Book of Exodus was correct, it would have begun *before* Moses was born, lasted during the eighteen or twenty years he was growing up, and continued during the years of his exile before his eventual return to lead the Exodus – a period of several decades, which seems an unduly long time to build the two store cities. The Oppression story in the Book of Exodus, in fact, links three separate events that happened at different periods – the first the plan to murder the Israelite male children; the second related to the religious upheaval caused by Akhenaten that was already in full flow at the time he was forced to build his new capital at Amarna to avoid further confrontation with the Theban priests; the third the rigorous Oppression of the Israelites by Horemheb after the final overthrow of Amarna rule.

It seems therefore that it was the scribes, working from what Cassuto has called 'an epic poem describing the enslavement of the Israelites in Egypt and their liberation' – whether it was oral or written, or partly oral and partly written, in Egyptian – who rearranged the chronology, especially in the opening chapter of the Book of Exodus, which was regarded as an introduction to that book as well as a link with the preceding Book of Genesis.

It is worth drawing attention at this stage to a few points in which this suggested outline of the historical events that lie behind the story in the Book of Exodus agree with what we know of the life of Akhenaten. As in the case of Moses, the childhood of Akhenaten is largely uncharted territory. Yet as soon as he appears on the scene at Thebes he is already bubbling with different ideas about art and rebellious ones about religion, suggesting that he must have been brought up in a manner that differed from the traditional upbringing of a future king. He had evidently not had the normal sport and warfare training common to his ancestors, nor does he seem to have known the sons of the Egyptian nobility, who were customarily educated at Memphis with the royal princes. It is more likely, as his new religion and rituals had many similarities with the solar worship which had developed in the lower end of the Eastern Delta, that it was there that he lived and was educated. The threats to the life of Moses in his early years also find an echo in Akhenaten's later life. The strange epithet 'Great in his Duration' ('He who Lived Long') that he applied to himself constantly has been interpreted by Gardiner as an indication that, as a child, he was not expected to live long. In addition, it is curious on two grounds that he allowed himself to be represented as an Osiris (god of the dead) in a large number of colossal statues placed in the massive Aten temple he built at Karnak early in his reign. Firstly, it was normally a dead king who was shown in this Osiride form, and, secondly, Akhenaten did not believe in Osiris or his underworld. The only possible explanation is that he saw himself as having escaped from death, supporting the idea that during his childhood his life, too, had been threatened.

Yet if, in outlining the story of Moses we are also outlining the story of Akhenaten, why is it that the world has remembered him as Moses rather than by the name under which he ruled Egypt, as coregent and alone, for seventeen turbulent years?

The Name Moses

It seems that neither the Bible nor the Koran gives us the proper name of the leader of the Jewish Exodus, but what on the evidence appears rather to be a codename.

In his last book, *Moses and Monotheism*, Sigmund Freud argued that Moses was an Egyptian, a follower of Akhenaten, who later led the Jews out of Egypt. Freud was first persuaded to take this view by the fact that Moses was itself an Egyptian name: 'What first attracts our interest in the person of Moses is his name, which is written *Moshe* in Hebrew. One may well ask: "Where does it come from? What does it mean?"'

The answer to Freud's question is found in Exodus, 2:10 when we are told how the mother-nurse returns the child to his royal mother who adopted him and called him Moses because, she said, 'I drew him out of the water.' For a Hebrew name, *Moshe* is a rare, even unique, formation. In fact, the Hebrew word *m sh a* does not mean what the biblical editor would like us to believe. As a verb it can mean either 'to draw' or 'one who draws out'. In order to agree with the explanation given by the biblical editor, the name should have been *Moshui*, 'one who has been drawn out'.

There are other questions to be raised about this explanation of why the name was chosen. How, for instance, can we expect the Egyptian royal mother to have sufficient knowledge of the Hebrew language to be able to choose a special Hebrew name for the child? Then again, as we can see from the case of the Patriarch Joseph, when Pharaoh appointed him as his vizier he bestowed on him an Egyptian name to go with his new Egyptian identity. How could we expect that the royal mother of Moses could still give her royal Egyptian son a Hebrew name at a time when the Israelites, in the lingering aftermath of the invasion by the Hyksos shepherds, were still regarded as 'an abomination' by the majority of Egyptians?

In Ancient Egyptian, the word meaning a child or son consists of two consonants, *m* and *s*. If we take away the two vowels *o* and *e* from Moshe we are left with only two consonants, *m* and *sh*. As the Hebrew letter *sh* is the equivalent of the Egyptian *s*, it is easy to see that the Hebrew word came from the Egyptian word. Short vowels, although always pronounced, were never written either in Hebrew or Egyptian, and using long consonants for long vowels, as we saw earlier in examining the identity of the royal mother of Moses, was a later development in both languages. A final point is that the *s* at the end of the name Moses is drawn from the Greek translation of the biblical name.

As a large number of scholars have noted, *mos* was part of many compound Egyptian names such as Ptah-mos and Tuth-mos, yet we also find some examples of the word *mos* used on its own as a personal pronoun belonging to the New Kingdom, which started with the Eighteenth Dynasty.[2]

After Akhenaten fell from power, the Egyptian authorities forbade any mention of his name. Consequently, it seems to me that an alternative had to be found in order that his followers could refer to him. Apart from that, Akhenaten's name was part of his royal power while he was king, but once he was no longer on the throne use of his royal names was forbidden to him, and he was referred to officially in latter days as 'The Fallen One of Akhetaten (Amarna)' and 'The Rebel of Akhetaten'. Faced with the accusation that Akhenaten was not the real heir to the throne, I believe the Israelites called him *mos*, the son, to indicate that he was the legitimate son of Amenhotep III and the rightful heir to his father's throne. We shall see how *mos* was used in a legal sense in a subsequent chapter where a protracted land dispute has added to the confusion and debate about the length of the reign of Horemheb, the Pharaoh of the Oppression.

Later, the biblical editor, who may not have had any knowledge of the original name of the greatest Jewish leader, attempted to put forward a Hebrew explanation of the Egyptian word Moses in order to sever any possible link between Moses and Egypt.

7

THE COREGENCY DEBATE (I)

IF Moses was born in 1394 BC, and if he was Akhenaten, according to the king-list of Gardiner (see p. 11) he would have been in his mid-forties when he fell from power in 1350 BC, not an unreasonable age. However, he would have been in his mid-eighties when he led the Exodus during the brief reign of Ramses I at the start of the last decade of the century. This is clearly unlikely – but the whole chronology changes into a more realistic one if it can be shown that the seventeen years Akhenaten spent on the throne included twelve years as coregent with his father, and that Horemheb ruled for less than half the twenty-seven or twenty-eight years assigned to him conventionally.

There is little dispute about the length of the reigns of the three Amarna kings who suceeded Akhenaten. To take them in reverse order, the king before Horemheb, who brought the Amarna era to an end, was Aye. The highest known regnal year for Aye, from the stele in the Louvre and the Berlin Museum, is Year 4. Tutankhamun preceded Aye. In the tomb of Tutankhamun wine dockets dating from Year 10 of his reign have been found, although it seems that he could have died early in this year, signifying that he reigned for only nine complete years. Before Tutankhamun there was Semenkhkare, who is known to have had a coregency period with *his* predecessor, Akhenaten.

At Amarna, Semenkhkare's name appears on many small objects enclosed within a cartouche, confirming his kingship, as well as on the wall of the tomb of Meryre II, High Priest of the Aten, Superintendent of the King's Harem, Royal Scribe and Steward, while in the North Palace Akhenaten's name is found in many examples, accompanied by the names of Semenkhkare and his queen, who was

Akhenaten's eldest daughter Merytaten, the heiress. His praenomen (coronation name) is Ankh-kheprw-re, meaning 'Kheprw-re lives', Kheprw-re being the praenomen of Akhenaten. Some reliefs found at Amarna showed Akhenaten and Semenkhkare together as kings, indicating that they ruled together. But did Semenkhkare rule alone for any period of time? From a graffito in the tomb of Pere, a Theban nobleman, at Western Thebes, the last date – Year 3 – was found and indicated that, at this point, Semenkhkare was sole ruler. The text does not mention Akhenaten at all and here Semenkhkare seems to have begun to number his own years. We also have a hieratic docket inscribed in Year 17 of Akhenaten, the last year of his reign, and later changed to Year 1 of Tutankhaten (Tutankhamun). The only possible conclusion is that Semenkhkare became coregent in Year 15 of Akhenaten and, after Akhenaten's fall from power, Semenkhkare, who was probably at Thebes at the time, became sole ruler for a few months, or maybe only days, before he met his death and Tutankhaten (Tutankhamun) followed him on the throne.

The question of whether Akhenaten (Amenhotep IV) shared a coregency with his father, Amenhotep III – important in trying to establish a precise chronology – is a vexed one. Many objects bearing the name of Amenhotep III were found at Tell el-Amarna (Akhetaten), the new capital city built by Akhenaten. This has led a large number of Egyptologists to believe that Amenhotep III was alive at the time the new city was built and may even have visited it in person. Others, who did not agree with this argument, have rejected entirely the notion of a coregency.

Both points of view have their distinguished supporters. Scholars who favour the coregency theory include Petrie, Pendlebury, Fairman, Engelbach, Seele, Steindorff, Aldred and Giles: those who dismiss it include Helck, Gardiner, Hayes, Campbell and Redford. The evidence that has been adduced in the argument on both sides includes wine-jar dockets, reliefs, cult objects, cartouches, temples, pylons, stelae, sarcophagi, statues, paintings, letters, praenomen, nomen (birth names) and the length of kings' reigns. Scholars who take the view that there was actually a coregency disagree among themselves about how long it lasted, with the duration put at anything from two to twelve years. In my view, the evidence pointing to a coregency of twelve years is overwhelming. However, so many counter-arguments have been put forward that it is, unfortunately, necessary to examine them in some detail to demonstrate their flaws. In order not to weary the reader, I propose to deal here only with some of the main points: a more detailed analysis can be found in Appendix B.

The Wine-jar Dockets of Amarna

If the notion that Horemheb had a long reign, which will be examined in Chapter Nine, is dismissed, the only king of the immediate period who ruled for more than twenty-eight years is Amenhotep III. The implication is that the wine-jars found at Amarna, dated Year 28 and Year 30 (Years 1 and 3 of Akhenaten), originated in Amenhotep III's Malkata palace at Western Thebes and were brought to Amarna by Akhenaten around the time that he began construction of his new capital and Amarna had no vineyards of its own. As Amenhotep III reigned for a total of thirty-eight years and died at the beginning of Year 39, this would argue a long coregency.

Amenhotep III's Soleb Temple in Nubia

The temple, begun and almost completed in the last decade of Amenhotep III's reign, possesses a few scenes on the pylon that were executed by Akhenaten in the year following his father's death. Professor Donald Redford of Toronto University, the most recent scholar to argue against the coregency theory, has dismissed all the scenes where Akhenaten or his name appears with his living father as of late date, after the death of Amenhotep III, when Akhenaten completed the work on the temple.[1] He cites Joseph M. Janssen, the 'scholar who has examined the [pylon] scenes most recently' and whose 'readings differ markedly from those of other scholars' before him. Two of his eight readings are of particular significance:

Number	Content	Royal Name
Scene 2	Coronation by Horus and Seth (figure of king and Horus hacked)	Nomen: Akhenaten over Amenhotep
Scene 8 (Cornice)	Cartouches	Akhenaten (original)

The cornice, according to Redford, is 'the only portion of the pylon that can be attributed beyond doubt to Akhenaten'. He agrees that Akhenaten's work on the pylon did not take place before Amenhotep III's death and was carried out within the following twelve months. He does not explain, however, the fact that, if there was no coregency, how is it that Scene 8 – the only original scene, according to Redford – gives the new king's name as Akhenaten, a name we know from a variety of sources that he did not adopt until Year 5–6 of his reign? It must therefore follow that the first year after Amenhotep III's death occurred *after* Year 5 of his son.

It is also surprising that Redford did not choose to comment on Scene 2. Here we have an original cartouche of Amenhotep (the original birth name of Akhenaten) in a scene that Redford agrees must have been completed by Amenhotep III before his death. Later the new king destroyed this birth name and imposed on it his new name, Akhenaten. The only possible explanation for this is that, while Amenhotep III was alive and busy decorating the temple, his son's name was still Amenhotep. By the time the old king died, the young king's name had already been changed, as we saw from Scene 8, and while completing the unfinished scenes he also replaced his Amenhotep name with that of Akhenaten. As Redford confirmed that the original Scene 2 was the work of Amenhotep III, this is again strong evidence for a coregency.

A Rock Relief At Aswan

The relief shows two chief sculptors, Men and Bek, father and son, each adoring an image of the king for whom he worked. Men bears the title 'Chief Sculptor' and 'Overseer of Works in the Red Mountain' to Amenhotep III: Bek has identical titles appertaining to the reign of Akhenaten. The relief was made during Akhenaten's reign and use of the late form of the Aten's name indicates that it cannot be dated before at least the second half of Year 8. At this time the name of the Aten received a new form to rid it of any therio-anthropomorphic or pantheistic ideas that may have clung to it. There is no indication that either Amenhotep III or Men was dead, nor that Bek, the younger official, was giving an account of his relations that justified mentioning his father's job. The fact that each of them is shown as holding an official position under a different king, with no indication whatever of any lapse of time, is a strong indication that the kings were contemporary.

The Panehesy Stela

A stela found in the house of Panehesy, the Chief Servitor of the Aten, at Amarna shows Amenhotep III with Queen Tiye, seated before a pile of offerings. As the Aten is shining over them in his later form, it cannot date from earlier than the second half of Year 8 of Akhenaten. The king is shown here in the realistic Amarna style with thick neck and bent head, indicating his age at the time. Neither in the scene nor in the text is there any indication that the king was already dead. On the contrary, as the queen is shown next to him – and she was still alive, with separate evidence that she visited Amarna before Year 12 of her son's reign – it would not have been possible for the artist to show her next to her husband if he were already dead. Furthermore, the artistic nature of the Amarna style used here gives a realistic portrayal of the couple in Amarna, under the Aten's rays, and not an abstract or idealized scene, drawn from memory, of a king who had died at Thebes a decade or so earlier.

Meketaten's Sarcophagus

A fragment of the sarcophagus of Meketaten, Akhenaten's second daughter, who died some time after his Year 12 and was buried in her father's royal tomb at Amarna, was found, with the praenomen of Amenhotep III beside the praenomen of Akhenaten. In another book Redford reports the first appearance of Akhenaten's daughter in the decoration of one of Akhenaten's temples at Karnak where 'possibly no earlier than the fourth year of the reign ... we first see two daughters toddling behind the queen'.[2]

If Amenhotep III was not alive in Year 4 of his son's reign when Meketaten had been born, it would not have been possible for his name to appear on his second grand-daughter's sarcophagus. Its presence indicates that he was alive when the sarcophagus was made, although this could have been at any time after the birth of the princess. Moreover, in this example the praenomen of Amenhotep III have been spelt differently. Instead of using the figure of the goddess Maat in writing the middle part of the word 'Neb-Maat-Re' – 'Maat' signifies 'truth' – Akhenaten spelt it phonetically, indicating an advanced stage in his rejection of the old religions, which did not take place until after he had left Thebes for his new capital, Amarna. The sarcophagus inscriptions cannot therefore be dated earlier than that.

The Amarna Rock Tombs of Huya and Meryre II

A scene and inscription in the tomb of Huya, steward to Queen Tiye, at Amarna has been interpreted as evidence that Amenhotep III was alive and in Amarna after the second half of Akhenaten's Year 8. The scene is drawn in two halves on the lintel of the doorway leading from the first hall of the tomb into the inner rooms.

The scene on the left shows the household of Akhenaten (Akhenaten, Queen Nefertiti and their four daughters), that on the right the household of Amenhotep III, Queen Tiye and the Princess Baketaten). Howard Carter, the British archaeologist who discovered the tomb of Tutankhamun, saw the juxtaposition of these two scenes as evidence that the old king was alive at Amarna: 'This equipoise of the two households not only confirms the coregency of the two kings, but gives reason to suppose that Amenhotep III continued to live for at least a year or so after the birth of Akhenaten's fourth daughter, Neferneferuaten Tasheri.'[3]

Redford, who does not agree with Carter, goes on to argue that, as Tiye is shown without her husband on the outer (south) wall of the hall in question, Amenhotep III must have already been dead when construction of the tomb began: 'Presumably, if the decoration of the tomb kept pace with its excavation, the scenes in the first hall showing Tiye alone would have been carved before the lintel jambs.'[4]

This is an over-simple approach. We have to examine the whole hall of Huya's tomb, as well as the neighbouring tomb of Meryre II, in order to establish which came before which of the tomb scenes. The argument is a somewhat complex one, but from the nature of the scenes, the number of princesses shown and their relative ages, it is possible to make the following deductions (see also Appendix B):

• The South and North Walls, where four daughters of Akhenaten are depicted, plus Baketaten, the daughter of Amenhotep III and Queen Tiye: Year 10;

• The East Wall, which does not show any of Akhenaten's daughters but depicts Baketaten, looking the same age as she is shown on the South and North Walls: Year 10;

• The West Wall is a unique scene showing celebrations that took place in Akhenaten's Year 12 and bears the date 'Year 12, the second month of winter, the eighth day'.

This dating has a further significance in the coregency argument. The temple scene shown on the East Wall shows a colonnade with a statue of a king and queen placed between each pair of columns. The inscribed names are now only partially preserved, but it seemed certain to N. de G. Davies, author of *The Rock Tombs of El Amarna*,[5] that here we have Queen Tiye's statue with alternating statues of her husband, Amenhotep III, and her son, Akhenaten. While Akhenaten is given his two names, Amenhotep III has only his praenomen, 'King of the South and North and Lord of the Two Lands, Neb-Maat-Re, given life'. This last epithet, 'given life', can appear only if the king was alive at the time the statue was placed in position and the inscription made.

Inside the sanctuary of the temple, statues – Queen Tiye alternating again with her husband and son – under the portico represent figures holding altars between their extended arms for the reception of gifts. In the centre is a naos (inner sanctuary of the temple) standing free from the wall. It is set on a platform to which three or four steps lead up. Here we see Queen Tiye drawn twice, standing on the steps, once with her husband, once with her son, and Amenhotep III himself, depicted inside the temple where the inscriptions have already made it clear that he was alive. A statue can sometimes be a representation of a dead person, but here, because they are shown on the steps, they are living persons.

Davies himself noted that it is not usual to erect statues on steps. Yet he refused to accept the clear evidence of the East Wall that we are not looking here at depictions of statues, but of real figures: '"Statues" I have said, but in truth there is nothing to prevent us from seeing in them four royal personages, except for the difficulty of granting the existence of two kings together at this time.'[6] He also chose to disregard the fact that the characters depicted are shown, not within the naos, facing outward, in a position of receiving offerings, which would have been the case if they were statues, but on the steps facing the naos, offering gifts to the Aten, which indicates that the royal characters were alive and worshipping.

As for Redford, he preferred to regard the old king as dead in the lintel scene and a statue on the East Wall, avoiding a real examination of the scenes that would date the decorations correctly and even relying on a misleading judgement by another scholar to obtain more support for his preconceptions. He quotes[7] the German scholar Alexander Scharff, who noted in his book *Archiv für Orientforschung* that Amenhotep III's accompanying jamb inscription to the lintel scene is not followed by the epithet 'given life'. Neither Scharff nor Redford seems to have examined the lintel scene carefully, for at the bottom of Amenhotep III's cartouche, which is shown behind his head, the signs for 'given life' are clearly visible, just as they are on the East Wall.

The Age of Baketaten

Redford next takes issue with Frederick J. Giles, the Canadian Egyptologist, who argued that Baketaten in the tomb scenes 'could not be older than fourteen at the most. On the assumption that Tiye married Amenhotep III in his second regnal year at the age of sixteen, Tiye would have given birth to Baketaten if there were no coregency, in the last year or so of her husband, when she was fifty-four. Since it is unlikely that Tiye was as young as sixteen at the time of her marriage, or as old as fifty-four at the birth of Baketaten, the assumption of a coregency of about twelve years is almost obligatory.'[8]

Redford complains that Giles's 'entirely unwarranted manipulation of numbers and his assumptions regarding Tiye's age at various times in her life do not command the respect of the uncommitted reader'.[9] However, he is using the inability of an opponent to present his case to try to persuade us that he has none.

Examination of the mummy of Amenhotep III suggests that he was about fifty when he died. As he ruled for a full thirty-eight years and died at the start of the thirty-ninth, he could only have been around twelve when he came to the throne and about fourteen when he married Tiye in or just before his second regnal year. As Tiye was not the heiress, whom he had to marry irrespective of her age, we should expect her to be younger than he, as this was the custom of the time, and it is thought that she was only eight years of age at the time of the wedding. This would not have been unusual in that era. The prophet Muhammad married a nine-year-old girl when he himself was fifty, and I think this custom of marrying young girls who had not yet reached puberty accounts for the number of 'barren' women who later give birth to children in a variety of biblical stories.

How old was Baketaten in the tomb scenes? Carter has made the point: 'Among many such scenes in El Amarna private mortuary chapels depicting these children [Akhenaten's] the relative age of each child is shown by her height. Careful discrimination of that kind excludes the possibility of twin births, and is therefore service-able when estimating their ages. A reckoning such as the above cannot, of course, be considered exact, but error cannot be more than say a year.'[10]

In Huya's tomb scenes Baketaten is shown consistently as being about the same age as Akhenaten's third daughter, Ankhsenpa-aten. Carter also noted the similarity in size of the two princesses: 'Judging from the stature of Baketaten figured in this picture [the lintel scene], she was about the same age as Ankhsenpa-aten.'[11] Merytaten, the eldest daughter of Akhenaten, was born towards the end of Year 1 of her father. The second daughter, Meketaten, was probably born in Year 3, as she appears as a very young child the following year in the decoration of Akhenaten's temple at Karnak. If we allow two more years for her birth, the third daughter, Ankhsenpa-aten, would be born around Year 5 of her father, thus making her five or six years of age when Huya's tomb was decorated in Year 10. (She is seen for the first time in Aye's tomb, dated by Davies to Year 9 of her father's reign, and was never depicted with her parents at Thebes.)

If this explanation is accepted as corresponding more closely to the facts, Baketaten must also have been five or six at that time. If there was no coregency between Akhenaten and his father, Baketaten could not have been Amenhotep III's daughter, being six years of age ten years after her father's death – yet the inscription in Huya's tomb confirms that she was. Furthermore, the very name Baketaten indicates that she was born during her brother's reign when he started relating his own daughters' names to the Aten. In this case Baketaten would have been born around Year 31 of Amenhotep III when her mother, Queen Tiye, was around thirty-seven, a late, but not impossible, age for giving birth.

Fragments from Amarna

Two objects bearing Amenhotep III's name, found at Amarna, indicate he was at Amarna at the time. The first is a fragment of a granite bowl with the late name of the Aten, the praenomen of Amenhotep III and the phrase "in Akhetaten"; the second a fragment of a statue of a kneeling person holding an offering slab. Between his outstretched hands is an inscription that includes the late Aten name, followed by the praenomen of Amenhotep III. The Aten's name is also found twice on the front edge of the slab with Amenhotep III's praenomen to the right and Akhenaten's name to the left.

. Redford rejects the possibility that Amenhotep III was either at Amarna or even alive at the time these objects were inscribed, which should be, according to the late Aten name, some time after the second half of Year 8. He writes: 'The most these miserable fragments allow is a cautious suggestion, and nothing more, that a cult of Amenhotep III continued after his death.'[12]

What Redford is suggesting, without any supporting evidence whatever, is that, in the city of the Aten, another god was worshipped by Akhenaten, a human god, his own father. Not only would the monotheistic beliefs of the king not allow this; the idea of a king being worshipped during or after his life is non-existent in the new city. No funerary temple has been found there for Akhenaten, who was himself the one and only prophet of the new God. The simple

explanation is that some time after the latter half of Year 8
Amenhotep came down from Thebes to visit his son and coregent,
during which time these objects were made, indicating that both
kings were worshipping the Aten. There are other indications that
Amenhotep III was converted to worship of the new god, although
he continued to worship the older gods as well.

8

THE COREGENCY DEBATE (II)

The Theban Tomb of Kheruef

A SCENE on the south side of the entrance corridor to the tomb of Kheruef, a high official of the period, in Western Thebes shows Amenhotep IV (Akhenaten) offering libation to his father, Amenhotep III, who stands, facing him, before Queen Tiye. Part of the accompanying inscription found fallen nearby has the cartouches of both kings facing each other. Although this was sufficient for H. W. Fairman, the British Egyptologist, to regard it as yet further evidence in support of a coregency, Redford is not convinced and regards Amenhotep III as already dead at the time.

In every case where the two kings are shown together, opponents of the coregency try to persuade us that either the elder king is dead or that what we are looking at is his statue. The argument at Amarna is that, although Amenhotep III was depicted as being alive *and* at Amarna, this was purely because he could not be represented as Osiris, the ancient god of the dead, who was banned from the city of the Aten: now here, in the tomb of a Theban official, who is himself seen addressing a long hymn to Osiris, when we find Amenhotep III depicted as a living king – and no traces of the phrase 'true of voice' that usually follows the cartouche of a deceased king – Redford argues that the libation scene belongs to 'the category of idealised portrayals. It is not a specific incident that is here being recorded. Nor can one argue that just because Amenhotep III is shown receiving an offering and about to eat – activities again reserved for the living – he must have been alive when the relief was carved. ...'[1]

What Redford is, in fact, saying is that there is no evidence in this scene to indicate that Amenhotep III was dead. However, as Redford is not prepared to agree that he was alive, he presents this new explanation – although the old king is not represented here as dead, the representation took place, in a formalized, stylized, abstract manner that has nothing to do with time, *after* he had died. This is incorrect.

Almost all the royal scenes in Kheruef's tomb are related to Amenhotep III's *sed* festival celebrations. This was a rejuvenation ritual and celebration that kings normally held for the first time after ruling for thirty years, then in shorter intervals after that. Amenhotep III celebrated three such jubilees in Years 30, 34 and 37, but Akhenaten is known to have celebrated two jubilees while still at Thebes during his first five years. The Aten, his God, also celebrated, as kings did, many jubilees. Here Amenhotep IV is presenting his father with libation on the same occasion. (See also Appendix B (ii).)

The Meidum Graffito

A graffito from the pyramid temple of Meidum, in Middle Egypt and dating from the time of Amenhotep III, persuaded Carter of the coregency between Akhenaten and his father: 'The graffito reads: "Year 30, under the majesty of the King Neb-maat-Re, son of Amun, resting in truth, Amenhotep (III), prince of Thebes, lord of might, prince of joy, who loves him that hates injustice of heart, placing the male offspring upon the seat of his father, and establishing his inheritance in the land." The "heir" referred to in this graffito can be no less than Amenhotep IV, who afterwards assumed the name Akhenaten. There was probably some reason for establishing this young prince upon the throne.'[2]

As usual, Redford does not agree with this view. He argues that the 'male offspring' referred to is not the king's son: 'The addition after the praenomen (coronation name) of 'son of Amun' is especially significant. In formal inscriptions it is Amun who is spoken of as establishing the king on his (i.e. Amun's) throne ... The inscription refers entirely to the king (Amenhotep III); it is he who is called the "male", and it is his own inheritance that is spoken of as being established. "His father" is none other than Amun, the epithet "son of Amun" in the first line being possibly a semantic antecedent.'[3] The point the author is making is that, as Amenhotep III was celebrating his first jubilee in Year 30, this inscription indicated the re-establishment of the king on his ancestral throne and the re-confirmation of his inheritance. Yet if we look back at the text we find first that the date given relates to the king himself, Amenhotep III, the son of Amun, and this is followed by three phrases:

1   Who loves (he, the king, loves) him that hates injustice of heart;
2   Placing (he, the king, who is placing) the male offspring (the heir) upon the seat of his father;
3   And establishing (he, the king, who is establishing) his (the heir's) inheritance in the land.

Nobody can say that, just because the king is called the 'son of Amun' or the 'son of Re' or of any other god, the statement that follows refers to the god rather than the king, and it is clear here that it is the king who is the subject of all the subsequent verbs. Then again, jubilee celebrations did not indicate inheritance, but rather rejuvenation of power.

To justify the use of the very strange epithet 'who hates falsehood' it is equally clear that the king must have been referring to some kind of opposition to a decision of his. The injustice he implies seems to be 'not placing the heir upon his father's seat', but, by placing his son there, the king was doing the just thing and securing the inheritance for him. Here Amenhotep III appears also to be defending an action that had taken place prior to Year 30. The only reasonable explanation would be that Amenhotep III felt that his son and heir, Amenhotep IV, whose mother, Tiye, had not been the heiress, might be challenged over inheriting the throne after the old king died. He therefore decided, while still alive, to appoint him as coregent to guarantee his inheritance. If a coregency of twelve years is accepted, this must have started in Year 28, with the priests of Amun being the almost certain source of protest. This protest could be the same as that mentioned on one of the border stelae at Amarna where Akhenaten referred to some critical comments he had heard about himself before he moved out of Thebes.

The king was regarded as the physical son of Amun. As Tiye was not the heiress when she and Amenhotep III were married, she could not be regarded as the consort of Amun and her son, Amenhotep IV, could not be considered the physical son of Amun. In the Eighteenth Dynasty that meant he would not be accepted as the legal heir and king. This same situation faced an earlier Pharaoh, Tuthmosis III, whose mother was not the heiress when she married. On that occasion an adoption ritual took place at Karnak where the image of Amun, carried by the priests, chose Tuthmosis III as Amun's son. Once Amenhotep IV had been rejected by the priests, he in turn rejected Amun, chose Aten as his father, first forced Amun out of his supreme position, then destroyed all the other gods, eventually establishing Aten as the only legitimate God of whom Akhenaten was the son. The real sense of Amenhotep III's statement in the Meidum graffito cannot be understood other than against this background.

The Tushratta Letters

After Akhenaten became the sole ruler of Egypt, Tushratta, King of Mitanni, wrote to him expressing the hope that they would enjoy the same friendship that had existed between him and Akhenaten's father, Amenhotep III. On its arrival the letter (No. EA27) was dated by an Egyptian hieratic docket which reads: '[Year?]2, first month of Winter, [day ...], when one (the king) was in the southern city (Thebes) ...; copy of the Naharin (Mitanni) letter which the messenger Pirizzi and the messenger [Puipri] brought.'

The German philologist Adolf Erman was the first to translate this docket. As the edge of the tablet was broken and he found tiny traces of ink ahead of the '2', Erman decided that it was possible to restore the date to '[Year1]2'. If this restoration was accepted, the letter, thought to have been the first sent to Akhenaten by the Mitannian king after his father's death, could be regarded as confirmation of a coregency of twelve years. However, another German philologist, J. A. Knudzton, contradicted Erman's restoration and preferred the reading '[Year]2'. Scholars have been divided since the start of the century over which restoration is correct, although Redford has admitted: 'Actually, on the evidence of the traces alone, both readings can be maintained.'[4] It has been argued by opponents of a coregency that, from the presence of Akhenaten at Thebes, to which the letter was addressed, it must have arrived during his first five years, when he was resident there before moving to Amarna, while supporters of a coregency make the point that he was already living in Amarna and had simply travelled to Thebes to attend his father's funeral. Redford has summarized the situation in the following terms:

'The letter to which this docket is appended, EA27, was written shortly after Amenhotep III's death ... Consequently the letter is rightly understood to be the first written by Tushratta to Akhenaten after the latter's entry upon sole rule. The allusion [in it] to "the great feast for mourning" shows that the funeral rites for Amenhotep III were either still in progress or had just been concluded. Now there are but two possible restorations of the date, Year 2 or Year 12. No other ... If Year 2 is restored, only a very short coregency amounting to but a few months at the most is possible. If Year 12 is restored, a coregency of not less than eleven years is as good as proved.'[5] We therefore have to seek elsewhere for evidence that might point to the correct dating of the letter.

Redford has made the point: 'Between the death of Amenhotep III and the writing of [letter] EA27 there occurred a short but well-attested exchange of letters between Tushratta and Tiye.'[6] This is not strictly accurate. In all, four letters from Tushratta form part of the coregency debate, but only one was addressed to Tiye: Akhenaten was the recipient of the other three. The letters are numbered from EA26 to EA29, but their contents indicate that they did not arrive in the order their numbering might suggest.

Redford, Gardiner and other scholars believe that letter No. EA26, addressed to the queen, was the first to arrive. The text begins: 'To Tiye, the Queen of Egypt ...' and goes on to make it clear that, before the sending of this letter, a Mitannian messenger named Giliya must have happened to be in Egypt at the time of Amenhotep III's death and Tiye had taken advantage of the fact to send back with him news of her bereavement as well as asking Tushratta to be as friendly with her son as he had been with her husband. Tushratta then goes on to complain: 'The present, which your husband commanded to be brought, you have not sent me; and gold statues ... Now, however, Napkhuriya (Akhenaten), your [son] ... has made (them) of wood.'[7]

The fact that Akhenaten had made wooden statues instead of the promised gold ones and sent them to Mitanni, where they had arrived before Tushratta's letter to Tiye was written, suggests that some time had elapsed between the death of Amenhotep III and the despatch of the letter of protest to the queen.

The first letter to Akhenaten (No. EA27) also dwells upon the gold issue. After mentioning the arrival from Egypt of a king's messenger named Khamashshi, seeking Tushratta's friendship, the Mittanian king complains: 'Your father ... wrote ... in his letter, at the time when Mani (the Egyptian messenger) brought the price for a wife (Tushratta's daughter, Tadukhipa)' that he had promised Tushratta two gold images, much other gold, lapis lazuli and 'implements without number'. Tushratta's messengers had actually seen the promised gifts 'with their own eyes'. Yet, he protests, on a return visit Mani has brought wooden images, not gold ones. The letter makes the point that, if Akhenaten has any doubts aboud the truth concerning the promised gold, he should 'ask his mother',[8] suggesting that it is Tiye rather than the young king who is *au fait* with the arrangements made by her late husband.

The remaining two letters from Tushratta to Akhenaten are Nos. EA28 and EA29. Redford believes that they are numbered in the order in which they arrived, but, because of the nature of their tone and contents, I believe the reverse to be the case.

Letter No. EA29, which I regard as the second from Tushratta to Akhenaten, delves even more deeply into the history of the friendly relationships between the two royal families in order to persuade the new king to continue them and to send the promised gold. He is also invited again to seek confirmation from his mother that Tushratta is speaking the truth: '... the images [of gold] ... for which I made request you have not given me ... my messengers for four years ... The images which I requested from your father, give; and now [when I have sent] my messengers for the second time [if he] does not prepare and give [them], he will grieve my heart ... Your mother Tiye knows all about these things, and (therefore) ask your mother Tiye ... [Now my brother said:] "Giliya ought to return to him. Because I should otherwise grieve my brother's heart, I will send Giliya back." [However, I said]: "Inasmuch as I have sent back quickly my brother's messengers, so let my brother always my messengers [send back quickly]". ... gives me word and sends Mani to me, then I will ... Giliya, with friendly intentions, to my brother.'⁹

From this letter it is clear that the messenger Mani is in Egypt because Tushratta is asking for him to be despatched with the gold. In letter No. EA28, however, we learn that Mani is not only in Mitanni, but being held hostage against the return of two of Tushratta's messengers. After the usual initial friendly formalities, Tushratta comes straight to the point: 'Pirizzi and Puipri, my messengers, I sent them to my brother at the beginning of his reign, and ordered them to express sorrow very strongly. And then I sent them again. And this message, on the former occasion, I gave to my brother: Mani, the messenger of my brother, I will retain until my brother sends my messenger, and until he arrives ... Now, however, my brother has in general not allowed them to go has retained them very much indeed.'¹⁰ The earlier letter containing 'this message' is missing. We therefore have no means of knowing what might have been the reason for Mani's third journey to Mitanni, but it was probably part of the ordinary exchange of messages between monarchs.

Much new information is revealed in letter No. EA28. Tushratta is no longer asking for gold or gold statues: he just wants the return of his two messengers, Pirizzi and Puipri. We also learn that they made two trips to Egypt – the first to 'express sorrow' at the death of Amenhotep III, the second when they brought the first letter we have to Akhenaten from Tushratta in Year 2 or Year 12 – and they have been detained 'very much indeed' by the time letter EA28 was written. The unfriendly tone of this letter, the presence of Mani in Mitanni and the fact that Tushratta seems to have lost all hope of obtaining gold, which he no longer mentions, makes it more probable that this, rather than letter EA29, was the last to Akhenaten from the Mitannian king.

From these communications we can establish the following chronology of events:

At the time Amenhotep III died, he had been arranging his presents for Tushratta, including two golden statues. Giliya, the Mitannian messenger, was in Egypt, probably waiting to take the gifts back to his master. These plans fell through on the death of Amenhotep III. Instead, Giliya left for home to inform Tushratta of his friend's death and carrying a message from Queen Tiye,

expressing the hope that the Mitannian friendship would continue in
the reign of her son, the new king. Either at the same time as Giliya's
journey home or shortly afterwards, Akhenaten sent Khamashshi
with a letter to Tushratta also asking for the Mitannian king's
friendship.

After this initial exchange of messages, Tushratta sent two messengers, Pirizzi and Puipri, to attend the funeral rites of Amenhotep
III. While they were still in Egypt, or not long after they had
returned home, Akhenaten despatched *his* messenger, Mani, with
two wooden statues instead of the gold ones Tushratta had been
promised by Amenhotep III. A disappointed Tushratta sent Pirizzi
and Puipri back to Egypt with two letters, one to Akhenaten (No.
EA27), dated by the Egyptian docket as arriving in Year 2 or Year
12, first month of Winter, and complaining about the wooden
statues: the second (No. EA26) to Queen Tiye, asking her to inform
her son of the friendly relationship between the Mitannian king and
his father and asking her to try to persuade him to send the gold.
Akhenaten for his part decided to keep the two Mitannian messengers in Egypt.

Tushratta sent another messenger with a letter (No. EA29) asking
again for the gold, complaining about the detention of his two
messengers and requesting the Egyptian king to send Mani to him.
Akhenaten must have agreed to this request and sent Mani with a
letter to Tushratta as we find him in Mitanni in what I believe to be
the third letter to Akhenaten (No. EA28), in which Tushratta states
that Mani is being held hostage against the release of Pirizzi and
Puipri.

Therefore, contrary to what Redford would have us believe, the
funerary rites of Amenhotep III were neither still in progress, nor
had just ended, when Letter No. EA27, the first to Akhenaten,
arrived; they had ended much earlier. Pirizzi and Puipri had attended
the funeral rites, returned home and were on their second visit when
they brought this letter. As Akhenaten's celebration of his sole reign
took place in the second month of Winter of his Year 12, their return
would have taken place some days before this occasion if the reading
for No. EA27 was Year 12.

Nor was Tushratta's letter to Queen Tiye sent before that first
letter from the Mitannian king to Akhenaten: Akhenaten had
already sent two messengers – Khamashshi and Mani, with the

wooden statues – to Tushratta before the first surviving letter to him, No. EA27, was brought, together with Tiye's letter. It is also clear that, as Mani was not in Mitanni when letter No. EA29 was written, yet we find him detained there as a hostage in letter No. EA28, these two letters must have been written in the reverse order to which they are numbered. Nor does the mention in letter No. EA29 of a four-year delay mean, as Redford understood, that the Mitannian ambassadors were detained in Egypt for that period: it is a reference to the fact that the Mitannian king had been trying for four years, without success, to obtain the gold that Amenhotep III had promised.

A more relevant point to the coregency argument, however, is the fact that we know from the evidence of the remains of the Malkata palace complex of Amenhotep III at Western Thebes that Akhenaten resided there before Year 30 of his father. Now, at the end of his father's reign at the start of his Year 39, how is it that the Crown Prince appears to be entirely unaware of the details of his father's relationship with Tushratta? Ask your mother, Tushratta keeps saying: Tiye knows all the details. Why would Akhenaten have no knowledge of the gold statues which, we know from Tushratta's letters, the Mitannian king's messengers had seen with their own eyes? The only explanation is that Akhenaten was totally in the dark about these events because he was not at Thebes when they took place. We know that from Year 4 of his reign Akhenaten, to avoid confrontation with the hostile Amun priesthood at Thebes, started to build his new city at Amarna and resided there in part until Year 8, when he made it his permanent home. If, as all the other evidence indicates, the coregency started in Year 28 of his father, then from Amenhotep III's Year 32 – shortly after the correspondence with Tushratta began – Akhenaten, having started to build his new capital, distanced himself increasingly, then finally, from the governing of Egypt and from its foreign affairs.

Thus all the implications support the reading of Year 12 rather than Year 2 for the arrival of letter No. EA27 of Tushratta to Akhenaten, who was staying at the time at Thebes before he moved, probably followed by the two Mitannian messengers, to Amarna to celebrate the assumption of his sole rule in Egypt. As the second-last letter we have from Tushratta to Akhenaten speaks of a four-year period during which he had been trying unsuccessfully to obtain the

promised gold, this would agree with the chronology if the coregency is established as having lasted until Year 12 of Akhenaten's
reign and was then followed by a period of five years during which
he ruled alone.

The Tomb of Aper-el

After this chapter had been written, it was announced that the tomb
of Aper-el, vizier to Akhenaten, had been discovered, almost intact,
at Sakkara by the French archaeologist Alain-Pierre Zivie. The
discovery, sixty feet beneath the sand, is the climax to ten years'
work and of great significance. The tomb makes it clear that
Aper-el, a figure previously unknown in Egyptian history, had been
a high priest of the Aten before he became Akhenaten's vizier. Zivie
was also able to retrieve from the tomb three skeletons and many
pieces of funerary furniture. The latter include a box given to
Aper-el by Amenhotep III and Queen Tiye. Amenhotep III's
cartouche and his praenomen, Neb-Maat-Re, were found in two
other cases in the tomb.

This is the most significant archaeological evidence yet unearthed
to point to a coregency between Amenhotep III and his son,
Akhenaten. The main points are: (1) Akhenaten would not have had
a vizier unless he was ruling, (2) his father would not have three
mentions in the tomb by his praenomen, Neb-Maat-Re, unless he
was still alive *after* his son, initially known as Amenhotep IV, had
changed his name to Akhenaten in honour of the monotheistic God
he had introduced in Egypt.

As I said earlier, a more detailed discussion of many of these points is
to be found in Appendix B, together with a rather complex
argument involving another tomb – that of Ramose, mayor of
Thebes and vizier of Upper Egypt. For the moment this somewhat
protracted analysis of the pros and cons of a coregency can best be
ended with the words of the American Egyptologist, William C.
Hayes: 'As it now appears that Akhenaten was elevated to the throne
as coregent in or about Year 28 of Amenhotep III and transferred his
residence to Tell el-Amarna in or about Year 33, this means that the

bulk of dated inscriptions from the palace at Thebes are contemporary with those found at Amarna. We can, indeed, establish a close correspondence in date, year by year, between the two groups of inscriptions, based on the equations: Year 28 of Amenhotep III = Year 1 of Amenhotep IV, Year 33 of Amenhotep III = Year 6 of Akhenaten, Year 38 of Amenhotep III = Year 11 of Amenhotep IV (Akhenaten), etc.'[11] Amenhotep III died in his Year 39, his son's Year 12.

9

THE REIGN OF HOREMHEB

As we saw before, Ramses I, already an old man when he came to the throne, did not reign for long. Manetho is quoted by Josephus as attributing one year and four months to the length of Ramses I's rule. The last year we have for him is Year 2, which comes from a stela found at Wadi Halfa in Nubia. He may not have survived to the end of that year, however, as the name of his son, Seti I, is found at the foot of the stela, indicating that it could be he who erected it after Ramses I's death.

It is when we come to examine the reign of Ramses I's predecessor, Horemheb, the Pharaoh of the Oppression, that we find ourselves facing considerable difficulties, summarized by Professor J. R. Harris, the British Egyptologist, in the following terms: 'Only three regnal years of Horemheb have survived intact in contemporary inscriptions – Year 1 in the temple of Ptah (the god of Memphis) at Karnak, Year 3 in the Theban tomb of Neferhotep (one of the nobles), and Year 8 in a graffito in the tomb of Tuthmosis IV. A further date is partially preserved on a fragmentary stele and could be 5 or 7 ... and Year 7 is later attested from two Ramesside ostraca, the year in each case being of Horemheb's actual reign. Beyond this there is uncertainty. The Manethonian tradition is clearly corrupt, but may conceal an original total of 12 years 3 months.'[1]

The uncertainty is such that estimates of the length of Horemheb's reign range from as low as eight years to as high as fifty-nine:

• Support for the above Manethonian tradition is provided by two large storage vessels, which bear hieratic dockets and were discovered in fairly recent times in Horemheb's Sakkara tomb. One of them is dated to 'Year 13, third month of Inundation' and is said to have contained 'very good quality wine from the vineyard of the estate of Horemheb, beloved of Amun ... in the house of Amun'.[2]

• A graffito from Madinet Habu at Western Thebes, given a date Year 27, has been interpreted variously as a) a visit by Horemheb to King Aye's mortuary temple, which Horemheb is known to have usurped, b) the date of Horemheb's death, c) a visit to Horemheb's tomb by Ramses II in Year 27 of his reign. The text goes: 'Regnal Year 27, first month of Shomu, day 9: the day on which Horemheb ... who loves Amun and hates his enemies ... entered ... '[3] The controversy centres upon two words at the end of the first line, which have been read either to mean 'the day of entry which Horemheb made' or 'the day of entering the domain of Horemheb'. Those who prefer the first rendering assume that it refers to a visit by Horemheb to the mortuary temple: those who prefer the second a visit by Ramses II in his Year 27 to Aye's temple that had been taken over and extended by Horemheb. The second reading was preferred by Fairman as it is supported by the first copy of the text printed from the original.[4] The style of writing also fits the Ramesside period quite well.

• Two fragmentary wine-jar dockets were found by British archaeologists, working at the site of Tell el-Amarna, the new capital which the Pharaoh Akhenaten built for himself and named Akhetaten. They bear only the dates Year 28 and Year 30. Although they most probably belonged to Amenhotep III, some scholars have argued that they might possibly have belonged to Horemheb. It is true that Horemheb's name has been found in Amarna, a city abandoned even before he came to the throne, but there is no reason to suggest that it was used as a place of residence for Horemheb or any of his officials, for otherwise we should have found more examples dating from different years of his reign as well as some archaeological remains.

A similar wine-jar label dated Year 31 was also found in the tomb of Tutankhamun, who had already been dead and buried for four years when Horemheb's reign began. In this case clearly the date could refer only to Amenhotep III.

• Year 59 in relation to Horemheb was found towards the end of the last century in the inscriptions of a tomb at Sakkara, the burial place for Memphis from the time of Ramses II. The tomb belongs to a scribe of Ptah named Khayri and the inscriptions give an account of a legal dispute about ownership of a piece of land that lasted over a long period of time during reigns of different kings of the Eighteenth and Nineteenth Dynasties.

Scholars faced with this figure of Year 59 looked upon it as too long for Horemheb's reign for a variety of reasons. He is known, before coming to the throne, to have been a high official during the nine years of Tutankhamun as well as the four years of Aye; he has not left much in the way of monuments other than those usurped from his predecessors or rebuilt using their materials; nor do we have any information about military activity by Horemheb in Asia that one would expect to be a feature of such an extended reign. In spite of these circumstances, scholars, without any supporting evidence, assumed that the reigns of the four Amarna kings – Akhenaten, Semenkhkare, Tutankhamun and Aye – had been added to those of Horemheb: 'It has been widely accepted that this is an inclusive date incorporating the reigns of Horemheb's four predecessors ... some 32 years in all, thus implying a minimum of 26/27. Neither the actual reading nor the broad conclusion is to be challenged, though *it should be emphasized that no other example of an inclusive date is known* (my italics). It is evident that the existence of the Amarna kings was ignored officially in the Nineteenth Dynasty (or at least under Seti I and Ramses II), but there is no indication that it was common practice to assign their regnal years to Horemheb.'[5]

It is true that Akhenaten and the three Amarna kings who succeeded him were omitted from the king lists of the time, and Akhenaten himself has been referred to as 'the rebel' or 'the fallen one of Akhetaten', but a date found on a fragmentary papyrus of the Nineteenth Dynasty, now in the British Museum, mentions 'Year 9 of the rebel' and, according to Gardiner 'the reference must surely be to the reign of Akhenaten',[6] indicating that the lengths of the Amarna kings' reigns were not, in fact, added to those of Horemheb.

The basic cause of the confusion that has arisen over the reference to Horemheb's Year 59 at Sakkara are two. Firstly, Egyptologists took it out of context and did not relate it to the rest of the information given in the Sakkara tomb inscriptions, which are not presented in strict chronological order; secondly, there is a missing word between Year 59 and the name of the king, which could radically affect the meaning that the scribe of the text intended to convey.

The inscriptions, which begin on the north wall of the tomb, relate to a piece of cultivated land, measuring thirteen arourae (about three hectares) and situated on the west bank of the Nile, somewhere to the south of Memphis. The land was given as a reward by Ahmosis (c. 1575–1550 BC), the first king of the Eighteenth Dynasty, to a shipmaster named Neshi. It passed down from generation to generation and became known eventually as 'the village of Neshi'.[7] Two centuries later, some time before Horemheb came to the throne, the heirs of Neshi consisted of six brothers and sisters who owned the land between them, with one of the sisters, named Urnero, appointed trustee over them. This trusteeship was subsequently disputed in the reign of Horemheb by another sister, Takharu. The tomb inscriptions, to place them in strict chronological order, recall:

1   An examination of witnesses (see also Appendix C), who gave evidence about events long before the reign of Horemheb, going back to the time of Akhenaten, who was not referred to by name but as 'the fallen one of Akhetaten', his capital city. At the end of these proceedings it was decided that the land which was the subject of dispute should be divided between the six heirs, with each one given his or her individual share.

2   Urnero was married to a man named Prehotep, by whom she had a son, Huy. Huy, who had been working in the land of Neshi since the reign of the king who preceded Horemheb, undertook cultivation of his mother's holding after the land had been divided among the Neshi heirs. The name of the king who preceded Horemheb has been lost from the inscriptions apart from the initial letter, 'A', but it can only have been Aye. Prehotep subsequently married another woman by whom he had a second son, Tjaui, and later, after Horemheb had ascended to the throne, Prehotep took steps to register the land of his first wife in the name of Tjaui, the son by his second marriage. This illegal transaction eventually became the subject of further litigation some years later in the reign of Ramses II, the third king of the Nineteenth Dynasty, when Huy died. His son, Khayri, tried to take over cultivation of the land, but found himself challenged by Tjaui's grandson, Khay.

3   It was the mother of Khayri who began legal proceedings in Year 14-plus – the number of months is missing – of Ramses II to establish his ownership of the land, arguing that he was the descendant of Neshi through his grandmother, Urnero. In the tomb account of the events that followed Khayri is referred to by name only once and is elsewhere called *mos* (the son and heir), to indicate his claim as the rightful inheritor.

4   In Year 18, Khay (the defendant in this action) went to court and presented the registration records showing that the land had been registered in his grandfather's name. He claimed, in addition, that Huy, the plaintiff's father, had merely been employed to work on it. The tomb account explains: 'Khay complained in the great court in Year 18. The priest of the (litter), Amenemope, who was the officer of the great court, was caused to come together with him, bringing a false land register in his hand. [Accordingly], I (Khayri) ceased to be the child of Neshi.'[8]

5   The plaintiff *mos* and his mother then appealed to the vizier in Heliopolis against the court's decision. The vizier ordered the land registers from Pi-Ramses, the residence of Nineteenth Dynasty kings in the Eastern Delta, and showed the mother of *mos* that they did not include her son's name. 'You are not in the documents,' they were told. However, after further protests by the plaintiff that he was indeed *mos*, the legal son and heir, the vizier instructed the court at Memphis to hear local witnesses to see whether the plaintiff could support his claim.

    In the subsequent testimony the word *mos* is again used, but in this case to establish that Huy, the father of the plaintiff, was the rightful heir of Neshi, the original owner of the land. The long tomb list of witnesses, for instance, begins with the testimony of the goatherd Mesman, who swore: '[As Amun endures and as the ruler endures], I shall speak truthfully to the Pharaoh ... I shall not speak falsely, and if I speak falsely cut off [my nose and my ears]; [let me (be banished) to Kush]. As to the scribe Huy, child of Urnero, it is said that he is the child (*mos*) of Neshi ... '

    After hearing these and other witnesses[9] the court decided that Khayri (*mos*) was, in fact, the rightful heir as a result of his descent from Urnero, his grandmother, and his father, Huy. The tomb inscriptions record: 'They gave me land, thirteen arourae, and land

was given to the heirs before the notables of the town,' said the
descendant *mos* at the successful conclusion of his case.[10] A copy of
the court's findings was placed in the Hall of Judgement, accompanied by a list of the judges who had made them.

The above account is given in chronological order. This,
however, was not the method followed by the scribe invited by the
tomb owner, who became known by the name of *Mos* after the case,
to relate this somewhat complex story in his tomb. It is important to
remember here that we are not dealing with a high official,
employing an official scribe to provide an autobiographical account
of his life, but with a private citizen employing a freelance scribe –
and, on the evidence, one with not very tidy thinking processes – to
record events that were significant in the citizen's own life.

The tomb inscriptions flit from one period to another. They begin
by stating that the litigation over ownership of the land began in the
reign of Ramses II. Then the scribe moved back to the time of
Horemheb and the conflict between Urnero and Takharu that ended
with division of the Neshi land between the six heirs. Having dealt
with this aspect of the story, he moved forward again to the time of
Ramses II, giving Year 14-plus as the date when Huy died and his
son, Khayri, was not allowed to possess and work the land that had
been worked by his father. From this point he largely followed
events in their chronological order until he came to the Memphis
court's decision to return ownership of the disputed land to Khayri.
The court's decision is followed by a list of judges, then the phrase
that has created all the confusion: 'Before the court this day, year 59
[. ? .] under the majesty of the king of Upper and Lower Egypt
Djeserkheprure-Setepenre, [son of Re], Horemheb-Meiamon.'[11]
Finally, the scribe ends his account by taking us right back to the
examination made by the priest Aniy at the time in the reign of
Horemheb when the dispute broke out between the plaintiff's
grandmother, Urnero, and her sister, Takharu.

The above date, Year 59, comes at the end of the court's ruling,
before the beginning of the examination of witnesses at the time of
Horemheb. It seems to be some kind of a flashback to the original
dispute between Urnero and Takharu. However, some scholars have
been confused into accepting Year 59 as an actual date in the reign of
Horemheb because they took the view that it relates to the text
which follows it. Yet, even if the scribe chose to give the Memphis

evidence and the list of judges *after* the actual decision of the court, the opening phrase 'Before the court this day ... ' at the end of this muddled section suggests that the date applies to the court's decision. Certainly one would expect a date referring to the successful conclusion of the case rather than events that were the subject of a different court hearing three generations earlier.

The question therefore remains: in what sense was the scribe linking two separate disputes – one in the reign of Horemheb, the other brought to a successful conclusion in the reign of Ramses II? The missing word that was placed originally between 'Year 59' and 'Horemheb' would certainly have changed the meaning of the phrase in question. Although this can only be conjecture, it seems reasonable to suggest that the scribe may have been indicating the time that had elapsed between the original dispute, involving Urnero and Takharu, and the end of the *mos*-Khay dispute over the same piece of land. In this case, the inscription, sandwiched between accounts of two separate court actions, that has caused all the confusion may have read: 'Before the court this day, Year 59 [since] under the majesty of the king of Upper and Lower Egypt Djeserk-heprure-Setepenre [son of Re], Horemheb-Meiamon' and then sketched in the distant origins of the dispute with a copy of the examination made by the priest Aniy at the time of Urnero and Takharu.

The *mos* inscriptions cannot be used, as we have seen, to prove that Horemheb had a long reign. Nor is there any justification, without any evidence, for saying that the total years of the four Amarna kings – Akhenaten, Semenkhkare, Tutankhamun and Aye – were added to the length of Horemheb's reign. It is not only pure supposition, but a course of action for which we find no other example in the history of Ancient Egypt and a course that is contradicted by the British Museum papyrus that mentions 'Year 9 of the rebel', a clear reference to Akhenaten. We have no record of any major military conflict by Horemheb in Asia when we know for certain from other sources that the situation created by the emergent Hittite power there called for urgent action. Nor has Horemheb left any major monuments – as one would expect if he had a long reign – other than the Amarna constructions he usurped, dismantled and re-used.

In the same *mos* text that refers to Akhenaten we find, as we have seen, the initial 'A' of another Amarna king, who must certainly have been Aye. Is it likely that the same scribe who identified these kings would ignore the length of their reigns in the very same text? In any case, it was the names of the Amarna kings that were banned from mention, not the length of their reigns.

In the circumstances, as Year 13 is the last sure date that we have for Horemheb and it agrees with Manetho's account, this should be regarded as being around the time that he died, already an old man who had been a general in the army as long ago as the start of Tutankhamun's reign twenty-six years earlier.

Acceptance of this date, and of a coregency between Amenhotep III and his son Akhenaten, also helps to throw some light on the obscure origins of Horemheb. A stela of Neby, the official of Tuthmosis IV, now in the Leiden Museum, is divided into three registers. The top register shows Neby, 'Troop Commander of Zarw' and his wife, and the central one depicts two offering scenes. The right-hand scene shows a figure identified as 'his son Horemheb' making libation offering to Neby, 'Troop Commander and Mayor of Zarw', and his wife.[12]

As Horemheb was a rare name at the time, Wolfgang Helck, the German philologist, suggested that the young figure shown on the stela was none other than the future king. The close relationship between Horemheb and the Ramesside kings who followed him and founded the Nineteenth Dynasty point to the likelihood of this identification's being accurate. It was Horemheb who appointed both Pa-Ramses (later Ramses I, first ruler of the Nineteenth Dynasty) and his son Seti (who succeeded his father as Seti I) as 'Troop Commander and Mayor of Zarw'. The connection between the god Seth and Horemheb, Ramses I and Seti I has also been proven by the remains of a sanctuary found at the Eastern Delta site of Tell el-Dab'a, dedicated to 'Sutekh (Seth), great of might' and bearing the names of King Horemheb.[13] Seti, while still Mayor of Zarw, was also the priest of Seth.

Helck's suggestion was rejected, however, mainly because it was thought that, if Horemheb had been born so early, there was no coregency and he had a long reign, he would have had to be more than a hundred years old when he died. There is a possibility that Neby died at some time during the reign of Amenhotep III. The stela would not have been made until after his death and as his son,

Horemheb, is not given a title in the stela he must have been very young at the time. Now, if we accept Year 13 of his reign as the year in which Horemheb died and a coregency of eleven years between Amenhotep III and his son, Akhenaten, it means that Horemheb, even if born in the first year of Amenhotep III, would have been only seventy – a possible age – at the time of his death.

10

A CHRONOLOGY OF KINGS

THERE is little dispute about the reign of Amenhotep III's father and predecessor, Tuthmosis IV. Here the archaeological evidence agrees with Manetho that his reign lasted eight years. We are therefore now in a position to present a chronology, working backwards, for the three-quarters of a century or so that preceded the Israelite Exodus:

	Years
Ramses I	2
Horemheb	13
Aye	4
Tutankhamun	9
Semenkhkare	–
Akhenaten (alone)	6
Amenhotep III	38
Tuthmosis IV	8
Total:	80

When did these kings actually reign? A convenient starting point in trying to answer this question is the reign of Tuthmosis IV's grandfather, Tuthmosis III, which is accepted as having lasted fifty-four years. However, two possible dates have been suggested for his accession. Those scholars who allotted a long reign to Horemheb and refused to accept the existence of a coregency between Akhenaten and his father favour 1504 BC while supporters of a short reign and a coregency prefer 1490 BC, which, because of the arguments put forward in the three preceding chapters, I, too, prefer.

Although the reign of his successor, Amenhotep II, has also been the subject of argument, the twenty-three years accepted by Gardiner seems on the bulk of the evidence available to be nearest to the truth. Amenhotep was succeeded in turn by his son, Tuthmosis IV, whose length of reign, together with those of Amenhotep III, the four Amarna kings, Horemheb and Ramses I, are given in reverse order in the table above. How long his son, Seti I, sat on the throne has been the subject of considerable controversy, with estimates of the length of his reign ranging from as high as fifty-nine years to as low as eleven. We are on safer ground, however, with his successor, Ramses II, who is known to have ruled for sixty-seven years, although here again two dates have been put forward for his accession, 1304 BC and 1290 BC. I prefer 1304 BC, the date favoured by supporters of a short reign for Horemheb and an Amarna coregency. If we subtract 1304 BC from 1490 BC we are left with a total of 186 years to be allotted between eleven kings as follows:

	Years
Tuthmosis III	54
Amenhotep II	23
Tuthmosis IV	8
Amenhotep III	38
Akhenaten (alone)	6
Semenkhkare	-
Tutankhamun	9
Aye	4
Horemheb	13
Ramses I	2
Seti I	?
Total:	157

Subtracting this total of 157 years from the 186 years to be allotted between these kings, we are left with twenty-nine years for the reign of Seti I.

The reason for the confusion surrounding the length of time he sat on the throne lies in the conflicting evidence available and, in some cases, the way it has been interpreted. Although the highest surviving date of Seti is Year 11, Manetho gave Seti a long reign (fifty-one years according to Africanus, fifty-five according to Eusebius and fifty-nine years according to Josephus). These dates were brought into question by a figure in the Karnak scene depicting Seti's campaign against the Shasu in his Year 1. The figure, which bore the name Ramses, was identified as the future king, Ramses II, shown here sufficiently grown-up to take part in his father's battles. Clearly, if this was the case and Seti had a long reign, Ramses II would have been well over a hundred years old when he died after his own sixty-seven years on the throne.

The impossibility of this prompted Gaston Maspero, the French Egyptologist, to shorten Seti's reign considerably: 'I had first supposed his reign to have been a long one, merely on the evidence afforded by Manetho's lists, but the presence of Ramses II as a stripling, in the campaign of Seti's first year, forces us to limit its duration to fifteen or twenty years at most, possibly to only twelve to fifteen.'[1]

James Henry Breasted, the American Egyptologist, took a different view. He began by pointing out that Ramses appears at Karnak 'in a scene of the Libyan war, without a date, far from the scenes of the Shasu war of Year 1, on the other side of the door. This appearance of Ramses with his father was therefore not necessarily in his father's first year, as has been so often assumed.' He then goes on to say: 'Furthermore, a close examination of the accompanying figures will show, first, that this scene is no proof that Ramses ever appeared in battle with his father at all, and, second, that Ramses was not the first heir to Seti's throne.' He bases his argument on the fact that a second prince, described as 'first king's son, of his body' – the name that follows is missing – is shown in the scene. ' ... The historical conclusion here is important: the "first king's son" of Seti I was not his successor, Ramses; that is, that Ramses II had an older brother, who did not reach the throne.'[2]

Breasted then went on to argue that the figure of the king's first-born son was not in the scene when it was completed, but was added by the elder prince at a later date. It was also clear that, at a later date still, probably after his elder brother's death and he had become the heir, Ramses chiselled out his brother's figure and the accompanying inscriptions and inserted his own figure 'for his own figure is not original in the scene'.[3]

The highest date we have for Seti is Year 11, on a stela from Gebel

Barakal in Nubia. This has been taken as his last year. Yet, in the light of the available evidence, the arithmetic doesn't work, whether one starts with the childhood of Ramses III and works forward or with his death and works backward. The essential facts are:

• Ramses has himself recorded the story of his childhood and accession in a narrative to be found in Seti I's temple of Abydos, and the account is confirmed by other evidence: 'From the time I was in the egg (a baby) . . . the great ones sniffed the earth before me; when I attained to the rank of the eldest son and heir upon the throne . . . I dealt with affairs, I commanded as chief the foot-soldiers and chariots. My father having appeared before the people, when I was but a very little boy in his arms, said to me: 'I shall have him crowned king, that I may see him in all his splendour while I am still on this earth!' . . . "Place the diadem upon his head," said he.'[4]

In many other inscriptions Ramses stresses that he was a mere child, not a young man of fighting age, while his father ruled the country.

• The precise identity of the heir whose inscription Prince Ramses usurped has since been established as someone named Mehy. He appears to have taken part in all of Seti I's campaigns, from the first against the Shasu, and to have enjoyed a favourable position, at least up to the king's Year 8 when his wars in western Asia came to an end. Moreover, as Seti's war reliefs were carved on the exterior of the northern wall of the Hypostyle Hall at Karnak some time after these wars had come to an end, it suggests that Mehy was regarded as Seti's heir up to that time. Yet, as Mehy himself was not included in these scenes originally and he is known to have inserted his figure at a later date, this could take us even to Seti I's Year 10.

The Abydos story tells us that Prince Ramses was about ten years of age when his father took the unusual step of appointing him as 'eldest son' and heir to the throne. This cannot have happened earlier than at least Year 9 when Mehy seems to have been regarded as heir to the throne.

• It is generally accepted, from examination of his mummy, that Ramses II was about ninety-four when he died, having ruled for sixty-seven years. This would point to his having come to the throne at the age of twenty-seven. If his father had ruled for only eleven years, Prince Ramses could not have been a child, as he claims, in the early stages of his father's rule and would have reached his tenth year before his father came to the throne.

• Seti gave his son wives, beautiful 'as are those of his palace', plus three of his heiress sisters, which – in the light of the above evidence of the time he was appointed 'eldest son' and heir to the throne – indicates that Seti ruled long after his Year 9 or 10.

• Later, Prince Ramses became an army commander and is thought to have been in charge of a campaign in the south at the time his father died.

Some further light is thrown on the length of Seti's reign by the career of a man named Bekenkhons, who, as a youth, worked for eleven years as an 'overseer of the training-stable' for Seti I before joining the priesthood. On his statue, now in Munich, he gives details of his priestly career, which lasted seventy years, during the last twenty-seven of which he was the High Priest of Amun. The statue was dedicated in the reign of Seti's son, Ramses II, while Bekenkhons was still alive.

From another source we know that Bekenkhons' successor as High Priest of Amun was a man named Rome-Roy, who also served under Ramses II. As we know that Ramses II ruled for sixty-seven years, even if we make the unrealistic assumptions that Bekenkhons died and was succeeded by Rome-Roy in the very last year of Ramses II's reign, the former's priestly career must have started no later than three years before Seti's death. Adding on the eleven years he served in the training-stable, and making another assumption, that he joined the king's service in Seti's Year 1, means that Seti's reign must have lasted at least fifteen years – and, on the balance of probabilities, even longer.

Another argument against a short reign is the fact that Seti I's mummy convinced Maspero that he was well over sixty when he died, which means, if he ruled for only eleven years, that he was well over fifty when he came to the throne. It is difficult to match such an advanced age with the figure of the mighty warrior who fought the Shasu in Sinai immediately after his accession and then proceeded to head further campaigns in south and north Palestine, Lebanon, Syria and Libya. Nor can we believe that, had he been that old when he came to the throne, his heir had not yet been born.

The amount of construction work in which he was involved is another indication of a substantial reign. Only Pharaohs who ruled for a considerable time – Tuthmosis III, Amenhotep III and Ramses II, for example – were able to leave great buildings. Seti I completed a funerary temple that had been started by his father, Ramses I, at Kurnah in Western Thebes. Although the pylon of the temple, which he dedicated to the cult of himself and his father, is no longer to be found, the façade, with lotus-bud columns, is still in perfect shape, together with a number of the chambers in front of the sanctuary. The decoration is very carefully executed.

At Abydos, the centre of worship of Osiris, god of the dead, Seti built a great and beautiful temple which Maspero describes in the following terms: 'The building material mainly employed here was the white limestone of Turah, but of a most beautiful quality, which lent itself to the execution of bas-reliefs of great delicacy, perhaps the finest in Ancient Egypt ... When the decoration of the temple was complete, Seti regarded the building as too small for its divine inmate, and accordingly added to it a new wing, which he built along the whole length of the southern wall; but he was unable to finish it completely ...'[5]

Another great architectural work, started by Seti and completed by his son, Ramses II, is the Hypostyle Hall at Karnak, described by Maspero as 'this almost superhuman undertaking': 'The hall measures 162 feet in length, by 325 in breadth. A row of 12 columns, the largest ever placed inside a building, runs up the centre, having capitals in the form of inverted bells. One hundred and twenty-two columns with lotus-form capitals fill the aisles, in rows of nine each. The roof of the central bay is 74 feet above the ground, and the cornice of the two towers rises 63 feet higher ... The size is immense, and we realise its immensity more fully as we search our memory in vain to find anything with which to compare it.'[6]

All of this great building work must have required a great deal of time in planning, the cutting and transportation of stone, and painting and decorating to a perfect finish, certainly longer than eleven years, particularly when Seti I was engaged in his many wars during the early part of his reign.

A further pointer to a substantial reign is the fact that evidence from the south shows that, while Seti ruled Egypt, there were two viceroys for Kush, Amenemopet, son of Paser I, and Yuni.[7] This is unlikely to have been the case had Seti ruled for only eleven years.

If the arguments in favour of a reign of twenty-nine years for Seti I are accepted, this would mean that he was born in Year 2 of his father, which seems possible from the above evidence.

We are now in a position to construct a chronology for the period that concerns us:

King	Length of reign	Dates
Tuthmosis III	54	1490–1436
Amenhotep II	23	1436–1413
Tuthmosis IV	8	1413–1405
Amenhotep III	38	1405–1367
Akhenaten (alone)	6	1367–1361
Semenkhkare	–	–
Tutankhamun	9	1361–1352
Aye	4	1352–1348
Horemheb	13	1348–1335
Ramses I	2	1335–1333
Seti I	29	1333–1304
Ramses II	67	1304–1237

On the basis of this chronology of Egyptian history and the chronology of the Sojourn set out in an earlier chapter, we can make the following deductions:

• Akhenaten was born in Year 11 or 12 of his father, 1394 BC;

• Akhenaten fell from power and fled to Sinai in 1361 BC at the age of thirty-four or thirty-five;

• If Akhenaten was Moses, he was around sixty when he returned to Egypt and led the Exodus in the reign of Ramses I.

Whether or not Akhenaten lost his life at the time he fell from power, which has been widely assumed, will be argued in a later chapter.

11

THE BIRTHPLACE OF AKHENATEN

IF Moses and Akhenaten are the same person, they must have been born at the same place at the same time.

From Old Testament and Egyptian sources we have mention of six Eastern Delta cities:

• **Avaris**, the old Hyksos capital, dating from more than two centuries earlier;

• **Zarw-kha**, the city of Queen Tiye, mentioned in the pleasure-lake scarab of Year 11 of her husband, Amenhotep III;

• **Zarw** or **Zalw** (**Sile** of the Greeks), the frontier fortified city, mentioned in texts starting from the Eighteenth Dynasty, whose precise whereabouts in the fourteenth nome is known;

• **Pi-Ramses**, the Eastern Delta residence of Pharaohs of the Nineteenth and Twentieth Dynasties, known as 'House of Ramses, Beloved of Amun, Great of Victories';

• **Raamses**, the city built by the Israelites' forced labour;

• **Rameses** (the same place as Raamses), where the Exodus began.

There is now general agreement among scholars that Pi-Ramses was situated on the site of the former Hyksos capital, Avaris, and that it was the same city as Raamses, the city built by the Israelites' harsh labour, and Rameses, named in the Old Testament as the starting point of the Exodus. The two questions at issue, therefore, are: are Pi-Ramses/Avaris to be found in the same location as Zarw? Was Zarw also Tiye's city, Zarw-kha? The answers to these questions are critical because of what we know of the birth of Moses and Akhenaten.

On their arrival in Egypt the Israelites settled at Goshen in the Eastern Delta, near to the known position of Zarw. As there is no evidence that they ever migrated to another part of the country, this must have been the area that provides the background for the Book of Exodus account of the birth of Moses. It is also implicit in the story that the ruling Pharaoh of the time had a residence nearby: he was in a position to give orders in person to the midwives to kill the child born to the Israelite woman if it proved to be a boy, and, according to the Book of Exodus, the sister of Moses was able to watch what happened when 'the daughter of Pharaoh came down to wash herself at the river' and noticed the basket containing Moses hidden among the reeds on the bank of the Nile. Later, when Moses and his brother Aaron had a series of meetings with Pharaoh there is no indication that they had to travel any distance for these meetings to take place.

In the case of Akhenaten, the pleasure lake scarab, dated to Year 11 (1394 BC) of his father, Amenhotep III, plus other evidence, points to his birth having taken place at Zarw-kha. Six versions have been found of the scarab, issued to commemorate the creation of a pleasure lake for the king's Great Royal Wife, Tiye. Although there are some minor differences, they all agree on the main points of the text, which runs as follows:

> Year 11, third month of Inundation (first season), day 1, under the majesty of Horus . . . mighty of valour, who smites the Asiatics, King of Upper and Lower Egypt, Neb-Maat-Re, Son of Re Amenhotep Ruler of Thebes, who is given life, and the Great Royal Wife Tiye, who liveth. His Majesty commanded the making of a lake for the Great King's Wife Tiye, who liveth, in her city of Zarw-kha. Its length 3700 cubits, its breadth 700 cubits. [One of the scarabs, a copy of which is kept at the Vatican, gives the breadth as 600 cubits, and also mentions the names of the queen's parents, Yuya and Tuya, indicating that they were still alive at the time.] His Majesty celebrated the feast of the opening of the lake in the third month of the first season, day 16, when His Majesty sailed thereon in the royal barge *Aten Gleams*.[1]

In my previous book[2] I argued that Pi-Ramses, Avaris and Zarw-kha were all to be found at one location – the frontier fortified city of Zarw, to the east of modern Kantarah, which is to the south of Port Said on the Suez Canal. To recapitulate what I believe to have been the correct sequence of events . . .

Here the kings of the Twelfth Dynasty are known to have built a fortified city (20th century BC). The autobiography of Sinuhi, a court official who fled from Egypt to Palestine during the last days of Amenemhat I, the first king of the Twelfth Dynasty (1970 BC), mentions his passing the border fortress, which at that time bore the name 'Ways of Horus'. The border city was rebuilt and refortified by the Asiatic Hyksos rulers who took control of Egypt for just over a century from the mid-seventeenth century BC. During this period it became known as Avaris. Later, when the kings of the Eighteenth Dynasty expelled the Hyksos, they in turn rebuilt the city with new fortifications, it was given the new name of Zarw and it became the main outpost on the Asiatic frontier, the point at which Egyptian armies began and ended their campaigns against Palestine/Syria.

During the time of Tuthmosis IV (1413–1405 BC), his queen had an estate and residence within Zarw. Subsequently, Amenhotep III, the son of Tuthmosis IV, gave this royal residence, Zarw-kha, within the walls of Zarw, to his wife, Queen Tiye, as a present. I explained this event as stemming from the king's desire to allow Tiye to have a summer residence in the area of nearby Goshen in the Eastern Delta where her father's Israelite family had been allowed to settle. (I regard Yuya, Queen Tiye's father, as being the Patriarch Joseph, of the coat of many colours, who brought the tribe of Israel from Canaan to dwell in Egypt.)

Later still, after the fall of the Amarna kings, who were descendants of both Amenhotep III and Yuya, Horemheb, the king who succeeded them, deprived the Israelites of their special position at Goshen and turned their city of Zarw into a prison. There he appointed Pa-Ramses and his son, Seti, as viziers and mayors of Zarw as well as commanders of the fortress and its troops. Pa-Ramses, the new mayor of the city, forced the Israelites into harsh labour, building for him what the Book of Exodus describes as a 'store city' within the walls of Zarw. Pa-Ramses followed Horemheb on the throne as Ramses I in 1335 BC, establishing the Nineteenth Dynasty, and it was during his brief reign, lasting little more than a year, that Moses led the Israelites out of the Eastern Delta into Sinai.

At the time he came to the throne, Ramses I already had his residence at Zarw, being the city's mayor. His son, Seti I, and the latter's son, Ramses II, later established a new royal residence at Zarw that became known as Pi-Ramses and was used as the Delta capital of the Ramesside kings of the Nineteenth and Twentieth Dynasties for about two centuries. The kings of the Twenty-first Dynasty established a new residence at Tanis, south of Lake Menzalah, and made use in its construction of many monuments and much stone from Pi-Ramses, which misled later scribes into the erroneous belief that Pi-Ramses and Tanis were identical locations.

The whole issue of whether or not Pi-Ramses/Avaris and Zarw are to be found at the same location has been clouded by the fact that, while we know the precise location of Zarw, scholars have in the course of this century canvassed the claims of no fewer than six other sites in the Eastern Delta, in addition to Tanis, as the location of Pi-Ramses/Avaris, and two alternative sites – one at Thebes, the other in Middle Egypt – as the site of Tiye's city. The Delta sites have been advanced even if they failed to yield the required archaeological evidence, were in the wrong nome and, in some cases, did not exist at the relevant time. Each was abandoned in turn to be replaced by a seventh site, Qantir/Tell el-Dab'a. Investigations at Tell el-Dab'a, just over a mile south of Qantir (one of the sites suggested earlier, and now revived), were begun by the University of Vienna and the Austrian Archaeological Institute in 1966 and are still continuing.

This location has achieved considerable acceptance as the site of Pi-Ramses/Avaris since Manfred Bietak, the Austrian Egyptologist in charge of the excavations, gave an interim report on the expedition's findings in 1979. Yet this site, too, does not withstand close scrutiny any more than the previous six in the Eastern Delta that had been put forward. Recent archaeological discoveries in the Kantarah area make it unnecessary to argue at this point the objections to the Qantir/Tell el-Dab'a location, which can be found in Appendix D: instead I am concentrating here on some of the mass of evidence that Pi-Ramses/Avaris is to be found on the same site as Zarw. From written sources we know that:

• Pi-Ramses was situated in a fertile wine-producing area and lay in the centre of a great vineyard: Zarw was in a wine-producing area, which is supported by two pieces of evidence. Remains of wine jars, sent from Zarw by its then mayor Djehutymes for celebrations of

Amenhotep III's first jubilee in his Year 30, were found in the Malkata palace complex at Western Thebes,[3] and a wine jar from the house of Aten at Zarw, belonging to his Year 5, was found in the tomb of Tutankhamun;

• Pi-Ramses was 'the forefront of every foreign land, the end of Egypt', located 'between Palestine and Egypt':[4] Zarw had an identical location, at the starting point of the 'road of Horus', leading to Palestine;

• Pi-Ramses could be reached by water from Memphis: Zarw could be reached by water from Memphis;

• Pi-Ramses was connected by water with the fortress of Zarw and the Waters of Shi-hor (north and north-west of Zarw), which fits exactly what we know of the Ramesside Delta residence;

• Pi-Ramses was supplied with papyrus by the Waters of Pa-Twfy, 'The Sea Of Reeds', which has been identified with Lake Ballah, to the south of Zarw;

• Pi-Ramses' boundaries were marked by some of its chief temples, with Seth the main deity worshipped there: 'Its western part is the house of Amun, its southern part the house of Seth, Astarte is in its Orient, and Buto in its northern part':[5] Seth was also the main deity worshipped at Zarw;

• An indication that Pi-Ramses was built originally as a royal residence within the walls of Zarw is to be found in the name Pi-Ramses itself. Instead of a usual determinative for a city, a cross inside a circle, we have a sign for a house, Pi (*Pr*) preceding the name. This term *Pr* is usually applied either to a temple area, a religious area or a walled area containing a royal palace as well as a temple and other administrative buildings.

• Pi-Ramses was located in the fourteenth Egyptian nome and to the east of the Pelusiac branch of the Nile Delta: so was Zarw;

• Pi-Ramses had strong military fortifications, and, according to Manetho, as quoted by Josephus, Avaris, which was on the same site, was very favourably situated, well-fortified and in a strategic military position: this was equally true of Zarw.

Abundant evidence exists to confirm that Pi-Ramses was heavily fortified. A stela at Abu Simbel of the thirty-fifth year of Ramses II has the god Ptah telling the king: 'I have made for thee a noble Residence in order to strengthen the boundary of the Two Lands, House of Ramses, Beloved of Amun,' thus confirming that the residence was both fortified and near the borders. Gardiner has pointed out that the special epithets attached to the city's name indicate its location near the border: ' . . . two epithets [are] frequently . . . added to the cartouche and its adjuncts; these, according to the habit of Egyptian names, express the precise aspect in which the king appears in the particular locality that they designate, and are the real distinguishing marks by which that locality could be differentiated from others owing their names to the same king. The original name of the city in its complete form was . . . The House of Ramses, Beloved of Amun, Great of Victories, and the boastful addition here made to the royal nomen conveys a significant hint as to the position of the city near the military road to Asia.'[6]

Another indication that Pi-Ramses was designated as being a 'mighty place' is provided in Ramses II's inscription at his father's temple in Abydos, while *Papyrus Anastasi III* describes Pi-Ramses as being 'the marshalling place of thy [Pharaoh's] cavalry, the rallying point of thy soldiers, the harbourage of thy ships' troops . . . '

All the sources we have about Avaris confirm – as one would expect if it is the same place – that, like Pi-Ramses, it was a fortified city. The Egyptian name of Avaris consists of two elements, *hwt-w'ret*, which are followed by a determinative, not of a city but of a walled area. The first element, *hwt*, indicates a settlement surrounded by a high brick wall, the second element, *w'ret*, as Alan Gardiner has explained, signifies a 'desert strip'. So the very name of the city indicates that it was both fortified and near the desert border, just as Zarw was. This was precisely what one would expect in the case of Asiatic invaders in order both to protect themselves against the natives and be near their escape road to Asia. The account of Manetho, as quoted by Josephus, agrees with this understanding: 'In the Saite [Sethroite fourteenth nome], he [the Hyksos ruler] founded a city very favourably situated on the east of the Bubastite branch of the Nile [the north section of the Pelusiac], and called Avaris after an ancient religious tradition. This place he rebuilt and fortified with massive walls, planting a garrison . . . to guard the frontier. Here he would come in summertime, partly to train them carefully in manoeuvres and to strike terror into foreign tribes ... '[7] This also agrees with the description of Avaris as a walled settlement in the Kamose Stela, which gives an account of campaigns against the Hyksos invaders by the brother of King Ahmosis, founder of the Eighteenth Dynasty, and the autobiography of Ahmose, a naval officer, who also took part in the war of liberation and describes in his tomb at el-Kab in Nubia how 'they [the Egyptian army] sat down [in siege] before the town of Avaris'.[8]

• Pi-Ramses was also called 'The Dwelling of the Lion': Zarw agrees with descriptions of Pi-Ramses in the fact that it is connected both with Horus and the lion: according to the text in *Papyrus Anastasi*,[9] Horus took the form of a lion at Zarw and a seated lion forms the second part of the city's name;

• Exodus 13:17 indicates that the city of Ramses was near 'the way of the land of the Philistines', known from Egyptian sources as the 'road of Horus', leading from Zarw to Gaza;

• The triumphal *Poem of Pe-natour*, recording the victories of Ramses II in his Year 5, and a letter describing the delivery of some stele identify Pi-Ramses and Zarw as being in the same vicinity, and the account of Seti I's return from his Year 1 campaign against the Shasu in Sinai indicated that the royal family had a residence in the area from the early days of the Nineteenth Dynasty;

• A reference was made in *Papyrus Anastasi* (vol. 24, pp. 7, 8) to 'the fortress of Ramses, which is in Zarw', indicating that the fortress of Zarw was sometimes referred to as 'the fortress of Ramses, *myr Amun*': this could also have been the case regarding the city;

• A channel through the Isthmus of Kantarah was first noticed by Napoleon's French expedition of 1798–1801. This channel was called the 'separating water' (*ta-dynt* in Egyptian), and is the canal represented on Seti I's war inscriptions in the Hypostyle Hall at Karnak. It connected Shi-Hor to the north and north-west with the Waters of Pa-Twfy in the south, and separated Zarw from the Eastern Delta. Access to the fortress was provided by a bridge, which became the origin of the modern name, Kantarah (bridge).

This mass of circumstantial evidence, which is by no means exhaustive, served to persuade some scholars that Avaris, Pi-Ramses and
Zarw occupied one and the same location: 'Dr Gardiner has told us
that Ramses, the capital, and Avaris are the same place. The question
is therefore: where was Avaris? I have no hesitation in agreeing with
M. (Jean) Clédat, (the French Egyptologist), that it was the region
and the city called Zarw, the present Kantarah, and its neighbourhood.'[10] Yet very few accepted this identification when it was first
put forward by Clédat in 1922.[11]

Basically it was the lack of archaeological evidence that caused the
failure of scholars to give proper attention to Clédat's views for,
although he was correct in identifying Pi-Ramses/Avaris and Zarw
as occupying the same location in the Kantarah area, he was wrong
in identifying the precise spot as Tell Abu-Seifah, just over a mile
south-east of modern Kantarah, where only monuments of a late
Graeco-Roman period were discovered. This error stemmed fundamentally from the assumption that the starting point of the ancient
'road of Horus' was the same as that of the modern road leading
from the Kantarah area to Gaza.

The fact that the ancient 'road of Horus' began elsewhere became
clear when Mohammad Abdel Maqsoud, a senior excavations officer
with the Egyptian Antiquity Organization, began to supervise
diggings at Tell Heboua, some two-and-a-half miles *north-east* of
Kantarah, three years ago. From the war reliefs of Seti I at Karnak
we know the names of different guarded military posts between
Zarw and Gaza, the first of which, from the Egyptian side, is called
the 'Dwelling of the Lion'. After two seasons of excavation,
Maqsoud gave an account of his findings to members of the Fifth
International Congress of Egyptology in Cairo in November 1988,
concluding his speech with the words: 'It is possible now to identify
the fortress of Tell Heboua with the "Dwelling of the Lion"
depicted in the reliefs of Seti I at Karnak.'

Maqsoud released some details of his findings at the end of the
third season, and on reading them in an Egyptian newspaper in April
1989 I realized that, without being aware of it, he had found the
location of Pi-Ramses/Avaris/Zarw, a view which was published by
the *Sunday Times* of London a month later and has since become the
subject of discussion by Egyptologists all over the world. What, in
fact, had Maqsoud discovered?

The site of Tell Heboua proved to be near the ancient Pelusiac branch of the Nile, between two lakes – north and south – on the western side of which are indications of an ancient canal, and it is at the start of what has now been established as the 'road of Horus'. Remains of massive fortifying walls, more than thirteen feet wide, enclose a square area of some 190,000 square yards. Inside the walls are the remains of at least two ancient towns – one Hyksos, the other dating from the Eighteenth Dynasty – with houses, streets, store-houses, bread and clay ovens, and burials of two different kinds on two levels. Maqsoud also found four identical stelae of Nehesy, the king of the weak Thirteenth Dynasty, two of which bear his cartouche. It was Nehesy (c. 1715 BC) who re-established Seth as the main deity of the fourteenth nome. Seth had earlier been discredited as a result of development of the myth that he had been responsible for the assassination of the good god Osiris. There was also a fragment of an architrave, belonging to a temple, with a cartouche of Seti I.

Although much of the site has not yet been excavated, scarabs and other small items found there point to the existence of temples and palaces. Skeletal remains of children also make it clear that this was not simply a fortress but also a non-military settlement during both the Hyksos and Empire periods. In addition, Maqsoud even found remains of an Asiatic community that had occupied the site before construction of the fortifying walls in the Hyksos period, indicating that the site had been occupied by a Canaanite community during the Thirteenth Dynasty which preceded Hyksos rule in the Eastern Delta.

The most important evidence, however, is provided by the fortifications themselves. This is the only fortified city ever to have been found in the Eastern Delta. Moreover, it has at least three different walls at three levels, confirming what we know from literary sources of Pi-Ramses/Avaris/Zarw.

Dr Eric Uphill, Hon. Research Fellow of Egyptology at University College, London, has accepted in a discussion at the Egyptian Cultural Centre that the city at Tell Heboua could be identified with Zarw, and even Maqsoud himself has changed the subject of the PhD thesis he is preparing at Lille University in France from having found the 'Dwelling of the Lion', accepting that what he has actually found is the fortified city of Zarw. I think that before long others will come to the same conclusion regarding the remains of the upper strata.

The next question that will have to be faced is: what about the fortified Hyksos city beneath Zarw? The textual information we have not only informs us that Avaris was fortified, but that it was the *only* fortified Hyksos city in Egypt – and none of the other locations suggested hitherto for the Hyksos capital so far reveals any kind of fortifications.

Archaeological work in Syria/Palestine has brought to light a number of Hyksos cities, all of which were almost identical. They featured a characteristic system of fortification whose most dominant feature was the use of glacis, a steeply-sloping inner wall of plastered limestone, encircling the sides of an ancient mound on which the city was built; a heavy retaining wall of battered stone at the foot of the inner wall, and a large city wall around the summit. In defence of the site of Qantir/Tell el-Dab'a being the location of Pi-Ramses, it has been suggested that the lack of massive walls and fortifications, which are essential evidence for such an identification, is to be explained by the fact that they were long ago washed away by the waters of the Nile: yet, if this were the case, one is entitled to ask how ordinary houses, much less strongly built, have managed to survive in the same layers and under the same conditions?

In the meantime, as the walled city of Zarw found by Maqsoud lies on top of a mound, it seems likely that the walls of Avaris lie beneath it; and Dr Ali Hassan, the head of the Egyptian Antiquity Organization, has admitted: 'The remains found beneath the city are the first Hyksos remains to be found in Sinai and raise a new doubt regarding the position – now generally accepted as Tell el-Dab'a – of the Hyksos capital in Egypt.' As there is complete agreement among scholars that the finding of Avaris would also mean having located Pi-Ramses, I do not think we are too far from establishing the truth now that both of those cities are located at Tell Heboua, particularly when the site yields further evidence in the planned fourth season of excavation.

Tiye's City

As the final part of the word Zarw-kha has the determinative of a
city – a circle including a cross – some early Egyptologists, such as
Petrie, Maspero and Clédat, having removed this final part of the
name, identified Tiye's city, Zarw-kha, with the border fortress and
city of Zarw.[12] In addition, Clédat demonstrated[13] that Lake Ballah,
to the south of Kantarah, is the pleasure lake mentioned in the scarab.
As Zarw was the frontier city on the road to Asia, the use of the
epithet 'who smites the Asiatics' in the scarab again points to Zarw as
the location of Tiye's city. More recently, however, two alternative
sites – distant from the frontier – have been canvassed as Tiye's city
(see Appendix D).

12

AKHENATEN: THE EARLY YEARS

THE early marriage between Amenhotep III and Tiye, the parents of Akhenaten, is attested by an issue of scarabs dated to Year 2 of his reign. Although we know of female descendants of this marriage, not much evidence survives about the birth and childhood of Amenhotep IV (Akhenaten). It seems, however, that he had an elder brother, Tuthmosis, who died before Akhenaten was born. Tuthmosis, we know, was being educated and trained at Memphis and held the title of the High Priest of Ptah, as did most heirs-apparent during the Eighteenth Dynasty, but then he disappeared suddenly from the scene.

Some additional light was cast on the youth of Akhenaten as a result of excavations on the site of Amenhotep III's royal palace complex at Malkata in Western Thebes by the discovery of hundreds of small inscribed fragments of great historical importance. Here it becomes evident that the Middle Palace of the complex was probably built for Akhenaten while he was still a prince and, as 'Regnal Year 1' occurs in the inscriptions, that he continued to live there during the early Theban years of the coregency with his father. The earliest dating for Amenhotep III is not earlier than Year 8, which indicates that Year 1 could not relate to him. The only mention of Akhenaten before his accession to the throne was found in Malkata in the form of an undated wine-jar seal with the inscription '... (of) the estate of the true King's Son, Amenhotep (Akhenaten)'. The use of the expression 'true son' indicates an early challenge to the prince's right to inherit the throne and that the coregency had not yet started. This therefore dates the wine-jar seal to some time between Year 20 of Amenhotep III, who spent most of his time in Memphis until then, and the start of the coregency in Year 28. It also suggests that at around this time Akhenaten was old enough to have his own establishment. It is, in fact, thought that he was in his mid-teens when the coregency started: 'His [Akhenaten's] brother, who ordinarily would have inherited the throne, had died in infancy, and Amenhotep IV was made coregent with his father ... He was perhaps sixteen years at the time.'[1]

Deducting sixteen years from the start of the coregency with his father, we come to Year 12 of Amenhotep III as the year of his birth. Furthermore, two commemorative scarabs issued by Amenhotep III point to the possible place of his birth. The first, dated to Year 10, relates 'a miracle, brought to His Majesty, the daughter of the prince of Nahrin [Mitanni], Sutarna [Tushratta's father], Gilukhipa and persons of her harem, 317 women'.

The last issue of these commemorative scarabs is the pleasure lake scarab, dated to Year 11 and, as we saw earlier, recording '. . . under the majesty of . . . Amenhotep III, given life; and the Great King's Wife Tiye, in her city of Zarw-kha . . . His Majesty celebrated the feast of the lake, in the third month of the first season, day 16, when His Majesty sailed thereon in the royal barge *Aten Gleams*.'

It seems that, after his first year with the Mitannian princess, Amenhotep III went back to Queen Tiye for a kind of second honeymoon in her Eastern Delta city of Zarw – the 'end of Egypt', where the desert and the road to Gaza began, and close to Goshen where the Israelites had settled – which must have become the summer residence for the royal family, as it became again during the Ramesside rule of the Nineteenth and Twentieth Dynasties. The Egyptians had three seasons, Inundation, Winter and Gathering, each of four months, with the year beginning in mid-July. The middle of the third month would therefore have been around 1 October. Thus it is possible that Akhenaten was born in 1394 BC, either towards the mid-July end of Year 11 or around the beginning of year 12.

Zarw had been rebuilt during the Eighteenth Dynasty as a conveniently situated military post for operations in Asia. It also seems that the harem of Tuthmosis IV, Amenhotep III's father, had a residence at Zarw as inscriptions of Neby, the city's vizier at the time, found at Sarabit el Khadim in Sinai, give his titles not only as 'Mayor of Zarw' and 'Troop Commander', but as 'Steward of the Harem of the Royal Wife'. If the queen in question was Mutimuya,

Amenhotep's mother, this could imply that even Amenhotep III must have spent some time during his childhood in this Eastern Delta residence of his mother, especially at the height of summer when the Delta was cooler than Lower and Middle Egypt.

Akhenaten was born in an era of peace and prosperity for Egypt. A combination of diplomacy, judicious marriages and equally judicious use of gold had secured a balance of power, at least temporarily, between Egypt and the neighbouring Hurrian State of Mitanni, the Hittites, the Assyrians and Babylonians; Palestine and Syria, conquered by Tuthmosis III in the middle of the fifteenth century BC, posed no threat; the southern frontier had been secured up to and beyond the Nile's Fourth Cataract. Luxuries from the Levant and the Aegean world poured into the country on a greater scale than ever before, more land was brought under cultivation, art flourished, prosperous State officials and priests enjoyed the pleasures of new town houses and country villas with large estates. How the common people fared is less clear, but they must have benefited from the general prosperity and the State projects that offered alternative employment during the long summer droughts.

Throughout the country, new temples were founded, old ones restored. One of the biggest temporal projects was Amenhotep III's splendid palace, the Malkata, in western Thebes, opposite modern Luxor, with an imposing mortuary temple beside it for the god Amun-Re. Thebes was also the seat of the State god, Amun-Re. While ancient cults of other gods continued to flourish locally, the cult of Amun-Re had received, and continued to receive, such favourable royal treatment – generous endowment for the great temple of Karnak at Thebes, munificent gifts of land and gold – that it had become virtually an arm of the State executive. Yet there was already a hint in the air of the enormous religious upheaval that lay ahead.

During the reign of Amenhotep II, the king's grandfather, and Tuthmosis IV, his father, a gradual but growing fusion had taken place between the cult of Amun, the patron god of the Eighteenth Dynasty, and the cult of Re, the sun-god, whose foremost centre of worship was far to the north at On (Heliopolis), north of modern Cairo and close to the important administrative and military capital of Memphis. Re was looked upon as the lord of the universe, the giver of all life, and the king ruled according to Re's divine plan by virtue of being his son. On an increasing scale during this period hymns and prayers to Re as the giver of life began to appear on a variety of monuments, including stelae and tomb doors. As a rule the name of the sun-god was given in the form common in Heliopolis, Re-Harakhti (Horus of the Horizon).

At a royal as well as a religious level a change took place during this period that must have seemed as strange to those aware of it as some of the wilder claims of today's ardent feminists. The name of Queen Tiye, unlike that of earlier queens, is placed regularly in a cartouche, a distinction previously limited to the ruling monarch, and is also included in royal titularies. Furthermore, she is represented as being of equivalent stature to the king.

As with Moses, we know very little of Akhenaten's early years beyond the fact that he had an extremely close relationship with his mother, Queen Tiye, who seems to have been his only confidante at this stage of his life. There is no evidence that he spent his early days at Memphis, where his father had his main residence at the time and where the heirs apparent were normally trained and educated with the sons of the nobles. His appearance at Thebes does not seem to have occurred until Year 20 of his father, Amenhotep III, when the evidence of the wine-jar seal has been interpreted as 'the true king's son, Amenhotep', indicates that he had a palace there. William C. Hayes, the American Egyptologist, comments on this inscription: 'The King's son, Amenhotep, referred to here was in all probability the future king Amenhotep IV before his elevation to the coregency, which is thought to have taken place in or about Year 28 of Amenhotep III.'[2]

It is from his behaviour and the kind of knowledge he seemed to have acquired at the time of his ultimate appearance at Thebes that we have to guess at where Akhenaten most probably passed the greater part of his childhood. His appearance does not suggest that he had any physical training, contrary to the custom among Eighteenth Dynasty kings, and he is never shown hunting lions or other wild animals. Nor is he depicted smiting an enemy or leading his army in combat. On the other hand he does not seem to have had the respect for Egyptian deities or customs evinced by other kings.

As many elements of Akhenaten's new religion had their origin in the solar worship of Heliopolis, this points to his having had some training and education at this city, especially as Anen, the brother of

Queen Tiye, was a high priest of Re, probably at Heliopolis. Yet his developed views about the Aten when he was still a young man suggest that he must have been involved in his early years in a monotheistic cult of the Aten at Zarw, his mother's city, which – if his life in early childhood, like that of Moses, had been under threat – would have been the safest place to conceal him.

A significant pointer to the existence of such a cult there even before the birth of Akhenaten is the fact that the vessel used by Amenhotep III when he sailed on the pleasure lake was named *Aten Gleams*. We also have evidence that the Aten temples which Akhenaten built at both Karnak and Luxor at the beginning of his coregency were not the first Aten temples in Egypt, and, again significantly, the very first shrine appears to have been in the city of Zarw. Another of the titles of Neby, the mayor of Zarw during the time of Tuthmosis IV, was *imyr hnt*, and, as the word *hnt* has been interpreted as meaning 'lake' or 'lake area', Gun Björkman, the Swedish Egyptologist, has taken this title to indicate Neby's control over the lake area of Zarw: 'This seems to agree very well with what can be concluded from the monuments of Neby. Considering the nature of Zarw and its neighbourhood, it also seems suitable that Neby should have the designation discussed.' Björkman also gave a footnote reference on the same page. 'Professor Yoyotte has drawn my attention to a photograph in the Archives P. Lacau (Photo A III, 63, F6) of a *talalat*, i.e. a small block from the time of Akhenaten (these are the stones that Akhenaten used in the building of his Theban temples), showing a procession of bowing officials. The accompanying inscriptions describe Neby as "The Overseer of the Foremost Water in the *hnt* of the Temple of Aten".'[3]

As this scene and inscription indicate a Temple of Aten already in existence at the time Akhenaten was constructing his first Aten temple at Karnak, it must have existed in the Zarw lake area of the Eastern Delta – what the Bible calls 'the land of Goshen' – before his rule began. In addition, we have the text on a wine-jar, placed in the tomb of Tutankhamun at the time of his death, that reads: 'Year 5. Sweet wine of the House-of-Aten [from] Zarw. Chief vintner Penamun.'[4]

Therefore, even before Akhenaten built his first temple for his new God and right up to at least the time of Year 5 of Tutankhamun, Zarw had a temple to the Aten. If Akhenaten was born there, for which there are strong supporting indications ... if his absence from Thebes and Memphis during his early years can be explained by the fact that, during this period of his life, he was living at Zarw, the city of his mother, whose Asiatic relatives had settled in the vicinity ... and if the first temple for the Aten in Egypt was at Zarw, then the inescapable conclusion has to be that he must have received his first inspirations regarding his new God and his new religion while he was at Zarw. This would explain the fact that his new religious ideas – including the Israelite idea of a God without an image – were already to a large extent developed when he came to the throne at Thebes as coregent. It is also worth noting that the name of the chief vintner, Penamun, resembles an Egyptianized form of Benjamin, and the vintner could have been a descendant of that tribe.

The section that follows immediately matches, in greater detail, the outline of the story of Moses given in Chapter Six and is repeated here to save the reader from having to refer back to it.

As her son reached his mid-teens, Tiye took the precaution of ensuring his right to the throne by marrying him to his half-sister, Neferneferuaten Nefertiti, daughter of Amenhotep III and *his* sister, Sitamun, and therefore the rightful heiress, whom the young prince succeeded in converting to his new religion. It has been suggested that because of her name, which can be translated as 'the beautiful one who is come', Nefertiti may have been the Mitannian princess Tadukhipa. Such a marriage would have been contrary to royal practice in Egypt at the time, however, since the new king established his right to the throne by marrying the royal heiress. Furthermore, the fact that Horemheb, the last ruler of the Eighteenth Dynasty, is generally believed to have established his right to the throne by marrying Nefertiti's sister, Mutnezmat, indicates that Nefertiti herself must at this earlier stage have been the heiress daughter of Amenhotep III.

As a further step towards ensuring that her son's right to the throne should be unassailable, Tiye subsequently persuaded Amenhotep III, whose health began to weaken as the years went by, to appoint him as his coregent at Thebes, but, in order to gain the acceptance of the priesthood, the stress in making the appointment was placed during the first Theban years upon the role of Nefertiti, the heiress.

On his accession to the throne as coregent, Akhenaten took the names Nefer-khepru-re Waenre Amenhotep – that is, Amenhotep IV – and from his very first year provoked the priests by his aggressive attitude. He had barely assumed his new position when he used some of the wealth amassed by his father to build at Thebes a large new temple to the Aten – a God for the world, not just for Egyptians – within the precincts of the existing Amun-Re temples at Karnak. This was followed by a second temple at Luxor. He snubbed the traditional priests by not inviting them to any of the festivities in the early part of his coregency and, in his fourth year, when he celebrated his *sed* festival or jubilee – usually, but not necessarily, a rejuvenation celebration that marked Year 30 of a monarch's reign – he banned all deities but his own God from the occasion. Twelve months later he made a further break with tradition by changing his name to Akhenaten in honour of his new deity.

To the resentful Egyptian establishment the Aten was seen as a challenger who would replace the powerful State god Amun and not come under his domination. In the tense climate that prevailed, Tiye arranged a compromise by persuading her son to leave Thebes and establish a new capital in Middle Egypt, on the east bank of the Nile, some two hundred miles to the north of Thebes.

13

HORIZON OF THE ATEN

THE climate of hostility that surrounded Akhenaten all his life – and one may wonder what could have been the causes were they not ethnic and religious – had surfaced as early as two years after his appointment as coregent. The Memphite inscription of his father's Year 30, as we saw in an earlier chapter, had sought to defend his action in 'placing the male offspring [the heir] upon the throne', suggesting that there had been opposition – undoubtedly from the Amun priesthood and the nobility – to his action in securing the inheritance for his son.

Further evidence of such opposition is found in the proclamation of Akhenaten on the boundary stelae, fixed before the start of the building of his new city of Amarna in his Year 4. Here he refers to what appears to be open opposition he had faced prior to that date: 'For, as Father Hor-Aten liveth, . . . priests [?] more evil are they than those things which I heard unto Year 4, [more evil are they] than [those things] which I have heard in year . . . more evil are they than those things which King . . . [heard], more evil are they than those things which Menkheperure (Tuthmosis IV) heard.'[1]

Akhenaten is referring to hostile comments he heard about himself prior to Year 4. Not only that: two kings who preceded him had been subject to similar verbal criticism. The missing name here can only be that of his father, Amenhotep III, whose Memphite inscription, referred to above, points to opposition over the steps he took to ensure Akhenaten's succession. But why should Tuthmosis IV have encountered similar hostility from the Establishment? We have no evidence on this point. I have argued in *Stranger in the Valley of the Kings*, however, that it was Tuthmosis IV who appointed Joseph (Yuya) as one of his ministers and the Old Testament indicates that, at the time, he was dissatisfied with his usual advisers, for which the Book of Genesis blames their failure to interpret Pharaoh's dream about the seven good years that would be followed by seven lean years: 'And it came to pass in the morning that his spirit was troubled; and he sent and called for all the magicians of Egypt, and all the wise men thereof; and Pharaoh told them his dream; but there was none that could interpret them unto Pharaoh' (Genesis, 41:8).

It would appear a reasonable deduction that priestly opposition to the king's behaviour went back to the time of Tuthmosis IV's appointment as his vizier of Joseph, one of the hated shepherds. Although the young Akhenaten would have known of the hostile comments directed at his father, he could have heard about criticisms of his grandfather, Tuthmosis IV, only through having been told about them, possibly by Yuya, his maternal grandfather, still alive when Akhenaten was born.

The criticisms levelled at Akhenaten himself included, according to other inscriptions on the boundary stelae at Amarna, the land the king had chosen for the building of a house for the Aten at Karnak: 'Behold Pharaoh ... found that it belonged not to a god, it belonged not to a goddess, it belonged not to a prince, it belonged not to a princess ... [There is no right for] any man to act as owner of it.'[2] The implication is that, as he made in Karnak and Luxor temples for his God, isolating the priests from running or taking part in any of the ceremonies of worship, they must have sought to remind him that the temples of Karnak and Luxor belonged to Amun and other traditional gods of Egypt and that he had no right to introduce there another God who would exclude their authority.

The building of his new city lasted from Akhenaten's Year 4 to Year 8, but he and his family and officials began to live there from Year 6. A fine city it was. At this point the cliffs of the high desert recede from the river, leaving a great semi-circle about eight miles long and three miles broad. The clean yellow sand slopes gently down to the river.

The modern name of the site of Akhenaten's city is Tell el-Amarna. In his book *Tell el-Amarna*, published in 1894, Petrie wrote: 'The name ... seems to be a European concoction. The northern village is known as Et Till – perhaps a form of Et Tell, the common name for a heap of ruins. The Beni Amran have given their name to the neighbourhood . . . But no such name as Tell el-Amarna is used by the natives and I retain it only as a convention . . .'

It was here that Akhenaten built his new capital, Akhetaten, The Horizon (or resting place) of the Aten, where he and his followers could be free to worship their monotheistic God. Huge boundary stelae, marking the limits of the city and recording the story of its foundation, were carved in the surrounding cliffs. The first of them date from about the fourth year of the coregency when Akhenaten had decided upon the site. A later set date from the sixth year and define both the city on the east bank and a large area of agricultural land on the bank opposite, apparently with a view to making the new capital self-supporting if it ever came under siege. The stela proclamation runs:

> As my father the Aten lives, I shall make Akhetaten for the Aten my father in this place. I shall not make him Akhetaten south of it, north of it, west of it or east of it. And Akhetaten extends from the southern stela as far as the northern stela, measured between stela and stela on the eastern mountain, likewise from the south-west stela to the north-west stela on the western mountain of Akhetaten. And the area between these four stelae is Akhetaten itself; it belongs to Aten my father; mountains, deserts, meadows, islands, high ground and low ground, land, water, villages, men, beasts and all things which the Aten my father shall bring into existence eternally forever. I shall not forget this oath which I have made to the Aten my father eternally forever.

A reiteration of his vows, made to his new capital, was added in his eighth year, which is thought the most likely time that the king, Queen Nefertiti and their six daughters – Merytaten, Meketaten, Ankhesenpa-aten, Neferneferuaten the younger, Neferneferure and Setepenre, all born before Year 9 of the king's reign – took up residence.

Akhetaten was a capital city possessed of both dignity and architectural harmony. Its main streets ran parallel to the Nile with the most important of them, known even today as *Sikket es-Sultan*, the King's Way, connecting all the city's most prominent buildings, including the King's House where Pharaoh and his family lived their private family life. Its plan was similar to that of a high official's villa, but on a grander scale and surrounded by a spacious garden. To the south of the house was the king's private Temple to the Aten. The

Great Temple of the Aten, a huge building constructed on an east-west axis, lay less than a quarter of a mile to the north along the King's Way. It was entered through a pylon from the highway and a second entrance gave access to a hypostyle hall called The House of Rejoicing of the Aten. Six rectangular courts, known as Gem-Aten, lay along a processional way and were filled with tables for offerings to the Aten. At the eastern end of the enclosure there was a sanctuary equipped with a great altar and more offering tables. Abreast the northern wall of the enclosure lay the pavilion where a great reception for foreign princes bearing tribute was held in Year 12, thought probably to have been the high point of Akhenaten's reign. The house of the high priest Panehesy lay outside the enclosure's south-east corner.

It was not just the form of worship that was new in Akhetaten. Queen Nefertiti, like her mother-in-law Queen Tiye, enjoyed a prominence that had not existed in the past. On one of his new city's boundary stelae her husband had her described flatteringly as: 'Fair of Face, Joyous with the Double Plume, Mistress of Happiness, Endowed with Favour, at hearing whose voice one rejoices, Lady of Grace, Great of Love, whose disposition cheers the Lord of the Two Lands.' The king gave tombs, gouged out of the face of surrounding cliffs, to those nobles who had rallied to him. In the reliefs which the nobles had carved for themselves in these tombs – showing Akhenaten with his queen and family dispensing honours and largesse, worshipping in the temple, driving in his chariot, dining and drinking – Nefertiti is depicted as having equal stature with the king and her names are enclosed in a cartouche.

Throughout this period changes took place in the nature of Akhenaten's belief. As we saw earlier, when he was shown in his Year 1 worshipping at the quarry of Gebel Silsila in Nubia, he called himself the 'first prophet' of 'Re-Harakhti, Rejoicing-in-the-Horizon, in his name the light (Shu) which is in the Aten'. Soon afterwards the name of the Aten was placed inside two cartouches so as to be represented as a ruling king. At this early stage the God was represented as a human shape, either with the head of a falcon surmounted with the sun disc or as a winged disc. These early representations were made in the conventional artistic style of the Egypt of the time.

Between the king's Year 4 and Year 5 a new style of art started to appear, part of it realistic, part distinguished by an exaggeration of expression. There was also a new representation of the God. A disc at the top of royal scenes extended its rays towards the king and queen, and the rays end in their hands, which sometimes hold the Ankh, the Egyptian symbol of life, to the noses of the king and queen, a privilege which only they enjoy. The disc and its rays are not to be seen, for example, in scenes showing officials in the doorways of their tombs, reciting the famous hymns to Aten found inscribed on Aye's tomb. The king and his queen are the major figures in the Aten cult: it is their colossal statues that surround the open courts of the temples, which contained no images of the gods although the walls were probably covered with scenes depicting the worship of the Aten. Pharaoh was Aten's channel of communication and only he had the power to interpret the divine will. In the longer hymn to Aten, thought to have been composed by the king himself, a long poetic passage credits Aten with the creation of all the phenomena of the universe and asserts that all creatures exist only by virtue of the sun's rising and infusing them with life each morning.

In Year 6 the Aten was given a new epithet, 'Celebrator of Jubilees', jubilees which coincided, significantly, with those of the king. Then, towards the end of Year 9 the name of the Aten received its new form to rid it of any therio-anthropomorphic and panatheistic ideas that may have clung to it. The falcon symbol that had been used to spell the word 'Re-Harakhti' was changed to abstract signs giving an equivalent 'Re, Ruler of the Horizon' while a phrase in the second cartouche was also altered, ridding it of the word for light, 'Shu', which was also a representation of the old Egyptian god of the void. This was replaced by other signs. The new form of the God's name read: 'Re, the living Ruler of the Horizon, in his name (aspect) of the light which is in the Aten'.

No evidence of burial, or even of sarcophagi, have been found in any of the nobles' tombs and their main interest remains in the vivid picture they give – in a manner previously unknown in Egypt – of life in the new city and of the intimate family life of Pharaoh himself. Pendlebury, who worked at the site in the 1930s, later had this to say, in his book *Tell el-Amarna*, published in 1935, of the tomb paintings and sketches: 'Carelessly and hastily carved as many of them are, the new spirit of realism is strikingly evident. The incidental groups of spectators are so alive, the princesses turn to one another with their bouquets so naturally. Almost more important, however, are the religious texts from which we can read the hymns to the sun written by Akhenaten and giving the theology and philosophy of the new religion.'

The ruling Pharaoh was regarded as being head of the priesthood, head of the army and head of the administration of the Two Lands of Egypt. By rejecting the gods of Egypt, Akhenaten ceased to be head of the priesthood and the temples of Egypt were no longer under his control. He also had no control over the running of the country while his father was still alive. But, from the time he moved to Amarna, Akhenaten relied completely on the army's support for protection and, possibly, as a future safeguard against the confront-ation that would be inevitable once his father died and he became sole ruler.

Alan R. Schulman, the American Egyptologist, was able to demonstrate that although, because of his physical weakness, Akhe-naten alone of the Tuthmosside House is not represented as an active participant in horsemanship, archery and seamanship – in which his forebears excelled – he seems to have been at pains to emphasize his military authority. In the vast majority of the representations, he is shown wearing either the Blue Crown or the short Nubian wig, both belonging to the king's military head-dress, rather than the traditional ceremonial crowns of Lower and Upper Egypt. Akhe-naten's use of these two types of headgear on almost every possible public and private occasion may then have been intended to identify him constantly in the minds of his people as a military leader: 'Scenes of soldiers and military activity abound in both the private and royal art of Amarna. If we may take the reliefs from the tombs of the nobles at face value, then the city was virtually an armed camp. Everywhere we see parades and processions of soldiers, infantry and chariotry with their massed standards. There are soldiers under arms standing guard in front of the palaces, the temples and in the watchtowers that bordered the city, scenes of troops, unarmed or equipped with staves, carrying out combat exercises in the presence of the king.'[3]

The military garrison of Amarna had detachments of foreign auxiliaries in addition to Egyptian units. Schulman goes on to say: 'Just as Amarna had its own military garrison which stood ready to enforce the will of the king, so the other cities of Egypt must also have had their garrisons and the army, loyal to the throne, carried out its will. That the army was so loyal to the throne and to the dynasty was almost assured by the person of its commander, the god's-father Aye, who somehow was related to the royal family. Though he does not give them great prominence in his inscriptions as a private individual, Aye held posts among the highest in the infantry and the chariotry, posts also held by Yuya, the father of Queen Tiye and possibly also the father of Aye.'[4] (The precise relationship of the four Amarna kings will be discussed later.)

It was again the loyalty of the army, controlled by Aye, that kept Akhenaten in power in the uneasy years that followed his coming to the throne as sole ruler in his Year 12 upon the death of his father. By that time Akhenaten had developed his monotheistic ideas to a great extent. If the Aten was the only God, Akhenaten, as his sole son and prophet, could not allow other gods to be worshipped at the same time in his dominion. As a response to his rejection by the Amun priests as a legitimate ruler, he had already snubbed Amun and abolished his name from the walls and inscriptions of temples and tombs. Now he took his ideas to their logical conclusion by abolishing worship of any gods throughout Egypt except the Aten. During the Amarna rule of Akhenaten his subjects were totally committed by the king to the worship of a monotheistic God, although at this time only the Levites among the Hebrews were involved in his new religion.[5] Akhenaten closed all the temples, except those of Aten, dispersed the priests and gave orders that the names of other deities should be expunged from monuments and temple inscriptions throughout the country. Units were despatched to excise the names of the ancient gods wherever they were found written or engraved, a course that can only have created mounting new opposition to his already rejected authority:

'The persecution of first Amun and then the other gods, which must have been exceedingly hateful to the majority of the Egyptians, would certainly also be hateful to the individual members of the army. This persecution, which entailed the closing of the temples, the despatch of artisans who entered everywhere to hack out his name from inscriptions, the presumed banishment of the clergy, the excommunication of his very name, could not have been carried out without the army's active support. Granting the fact that the theoretical fiction of the divine kingship was accepted by the mass of the Egyptian people, it is, nevertheless, hardly credible that they would just sit by and acquiesce silently to the persecution of Amun. Some strong backing had to support the royal dicta. Each time a squad of workmen entered a temple or tomb to destroy the name of Amun, it must have been supported by a squad of soldiers who came to see that the royal decree was carried out without opposition. Ultimately the harshness of the persecution must have had a certain reaction even upon the soldiers who, themselves, certainly had been raised in the old beliefs, and rather than risk a wholesale defection and perhaps even a civil war, the army, through the agency of Aye, probably put pressure upon Akhenaten, not only to cease the persecution, but to compromise with the old order by the elevation of Semenkhkare to the coregency.'6 In fact, when even this compromise failed, the clamour grew, as we shall see, for the king's abdication.

More information about the extent to which Akhenaten went in trying to eliminate the old forms of worship, as well as the consequent sense of complete loss felt by Egyptians, can be gathered from Tutankhamun's Restoration Stela, which he erected in the Temple of Amun at Karnak and which was later usurped by Horemheb: '... The good ruler, performing benefactions for his father (Amun) and all the gods, for he has made what was ruined to endure as a monument for the ages of eternity ... Now when his majesty appeared as king, the temples of the gods and goddesses from Elephantine [down] to marshes of the Delta [had ... and] gone to pieces. Their shrines had become desolate, had become mounds overgrown with [weeds]. Their sanctuaries were as if they had never been. Their halls were footpaths. The land was topsy-turvy, and the gods turned their backs upon this land. If [the army was] sent to Djahi (Palestine-Syria) to extend the frontiers of Egypt, no success of theirs came at all. If one prayed to a god to seek counsel from him, he would never come [at all]. If one made supplication to a goddess similarly, she would never come at all.'7

It is certain that it was the strength of opposition to Akhenaten's religious reforms, and his own unwillingness to change his attitude, that forced him to appoint Semenkhkare as his coregent around Year 15 after giving him his eldest daughter, Merytaten, as his wife. The precise identity of Semenkhkare has been the subject of considerable scholarly debate. Suffice to say for the moment that it has been suggested that he might have been the son of Amenhotep III or of Akhenaten himself. They are shown together on some monuments and inscriptions have been found, including some on the pleasure pavilion at the south of Amarna, the Maruaten, in which the name of Nefertiti had been erased and the name of Merytaten inscribed in its place. One curious feature of the period is that, soon after his accession, Semenkhkare was given Nefertiti's official name – Neferneferuaten, beloved of Waenre (Akhenaten).

Initially, Semenkhkare and his queen lived with Akhenaten in the royal palace at Amarna. In face of the continuing hostility throughout the country, however, Semenkhkare left Amarna for Thebes where he reversed the trend of the religious revolution, at least in the capital, by establishing a temple to Amun, an action by his coregent and son-in-law that indicates the extent to which Akhenaten was isolated in his attempt to force his religious ideas upon his country. A hieratic document found in the Theban tomb of Pere, the Theban nobleman, indicates that the Amun temple existed in Year 3 of Semenkhkare and that the young king was in the old capital at the time.

At around the time that Semenkhkare became coregent, Nefertiti also disappeared mysteriously from the palace. There is no evidence that she was buried in the royal tomb to suggest, as some scholars believe, that she must have died around that time. On the contrary, there *is* evidence that she lived for a period after that date in the North City of Amarna where Tutankhamun was also resident and where objects inscribed with the queen's name have been found. This suggests that she may have disagreed with her husband over his religious policy on the grounds that it endangered the whole dynasty and wished him to agree to a compromise that would allow the old gods to be worshipped alongside the Aten. If this is the correct interpretation, her views proved to be right. In his Year 17 Akhenaten suddenly disappeared, followed shortly afterwards – perhaps only a few days afterwards – by the equally sudden death of Semenkhkare, both of them to be succeeded by the boy prince, Tutankhamun, after his marriage to Akhenaten's third daughter, Ankhsenpa-aten. The parentage of Tutankhamun will be discussed in Chapter Fourteen. (Akhenaten's second daughter had already died – around Year 12 of her father – and been buried in the royal tomb at Amarna. No trace of her remains have been found, but that may be because her mummy was transferred to Thebes after Amarna was abandoned.)

There remains one further important question to be asked about Akhenaten: did his life as well as his reign come to an end when he fell from power?

14

THE TOMB OF AKHENATEN

ALTHOUGH not a shred of evidence has been found to confirm the date of Akhenaten's death, Egyptologists have assumed that it must have taken place at the end of his reign in his Year 17. There is evidence, however, indicating that – as in the Talmud account of the reign of Moses as a king in Nubia (Ethiopia) – he simply fell from power in the course of this year, but did not die. This evidence comes from archaeological, philological and historical sources.

The Archaeological Evidence

The Royal Tomb of Akhenaten was desecrated originally in the wave of anti-Amarna feeling that followed his disappearance from the scene and the subsequent brief reigns of Tutankhamun and Aye. Later, it was further plundered by local inhabitants before it was first discovered officially by the Italian archaeologist Alessandro Barsanti in December 1891 during an expedition carried out on behalf of the Egyptian Service des Antiquités.

The Amarna city of Akhenaten was built halfway between Luxor and Cairo where the high barren plateau stretching 200 miles from the Red Sea recedes, leaving a crescent-shaped plain to the east of the Nile, about eight miles long and three broad. Three main valleys break into the rocks to the east of Amarna. The north and south valleys were used for the tombs of Amarna nobles and officials, the middle valley, Wadi Abu Hassan el-Bahri, for Akhenaten's tomb. It was dug inside the rocks of a small side valley that branches out from the north side of the main valley.

DESCRIPTION OF THE TOMB

The entrance of the tomb is cut into the floor of the Royal Valley with the doorway facing roughly east.[1] Then there is a smooth, inclined plane for the lowering of the sarcophagus with, on each side, a flight of steps descending to the entrance. This leads to a sloping corridor, neither decorated nor inscribed.

At the end of the corridor is another flight of steps that leads to a platform giving abruptly on to a shaft some ten feet deep. In the wall opposite the shaft is the doorway of the royal burial chamber, some thirty-two feet square. The left third of the room is taken up by a dais and two columns that support the roof while the remaining two-thirds on the right has an emplacement, raised half an inch or so above the floor, for the sarcophagus. All the walls of the royal chamber had been smoothly plastered for the artists to do their work, but Akhenaten's enemies, determined to destroy all traces of him, made sure that there is nothing left of whatever scenes or inscriptions the walls may once have borne.

If we go back to the corridor at the top of the stairs we find an opening on the right-hand side, near the royal chamber, leading to three rooms, two of which were used for the burial of Akhenaten's second daughter, Meketaten, who died some time after his Year 12. Mourning scenes for the princess decorate the walls. A short way along the corridor is another doorway leading to six unfinished rooms that could have been intended for the other members of the royal family. So, in fact, we first have the entrance, then the corridor off which are found the six unfinished rooms, then the Meketaten suite before the steps leading to the royal chamber area.

EXCAVATING THE TOMB

Barsanti's main objective on his first visit at the end of 1891 and another eight months later was to clear the tomb, whose entrance was blocked by debris. Once that had been done it seems he gave most of his attention to the royal burial chamber. However, his second visit yielded some fragmentary *ushabti* (small funerary statues normally placed in a tomb *before* the owner's death) of Akhenaten and one small stela, in good condition, that had apparently escaped the attention of previous tomb plunderers.

More than a year passed before the arrival in January 1894 of a third expedition, led by Urbain Bouriant, director of the Mission Archéologique Française. Bouriant's team concentrated largely on making a plan and section of the tomb and recording the inscriptions and reliefs in all of the rooms apart from the badly damaged royal burial chamber. Then followed a long gap before the Egypt Exploration Society – the first British organization to be invited to carry out work on behalf of the Service des Antiquités – was asked to re-examine the tomb as well as excavating the area outside it. Pendlebury, the director of the expedition, which began work on 18 December 1931, wrote later: 'Outside the tomb was a large dump, some seventy metres long and varying from five to ten metres broad. The depth was, in places, as much as four metres. The dump consisted of three layers. Above lay the debris thrown out of the tomb by Barsanti; below this came the deposit left by the original desecrators of the tomb, while at the bottom was a layer of chips from the cutting of the tomb itself.'

It took more than three weeks to make a thorough examination of the dump. Three days after Christmas excavation was also begun in the shaft of the tomb. The result was that from both the dump and the shaft came many more fragments of the sarcophagi and some broken *ushabti* figures. The expedition also found part of Akhenaten's alabaster canopic chest, a box with four compartments, used to hold the four canopic jars. These jars, made of pottery or stone with a head for a stopper, were used in the course of mummification to keep the viscera of the dead after they had been removed from the body, but no fragments of the jars themselves were found.

After the departure of the Egypt Exploration Society team the site continued to be the focus of attention for local predators. Robbers broke into the tomb and made off with a large number of fragments of the plaster reliefs that adorned the walls of the Meketaten rooms. In May of that year, therefore, the Service des Antiquités organized a sondage (excavation) that produced another dozen *ushabti* fragments.

Part of the attraction of the area for the predators lay in persistent rumours that it contained yet another tomb, so far undiscovered. This resulted in the mounting of another expedition – by an Egypt Exploration Society team led by Pendlebury and his wife – to prove or disprove the rumour. The result of six weeks' work was a blank, and Pendlebury wrote in his subsequent report: 'All we can say for certain is that the cutting of the tomb began later than Year 6 of Akhenaten's reign, since the ostracon ... found in one of the dumps of chips bore that date, a conclusion to which we should have been forced in any case since the city itself was not founded until that year. Since many of the fragments, both of the canopic chest and of the sarcophagi were found in the shaft inside the tomb, it is probable that they were broken up *in situ*.' In addition to searching unsuccessfully for a second tomb, the Pendlebury team made a plan of the Royal Tomb, photographed the walls and copied all the wall-scenes and inscriptions. Once this work was completed the tomb was sealed off from the attentions of further predators by closing the entrance with a wall containing a steel door.

More recently, in 1974, the Egypt Exploration Society published the first part of an account by Geoffrey T. Martin, Professor of Egyptology at University College, London, with details of the small items that were found during the different stages of excavation at Akhenaten's tomb.[2]

Out of the many small sarcophagi fragments, which are no more than a few centimetres each, it was possible to reconstruct one sarcophagus of pink, grey and white granite. It is too large to have been Meketaten's. On the other hand, as Nefertiti is shown at each corner of the sarcophagus in place of the four protecting goddesses – Isis, Nephthys, Neith and Silket – it could not have belonged to the queen herself. It is safe in this case to attribute the reconstructed sarcophagus to Akhenaten.

The remaining sarcophagi fragments proved to have come from:
a) the reconstructed sarcophagus of Akhenaten;
b) the lid of Akhenaten's sarcophagus;
c) the sarcophagus of Meketaten;
d) the lid of Meketaten's sarcophagus.[3]

The great size of Akhenaten's sarcophagus indicates that this was the outermost of a series of coffins that would protect the royal mummy (the mummies of both Yuya and Tutankhamun were enclosed in three coffins). Nevertheless, no remains of other coffins were found, nor any remains of the usual shrine or canopy that were part of the normal burial furniture, thus raising the possibility that Akhenaten was never buried in this tomb. What reinforces this idea is the fact that, although the evidence indicates that Akhenaten's enemies smashed everything in the tomb, no matter how large or solid, into small pieces after the end of the Amarna regime, the fragmented funerary remains found in the tomb could not be considered sufficient in quantity to indicate the burial of Akhenaten and his daughter Meketaten – or for that matter burial of the king alone. Apart from the absence of the additional coffins there was no trace of other items – chariots, chairs, boxes, magic bricks and amulets – that were normally buried in royal tombs only *after* the king's death. The sole remains that can be said with certainty to have belonged to Akhenaten are the sarcophagus lid, the *ushabti* and the canopic chest, all objects that were normally placed in the tomb *earlier* than the time of actual death.

Martin, one of the few scholars who believes that Akhenaten was actually buried in his tomb, tries to justify this view by arguing: 'Possibly the mummy of Meketaten, together with the funerary trappings – which probably would not have been extensive – were transferred to Thebes after the abandonment of el-Amarna.'[4] Although evidence from the tomb confirms that Meketaten was originally buried there during her father's reign, there is nothing to indicate that these funerary objects were removed to any other place, and Martin, who took no part in any of the excavations at Akhenaten's tomb, gives us no reason for suggesting the possibility that they were.

It is possible, of course, to suggest, even if supporting evidence is lacking, that it was considered unsafe to leave Meketaten unguarded in the Royal Tomb once Amarna was abandoned about Year 4 of Tutankhamun. But if, as Martin suggests, Akhenaten was buried there as well, why would they move the princess and leave the king? Then there is the difficulty of the absence of funerary objects that would in the normal course of events have been placed in the tomb *after* the king's death. Martin attempts to deal with this point, again without putting forward any evidence, by suggesting that there was a second exodus of objects from the tomb: 'Most of the valuable items were doubtless carried off by the despoilers ... This is unlikely to have taken place in the reigns of Tutankhamun or Aye, who were closely linked to Akhenaten's family by marriage. The spoliation was probably ordered under Horemheb or conceivably later, in the Ramesside period.'[5] However, the archaeological evidence not only does not support Martin's theory: it contradicts it.

After his first season of excavation at the tomb in 1931, Pendlebury made the important observation: 'In view ... of the demonstration that the so-called body of Akhenaten found in the cache of Tiye at Thebes' – he was referring to Tomb No. 55, discussed below – 'is in reality not his at all, it was imperative to try and collect all the evidence as to whether Akhenaten was ever buried at el-Amarna, and, if so, whether in the Royal Tomb or elsewhere.'[6]

After giving a short account of what was found in the tomb, he went on to say: 'From both dump and shaft came many more fragments from the sarcophagi, similar to those already in Cairo Museum, as well as broken shawabti-figures (*ushabti*). In addition there were found parts of Akhenaten's magnificent alabaster canopic chest, with protecting vultures at the corners, together with pieces of the lids capped with the king's head. The chest gives evidence of never having been used, for it is quite unstained by the black resinous substance seen in those of Amenhotep II and Tutankhamun, and is additionally interesting in that it is inscribed with the early form of the Aten name, while the sarcophagi all have the later.'

Pendlebury is here remarking that as the burial rituals required some parts of the funerary furniture, including the canopic chest, to be anointed by a black liquid, and he was unable to see any traces of such staining on the fragments he found, he concluded that the tomb had never been used. This would mean that Akhenaten was never buried in his Amarna tomb. This view was supported by the fact that no trace was found of any fragments of the canopic jars themselves, usually placed in position at the time of burial. This idea is further reinforced by the use of the early Aten name, which suggests that the canopic chest was made and placed in position very early in the king's reign, before Year 9 when Aten received his new name.

Pendlebury's conclusions were later confirmed by the Egyptian archaeologist Muhammad Hamza, who in 1939 was able to restore Akhenaten's canopic chest from the fragments found by Pendlebury: 'As the box is quite unstained by the black resinous unguents to which those of Amenhotep II, Tutankhamun and Horemheb were subjected, it seems probable that it has never been used for the king's viscera.'[7]

As a result of the archaeological evidence presented by Pendlebury and Hamza, most Egyptologists accepted the conclusion that Akhenaten could not have been buried in his Amarna tomb, but still believed that he died in his Year 17, the year he fell from power. Some, like Gardiner, took the view that he had never been buried at all and his 'body had been torn to pieces and thrown to the dogs': others, like Weigall and Aldred, thought that he must have been buried at Thebes, in Tomb No. 55, or somewhere else. Only Martin was not convinced: 'Akhenaten was buried in the Royal Tomb in or shortly after Year 17.'[8]

Where did he obtain this information? The only actual date found in the tomb, as remarked by Pendlebury, was Year 6. Then, as the late name of the Aten was found on the reconstructed sarcophagus and other objects, we can draw the deduction that some work in the tomb was carried out after Year 9. Furthermore, as Meketaten died some time after Year 12, probably in Year 14, her burial could have taken place then. But which evidence found in the Royal Tomb provided Martin with his Year 17 and persuaded him, against the evidence, that Akhenaten had been buried there?

He makes the point: 'The suggestion that the canopic chest was never used is open to serious question.'[9] What are his grounds for taking this view? 'The absence of bitumin or resin in the canopic chest from the Royal Tomb has been alluded to by several writers, and the assumption made that the chest was never used, and that Akhenaten was therefore never buried in the tomb prepared for him.'[10] He then goes on to put forward three arguments in support of his view.

1   'The actual canopic coffins or jars which would have contained the viscera have not been found. These were presumably of a precious material, and were placed inside the cylindrical compartments of the canopic chest, as in the Tutankhamun examples.'

Thus the first of Martin's 'serious questions', being used to confirm Akhenaten's burial in the Royal Tomb, turns out to be a serious point of evidence that he was not buried there at all. The four jars in which the viscera of the dead were placed have separate names: Imset, for the liver, Hapi (lungs), Duamutif (stomach) and Qebehs (intestines). These organs were removed in the first stages of mummification and brought to the tomb with the funerary procession at the time of burial. The absence of these jars from Akhenaten's tomb, far from proving that he was buried there, as Martin would have us believe, is strong evidence that he was not.

Furthermore, as those responsible for the tomb's mutilation in ancient times were not thieves, but political enemies who wanted to ensure the complete destruction of Akhenaten by removing his name, image and memory – and thus ensuring his spiritual death – they would not have removed the canopic jars from the tomb because they were precious in terms of value: rather would they have destroyed the jars and their contents for vengeance *in situ*, as they did with all the other tomb objects they found. They would not have risked the possibility of any part of him surviving for the sake of the value of the containers. The four vases were usually covered with tops that were decorated with the head of the dead king and the vases themselves were usually inscribed with his name and other personal details. To preserve his image or his name, according to ancient Egyptian beliefs, was to allow the spiritual part of him to live. Therefore, by removing his image, his name or any objects belonging to him, his enemies believed they were condemning him to eternal death.

2   'It cannot automatically be assumed that the ritual feature of pouring bitumin or resin over or in the canopic jars was a regular feature of the funerary rites of the Amarna royal family.'

This second 'serious question' is an assumption, not supported by any evidence. Martin is saying: what if Akhenaten didn't follow the usual ritual? Yet we know that his successor, Tutankhamun, did, and, if Akhenaten had died in his Year 17, Tutankhamun would have been responsible for his burial. Martin is here putting forward a possibility, then using what is only a possibility to support his view. This line of argument is invalid. To suggest a possibility either requires supporting evidence or a situation where the possibility makes sense of other evidence. Neither of these conditions exists in this, the second of Martin's 'serious questions'. Yet he asks us to accept it as a reason for rejecting what the majority of scholars have regarded as solid archaeological testimony.

In addition, the evidence from the Royal Tomb and from Amarna as a whole confirms that Akhenaten rejected the old customs and rituals only when they had polytheistic implications that contradicted his monotheism: 'In the Aten period, great as was the spiritual reform which Akhenaten imposed upon his subjects, the outer forms prevailing in earlier ages could not be discarded; the king's own sepulchre at el-Amarna still contained *ushabti*-figures though no longer bearing the time-honoured summons to field-labourers to till the fields as substitutes for their lord, and there exist large scarabs of the period which no longer appeal for mercy in the weighing of the heart before Osiris.'[11]

Why should Akhenaten have rejected the ritual of anointing the canopic chest and other funerary objects with bitumin or resin when this normal practice did not contradict his religious beliefs in any way? This is what Martin did not attempt to explain.

3   'The canopic chest, as it now exists, is largely a skilful reconstruction in plaster.'

In his third 'serious objection', as he regarded it, Martin complains that too few of the original fragments were used in the reconstructed chest for the stains to be seen and even some of those are covered with plaster. This leads him to argue: 'It follows that any conclusion drawn from the absence of resin or bitumin in these compartments or on the canopic chest must be tentative in the extreme. There is no certain evidence to prove that the chest was never used.'

Both Pendlebury and Hamza, who saw all the found parts of the canopic chest before it was plastered and reconstructed, confirmed that it was not stained with resin or bitumen. Yet Martin, without himself having any first-hand knowledge of the chest fragments, and without putting forward reasons why the two earlier archaeologists were either misled by the evidence or themselves gave a misleading account of it, wants us to reject their conclusion. Then, if he were able – which he was not – to make us suspect the accuracy of the earlier conclusion, the best he could have hoped for is to be able to say: 'There is no certain evidence to prove that the chest was never used.' However, he goes further than that and states confidently: 'There can no longer be any room for doubt that Akhenaten was buried there [in the Royal Tomb].'[12]

From the following details of the fragments that were used in the reconstruction of the canopic chest given by Martin himself,[13] we can see that they were more than enough to show whether it was stained or not: 'Canopic chest of Akhenaten, with separate cover ... Reconstructed in 1939 by M. Hamza from various fragments, with the missing portions supplied in plaster ... Height of chest 76.5cm. Height of lid (front) max. 22cm. Height of lid (back) 18cm. Width (front) 60cm. Depth 60cm. Height of supporting falcons at the corners (including disk) 47.3 cm. Height of base and frieze of tyet and djed amulets [sacred ritual objects related to the dead] 23cm. Height of large cartouches 14.2cm. Height of inscription around lid 5.5cm., measured from the bottom of the lid to the border immediately above the cartouches.

'In the reconstructed canopic chest, the front and both sides of the cover each have 26 cartouches, the back 29. The surviving inscriptions, which are all incised, consist of the early "didactic" names of the Aten. None survives on the front or on the left side of the cover ...

'The canopic chest conforms in most particulars to the other extant royal canopic chests of the Eighteenth Dynasty, which appear to have been used only for Pharaohs and not for their consorts or families. In the reconstruction the following original material is incorporated:

Front:

1   On the left side, a fragment of the feathering of the upper part of the falcon's wing;
2   A fragment from the point where the wings of the two falcons meet;
3   Lower part of the tail of the right falcon and the tips of the wings of the left falcon;
4   Part of the base with frieze of tyet and djed.

Back:

5   Fragments of the feathering of the wings of the left falcon, and part of the tips of the wing of the right falcon;
6   Fragments of the base, including the upper border and tyet and djed elements.

Left side:

7   Fragments of the rim and much of the base, including the upper border and tyet and djed elements.

Right side:

8   Part of the base of the cartouche on the right side;
9   Tail and part of the feathering of the left falcon;
10 Part of the claw and shen amulet (for protection of the dead) of the right falcon;
11 Fragments of the base, including the upper border and tyet and djed elements.

Cover:

Largely reconstructed in plaster, presumably over wood.'

As we can see from Martin's own account, enough original fragments were found of the canopic chest, and have been used in the reconstructed chest in Cairo Museum, to be able to judge whether it was anointed with resin or bitumen or not. And as both Pendlebury and Hamza have confirmed the complete absence of such stains, I do not take Martin's unsupported 'serious questions' seriously.

WHOSE BODY IN THE VALLEY OF THE KINGS?

In January 1907 a small tomb – now known as Tomb No. 55 – with only one burial chamber was found in the Valley of the Kings. The tomb is one of only three discovered closed in the Valley, with both mummy and funerary furniture inside, the other two being that of Yuya and his wife Tuya, which first came to light in 1905, followed by Tutankhamun's in 1922. The excavation was sponsored by the rich, retired American lawyer and amateur archaeologist Theodore M. Davis, who employed the British archaeologist Edward R. Ayrton to conduct the digging under the supervision of Arthur Weigall, another Briton, appointed two years earlier to the post of Inspector-General of the Antiquities of Upper Egypt.

Although numerous fragments of small clay seals were found with the cartouche of Neb-kheprw-re (Tutankhamun) used only during the Pharoah's lifetime, it seems that the tomb had been re-entered at a later date as the outer door had been sealed with the same style of seal (a jackal above nine foreign prisoners) used to close the tomb of Tutankhamun.

The tomb is near the entry of the inner Valley, close to the site where the tomb of Tutankhamun was subsequently found. It consists of a small, rock-cut chamber approached by a sloping passage, and does not seem to have been intended originally for a royal burial. The burial also appeared to have been carried out in haste, with a minimum of equipment. What made the situation worse in trying to establish ownership of the tomb was the fact that it had deteriorated as a result of a great deal of rainwater dripping into it through a fissure in the rock.

The debate about ownership of the tomb has rumbled on for the greater part of this century and still surfaces from time to time. Initially it was thought that the decayed mummy was that of Queen Tiye, then that of Akhenaten. This, allied to an apparently nude statue of the king at Karnak – one of four colossi – which showed him seemingly deformed and without genitalia, led to elaborate pathological attempts to try to discover what disease he suffered from. At the end of the day this proved to be something of a storm in a canopic jar: it was demonstrated eventually that the mummy was not that of Akhenaten, but of his coregent, Semenkhkare, and, in addition, that the seemingly nude colossus at Karnak was actually an unfinished statue, awaiting, like the completed three, the addition of a kilt. It is worth examining this debate, however, because it indicates the lengths to which some of those who do not find Akhenaten to their taste are prepared to go to try to discredit him (see Appendix E). The contents of Tomb No. 55, which have prompted a protracted debate over the original ownership of the tomb, and some of the items found in the tomb of Tutankhamun, provide further evidence that Akhenaten's life did not end when he fell from power, but in order not to weary the reader at this point I have put them in Appendix F. Here it is perhaps worth making the point briefly that some magical bricks of Akhenaten, essential for his burial, were found in Tomb No. 55, whose incumbent has been established as Semenkhkare – indicating that Akhenaten himself did not need them.

THE AMARNA FAMILY

Both Professor D. E. Derry, then Professor of Anatomy in the Faculty of Medicine at Cairo University, who restored the skull of the occupant of Tomb No. 55 and concluded that the remains were those of a man no more than twenty-three or, at most, twenty-four years of age at the time of death, and Professor R. G. Harrison, the late Derby Professor of Anatomy at the University of Liverpool, who confirmed Derry's conclusion that the remains were those of Semenkhkare (see Appendix E), found a striking similarity between the facial characteristics of Semenkhkare's skeleton and the artistic impressions we have of Akhenaten, suggesting that they must have been brothers or close relatives. Grafton Elliot Smith, at the time Professor of Anatomy at Cairo Medical School, also found similarity between Semenkhkare's remains and the mummies of both Amenhotep III and Yuya, sufficient to make him a descendant of both. As Queen Tiye was Yuya's daughter, this suggests that Semenkhkare could have been a son of Amenhotep III and Queen Tiye, a full brother of Akhenaten. At the same time he could also have been the son of Akhenaten, who was a descendant of both Amenhotep III and Queen Tiye. However, as Harrison's examination proved that he died in his twentieth year, and that was Year 17 of Akhenaten's reign, this would mean that he was born about three years before Akhenaten came to the throne as coregent. As we know that Akhenaten was not married until around the time the coregency started, this rules out the possibility that Semenkhkare was his son, and it is most likely that he was Akhenaten's full brother.

As for Tutankhamun, who certainly belonged to the same family, he was about nine or ten years of age when he succeeded Akhenaten on the king's fall from power and the sudden death of Semenkhkare. This means that he was born during Year 7 of Akhenaten, which was Year 34 of Amenhotep III. As we saw earlier, Baketaten, the youngest of Queen Tiye's daughters, was probably born in Year 4 of Akhenaten, Year 31 of Amenhotep III. In Year 7 of her son, Akhenaten, Queen Tiye was about forty years of age and Amenhotep III about forty-five, in both cases a possible age for them to produce a son. Yet it is more likely that Tutankhamun was the son of Akhenaten and Nefertiti.

In Tutankhamun's tomb a figure of a recumbent jackal was found upon a shrine containing pieces of jewellery. The figure, which had been carved from wood, was overlaid with a thin layer of plaster and painted with black resin. The body of the jackal was covered almost completely with linen draperies, one of which proved to be a shirt dated to Year 7 of Akhenaten, the same year that Tutankhamun was born.[14] This dated Akhenaten shirt was surely used for Tutankhamun at the time of his birth, strongly indicating the parental relationship and the place of birth as Amarna. His original name at the time of his birth, Tutankhaten, also suggests that he was born at Amarna. In addition, there is evidence that, while still a prince, he lived at the northern Amarna palace, the very same place where Queen Nefertiti lived during the last years of Akhenaten's reign. Why would he have lived at Amarna with Queen Nefertiti if he were the son of Queen Tiye?

It is true that he describes Amenhotep III as his 'father' on a statue of a lion, now in the British Museum, and that a small golden statue of Amenhotep III as well as some of Queen Tiye's hair, in a small coffin, were found in Tutankhamun's tomb, but it was customary among Egyptians, as with the Hebrews, to use the word 'father' as a synonym for 'ancestor', and if Queen Tiye were Tutankhamun's grandmother, it would be normal to find some of her belongings as well as Amenhotep III's in his tomb.

What is the correct sequence of events? It would seem that the political struggle must have reached a point where the old priesthood and some factions of the army were in open revolt against Akhenaten's regime as a result of his attempt to impose his new God on his people. Aye, who was responsible for the army and must have been the most powerful man in Egypt at the time, either convinced, or even forced, Akhenaten to abdicate in order to save the Amarna Dynasty, and replaced him with Semenkhkare. It seems that, shortly after the fall of Akhenaten, Semenkhkare died suddenly at Thebes, most probably from unnatural causes because he was not regarded as a suitable replacement for Akhenaten.

While the country was still in turmoil it was not possible to bury Semenkhkare in the proper way – especially as it seems that his death occurred at Thebes – using his own funerary equipment which had been prepared for him (and some of which was later used by Tutankhamun). Aye therefore had to do the best he could with whatever material was available. He buried Semenkhkare secretly, and in a hurry, using some objects meant to be used by Akhenaten, who had already fled from Amarna.

The presence of a shrine of Queen Tiye's in the tomb (see Appendix F) is not easy to explain, but it is possible that she was either still alive or, as Weigall thought, had died and been buried in the same tomb prior to the death of Semenkhkare, in which case her mummy and most of her objects would have been moved away when the time came to bury the young coregent. It is also clear that, as Tutankhamun's priests would not have erased Akhenaten's name from the shrine and coffin, the tomb was re-entered later, probably during the reign of Horemheb when the campaign was mounted to try to wipe out all traces of the Akhenaten regime from Egypt's memory.

15

THE FALLEN ONE OF AMARNA

It is now generally accepted that Akhenaten ruled for only seventeen years, although there is no evidence pointing to which month of this final year his rule ended. However, although he was no longer on the throne, did his followers believe that he was still alive – and would perhaps return one day to take power again?

The Philological Evidence

The main reason for accepting Year 17 as Akhenaten's last in power is that a docket, No. 279, found by excavators at Amarna, bears two different dates – Year 17 and Year 1. This was explained by Fairman in the following terms: 'It records, therefore, the first year of an unnamed king which followed the seventeenth year of another unnamed king. There cannot be any doubt that the latter was Akhenaten. Year 1 can hardly have been that of Semenkhkare since ... his Year 1 was probably Year 15 of Akhenaten. Thus the docket must be assigned to the first year of Tutankhamun.'[1]

Fairman dismissed the possibility that these two dates might be construed as pointing to a coregency between Akhenaten and Tutankhamun: 'This docket does not contain a double-dating since "Year 1" is written over "Year 17".' Yet a few pages earlier Fairman had given us a different account of how the dates were written: '"Year 1" is written partly over an earlier "Year 17". And if the copy of the text on the docket was correctly produced (No. 279 in plate xcv), then the second date is written neither completely over nor partly over the earlier date, but underneath it.'[2]

This is the first time, as far as I am aware, that a king placed his own date on the same text as that of a predecessor after the latter's rule had come to an end. However, as no other evidence was found to support a coregency between Akhenaten and Tutankhamun, Fairman's explanation was taken for granted. Yet, in the light of Egyptian custom, the evidence of docket No. 279 is confusing. Egyptians calculated the years of each king separately and, if there was no coregency, the first year of the new king began only after the last year of his predecessor. How, therefore, is it that Akhenaten's Year 17 was also regarded as Year 1 of Tutankhamun unless there was a coregency?

No attempt was made to erase or cross out the earlier date before the later one was written. For this there can be only one convincing explanation. When we say that Akhenaten abdicated his power, we use a modern term expressing a modern practice. However, Egyptian Pharaohs did not gain power from the people or the parliament, but from the gods. From the time of his birth the king was regarded as the son of Amun-Re and destined to rule, and on being crowned he took possession of his inheritance, the lands given to him by the gods, and retained possession until the day he died. As long as he was alive Pharaoh was regarded as being the lawful ruler of his lands, even if he was weak and had no authority.

The abdication of Akhenaten must have been the first in Egyptian history. It is true that Aye and his army stopped him from exercising his power, but he was still regarded as the legitimate ruler. Semenkhkare was not accepted by Egyptians as a successor and was most probably assassinated at Thebes a few days after Akhenaten gave up his throne. When Tutankhamun became ruler, he was still called Tutankhaten, and as his Year 1 – although not as coregent – started while Akhenaten was still regarded as the legitimate ruler, in a way he took his authority from the old king until such time as he abandoned his allegiance to the Aten.

Akhenaten had ruled in the name of the Aten, whom he regarded as his father, having rejected, and been rejected by, Amun. The only legal way the new young king was able to establish himself on the throne was to renounce the course of action taken by his predecessor. In his Year 4, therefore, he rejected the Aten and returned to being the son of Amun. The Amun priesthood accepted this return in a new crowning celebration. Thus, at this point the Aten had no power in Egypt, no land to give. It was only then, as we shall see later, that Akhenaten, who was still alive, stopped being king and Tutankhamun became regarded as the sole heir of the god Amun.

TESTIMONY OF SURVIVAL?

Another hieratic docket found at Amarna recorded another date that has been the subject of long arguments and has even resulted in a charge of dishonesty being levelled at certain scholars. The essence of the dispute is whether this docket refers to Year 11 of Akhenaten or – despite the fact that we know he ruled for only seventeen years – to Year 21.

A facsimile of this docket, made and published by Battiscombe Gunn, the British archaeologist,[3] persuaded the American scholar Keith C. Seele to believe that 'the hieratic date is certainly "Year 21"'.[4] He even went as far as to accuse British scholars of avoiding the evidence intentionally: 'While the actual fate of Akhenaten is unknown, it is evidence that he must have disappeared in his twenty-first year on the throne or even later. Some Egyptologists, including the Egypt Exploration Society's excavators at Amarna, allow him but seventeen years.'[5] As many scholars all over the world became convinced by Seele's arguments, Fairman, who had been one of the society's excavators at Amarna, felt he had to rally to their defence: 'It seems appropriate to state the true position and at the same time vindicate those members of the Egypt Exploration Society's expeditions at Amarna who have been quite unjustly accused of dishonesty.'[6]

Although Fairman has to be regarded as one of the most trusted British Egyptologists of this century, the way he tried to dispose of Seele's opposition makes it clear why Seele had grounds for feeling suspicious: 'Year 21 occurs "certainly", according to Seele, on a hieratic docket published by Gunn. Seele has not seen this docket, but he is quite satisfied to reject Gunn's reading on the evidence of the published facsimile. The first comment that occurs to one is that no one knowing the very high standards set and maintained by Gunn can believe that he would have advocated a reading he knew to be false simply to support a theory.'[7]

This was Fairman's first attempt to avoid the facts, for, contrary to what he said, Gunn translated the date as 'Year 11' only because of

This statuette of Akhenaten and Nefertiti, now in the
Louvre in Paris, offers a more realistic view of the King
and Queen than do the exaggerated representations of
other, more romantic styles of Amarna art. No physical
defect mars Akhenaten's appearance.

Right: Yuya's mummy, found in his small tomb in the Valley of the Kings in 1905, now lies inside his coffin in the Cairo Museum. I have been able to identify this minister of both Tuthmose IV and Amenhotep III as the Patriarch Joseph of the coat of many colours, who brought the Israelite family into Egypt. His importance was enhanced when Amenhotep III married his daughter Tiye and made her the Queen of Egypt.

Below: Akhenaten and Nefertiti make an offering to Aten. The royal family worshipped in the open. This scene, which was found in the Amarna house of Panehesy, the Chief Servitor of the Aten, portrays the latest symbol of the Aten, the disc at the top, sending its rays over the members of the royal family. These rays are directed at the key of life, held in front of their eyes. The name of the God (the same as that of the King) appears inside a cartouche.

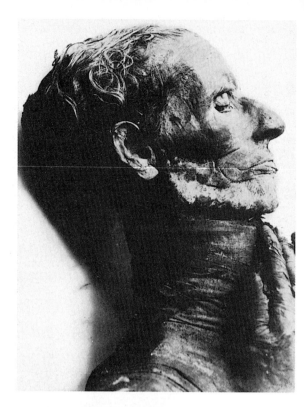

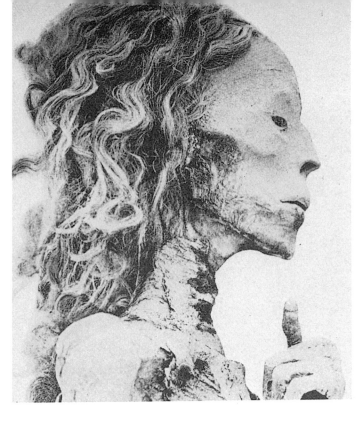

Left: This mummy of a woman, found in 1898 with other members of the royal family in the tomb of Amenhotep II in the Valley of the Kings, has now been identified as Queen Tiye.

Below: Queen Tiye, daughter of Yuya/Joseph, wife of Amenhotep III and mother of Akhenaten. This small head of Tiye was found by Petrie, the father of modern archaeology, in the cave temple of Sarabit el Khadim in Sinai. The presence of the head of Akhenaten's mother in this remote area is one of the indications that the young king himself could have been living there for some time after he had been forced to abdicate the throne.

Above: Aye (right) and Tiy. Tiy, Nefertiti's childhood nurse, also nursed Akhenaten during his childhood. She was married to Aye, second son of Yuya and brother of Queen Tiye. As the strongest military figure in Egypt, Aye protected Akhenaten's rule and helped him during his religious revolution. Aye himself became the fourth and last of the Amarna kings when he sat on the throne after Tutankhamun's death.

Below: Akhenaten and Semenkhkare. This sculptor's model found at Amarna is another indication of a co-regency, this time between Akhenaten on the left and his brother Semenkhkare on the right. Semenkhkare died shortly after Akhenaten's fall from power, and it was Tutankhamun, the latter's son, who followed him on to the throne.

Above: Akhenaten, Nefertiti and three of their children. This stela in Cairo Museum shows the royal family in kissing and relaxing mood, something that was never allowed to be shown in Egypt either before or after the Amarna rule. Scenes showing different aspects of the life of the royal family took the place of the old deities of the dead on the tomb walls of the Amarna nobles.

Right: The Israel Stela. This stela of Merenptah, Ramses II's son and successor, contains the only mention of Israel in ancient Egyptian sources. Although the stela was made in Merenptah's fifth year to commemorate his victory over invading Libyan tribes, the fact that the text concludes with the mention of some already subdued nations in western Asia (including the Israeli people) has misled some scholars into believing that this king was the Pharaoh of the Exodus who followed the Israelites into Canaan.

Above: Amenhotep III and Queen Tiye. This stela was found in the house of Panehesy at Amarna. The fact that Amenhotep III is represented in a clearly realistic style at Amarna indicates that the old King was living at the time and confirms the existence of a co-regency between him and his son Akhenaten. Neither the scene nor the text indicates that Amenhotep III was dead at the time. The stela is now in the British Museum.

Right: This unfinished statue of Akhenaten kissing one of his daughters was also found at Amarna. Again this was claimed by some scholars as evidence of Akhenaten's homosexuality; without any justification they stated that the younger figure represented Semenkhkare, the King's brother and son-in-law.

Opposite page: Akhenaten's Osiride statues. These statues are two of the four colossal figures that were made to stand at the entrance of the temple Akhenaten built for his God inside the Karnak complex. They are now in Cairo Museum. In three of the statues the King is shown wearing a kilt, while the fourth, which has larger lower parts, has no kilt. This persuaded some scholars to claim that Akhenaten lacked any signs of genitalia. This proved to be an incorrect assumption; the statue is in fact unfinished, and the lower part would have been cut back later to make the kilt.

This figure of the guardian of the dead, Anubis, was found in the tomb of Tutankhamun. The jackal was sitting on a shrine containing pieces of jewellery. A linen shirt covering Anubis was dated in year 7 of Akhenaten, the birth year of Tutankhamun. The dating of Tutankhamun's birth in this manner indicated that Akhenaten was his father.

the belief that Akhenaten ruled for seventeen years. He even stated this reason himself: 'In the absence of other evidence as to the reign extending beyond Year 17, no one will want to read the dating of I, plate lxiii, as "Year 21".'[8]

The hieratic sign for the figure ten is an upside-down 'V' and for 'twenty' two upside-down 'Vs' one above the other. The hieratic docket, as can be seen from the facsimile published by Gunn, shows a complete ' Λ ' with the remains of another ' Λ ' above it, which convinced Seele, correctly, that the date should be read as 'Year 21'. But Fairman disregards that, and Gunn's statement that he read the sign as 'Year 11' only because Akhenaten's reign was thought to have lasted only seventeen years in all, and goes on: 'In editing the inscriptions for *City of Akhenaten*, III, Jaroslav Černý, the Polish Egyptologist, and I had hoped to include some detailed and critical study of Amarna hieratic. In preparation for this, in 1937–39 Černý studied all the Amarna dockets he could find at the British Museum, the Ashmolean Museum and University College, London, in addition to several hundreds that I handed over to him. It is important to note that it was Černý's invariable method never to use or refer to any previous publication when copying and his work on the dockets ceased before he could attempt identification. His notebooks were handed over to me and I worked through them methodically, identifying all that in part or whole had previously been published. In the course of this work I discovered that the docket published by Gunn was in the British Museum (BM55640) and that Černý had unhesitatingly transcribed the date as (eleven) without a single query or note.

'Černý was unaware of the identification of this docket until after the publication of Seele's article when I informed him of the facts and asked him to re-examine BM55640. Černý not only did so, but called in Edwards and James (of the British Museum) and they all three declared that the reading was "Year 11". Černý reported to me at the time that the docket had faded seriously, but that the hieratic sign bore no resemblance to the normal form of (twenty) and was certainly in his opinion (ten): he thought that perhaps either a piece of ink had flaked off, or that a piece of ink had fallen on the end of the sign, but the condition of the docket did not permit him to decide which. I have since examined the docket myself, and I have nothing to add to Černý's statement. In short, there is no evidence of a regnal Year 21.'[9]

So, although in referring to Černý's statement, Fairman admits that 'the docket had faded seriously' between 1937–9, when Černý made his copy, and 1955 when, after Seele's article, he re-examined the docket, Fairman does not even publish a new facsimile to enable us to compare it with the earlier one made by Gunn in 1923. As if trying to avoid committing himself, he calls many other witnesses, in a way asking us to trust a group of wise men rather than giving us the evidence so that we can decide for ourselves. We have not even been told whether Fairman and his witnesses accept Gunn's facsimile, which was the basis for Seele's comments.

Even some of those who have changed their minds, such as Redford, and come round to accepting 'Year 11' as the correct reading, have proved not to be really convinced by Fairman's argument: '. . . those who have only Gunn's facsimile before them will be forced to admit that the prima-facie probability lies with the reading "21". If the present writer returns to the reading "regnal Year 11", it is solely because of an awareness of the increasing weight of the *argumentum e silentio*: if Akhenaten did attain a twenty-first year it is inconceivable that Years 18, 19 and 20 should be entirely absent from the Amarna dockets, especially in view of the large number of dockets dated to Year 17 and before.'[10]

But is this true? Were there no other records for these years? According to Fairman himself, Bennett, a member of the Egyptian Exploration Society team that worked at Amarna during the years 1930–31, was able to read the date 'Year 18' on one of the ostraca he was responsible for copying. However, Fairman took the view: 'Bennett's ostracon of Year 18 . . . may be dismissed as being untrustworthy, and without value.'[11] Then Fairman declares, on the following page of the same book, that 'the ostracon was not kept, but according to a rough facsimile this reading is certainly wrong'. This is even more serious, for Fairman is not telling us that the disputed ostracon was lost: he is saying that it was 'not kept', that it was thrown away. One would have expected that, as this ostracon gives an anomalous reading, it would have been guarded carefully for further examination. Instead, we now have only Fairman's judgement to rely on for whether Bennett's reading was right or wrong. No wonder Seele was convinced of a deliberate attempt by some scholars to discard any evidence that did not agree with their preconceived ideas.

However, there is still other evidence to indicate that Year 17 was not the end of the Akhenaten story. Derry has made the point: 'Akhenaten is known ... to have reigned for at least seventeen years, a period which has been extended to the nineteenth year by Pendlebury's recent discovery at el-Amarna of a monument bearing that date and with the further possibility that this may be lengthened to the twentieth year. Mr Pendlebury has very courteously permitted us to make use of these hitherto unpublished facts.'[12] Pendlebury died a few years later without publishing the source of his information and, as with Bennett's ostracon, Pendlebury's monument cannot be found anywhere.

In the course of his article on the correct date of Gunn's facsimile of the disputed hieratic docket as being 'Year 21', Seele gave a list of four scholars who believed that Akhenaten's reign lasted for eighteen years and one, Derry, who favoured nineteen. However, as long as nobody is able to discredit Gunn's original facsimile, Year 21 has to remain a certainty. As we said before, this does not mean, though, that Akhenaten actually reigned for twenty-one years.

If my hypothesis is correct, he abandoned Amarna and fled to Sinai. However, as long as Tutankhaten continued to reside at Amarna and as long as the Aten was regarded as the God of the throne, who owned the land of Egypt, Akhenaten, his son, was still looked upon as the legitimate Pharaoh. Therefore his followers kept up the practice of using a date relating to him as if he were still in power. It was only when Tutankhamun left Amarna, which soon became an abandoned city, for Thebes and Memphis in his Year 4 – Year 21 of Akhenaten – that this practice came to an end.

Those Egyptologists who had all the evidence indicating that Akhenaten ruled until only his Year 17 were confused to find further evidence of later dates for him, and had even to dispose of the evidence rather than be embarrassed by a contradiction they were unable to explain. It is true that Akhenaten ruled only until his Year 17, but it is also true that he was still regarded as the legitimate ruler until the change of the supreme god in Year 4 of Tutankhamun, Year 21 of Akhenaten. After that he had no legal status and, as we shall see, had to try to prove that he was the heir of his father, Amenhotep III, when he returned later to try to reclaim his throne.

SEMENKHKARE'S NAME AND EPITHETS

It is now generally accepted that Semenkhkare was appointed as coregent by Akhenaten in his Year 15. Yet we do not have any firm proof that Semenkhkare started numbering his own regnal years from that date as we do not have a Year 1 or Year 2 that can be said with certainty to have belonged to him. It seems that the years after his appointment continued to be dated according to Akhenaten's old system as Year 16 and Year 17. Nevertheless we have one case of a Year 3, found on a graffito at the tomb of Pere, a Theban nobleman: 'Year 3, third month of Inundation, day 10. The King of Upper and Lower Egypt, Lord of the Two Lands, Ankh-khepru-re beloved of [Nefer-khepru-re?], the son of Re Neferneferuaten beloved of Waen[re?].'[13]

This graffito is simply dated to Year 3 of Semenkhkare: no date of Akhenaten can be found on it. This is strong evidence that Semenkhkare was a sole ruler at the time the graffito was made. Yet, as we saw before, Tutankhamun's reign started during Year 17, the last year in which Akhenaten held authority. When, therefore, did Semenkhkare rule? The only acceptable explanation, as we saw before, is that he must have ruled for only a very short time, died and was followed in the same year by Tutankhamun. In this case, according to those who claim that the end of Akhenaten's rule coincided with his death in his Year 17, he would already have been dead when the graffito from Year 3 of Semenkhkare was made. Yet the epithets of Semenkhkare that indicate Akhenaten's affection towards him, which the young king had always used in his inscriptions and refer to the living Akhenaten, are also to be found in the Theban graffito, a fact that can be interpreted as meaning that, although his rule had ended, Akhenaten was still alive at that time. Redford confirms this understanding of the situation: '"Beloved of Nefer-Kheprure" and "beloved of Wa-enre", note that the praenomen of Semenkhkare, Ankh-Kheprure, i.e. "Kheprure (Akhenaten) lives", may indicate that at the time it was formulated Akhenaten was still alive.'[14]

THE FALLEN ONE OF AMARNA

No record has reached us about Akhenaten after the end of his rule. Tutankhamun left Amarna for Thebes and Memphis in his Year 4 and, at the same time, changed his own name and that of his queen, substituting 'amun' for 'aten'. A compromise was also reached by means of which all the ancient temples were reopened and worship of the old gods of Egypt restored, but worship of the Aten was not banned: the Aten was now regarded as just one god among many. No damage was done to Akhenaten's name, objects or memory until the end of the reign of King Aye, the last of the Amarna kings, who followed Tutankhamun. However, with the accession of Horemheb and the Ramesside kings who succeeded him, all standing monuments of Amarna were pulled down and worship of the Aten was forbidden. Horemheb and his followers also ensured that all memory of Akhenaten was wiped out of Egypt's official records, even to having his name and those of the three Amarna kings who succeeded him erased from the official king lists. Nevertheless, private texts referring to events that had taken place during Akhenaten's reign, while not mentioning him by name, used synonyms. A papyrus in the Berlin Museum, dating most probably from the time of the Nineteenth Dynasty, contains remains of a letter that gives the date of someone's death during the period of Akhenaten's rule in the following form: '. . . he died in Year 9 of the rebel.'[15] As well as avoiding mention of his name, this text shows us that he was regarded as an outlaw by the Ramessides, which would justify all the vengeful actions they were taking against his memory.

In a legal text from the tomb of Mos, which we discussed earlier, in referring to events that had taken place during Akhenaten's reign, some of the witnesses used another expression – *Pa-kherw-n Akhe-taten*.[16] This phrase was translated early in this century by Gardiner as 'the enemy of Akhetaten (Amarna)', a translation which the majority of scholars have since taken for granted to be correct. This is not the case if one breaks the phrase down into its constituents: *Pa* is the Egyptian definite article; *kherw* means literally 'fallen', and the *n* represents the preposition 'of'. Although enemies of Egypt were described as having fallen, the word itself, which is derived from the verb 'to fall', means 'the fallen' and could not mean 'enemy'. Even the little figure of a fallen person that comes after the word as a determinative confirms the 'fallen' sense. Furthermore, we could understand if Akhenaten was called the enemy of Amun or Thebes, but how would it be possible even for his opponents to call him 'the enemy of Akhetaten (Amarna)', the new capital city which he himself established? In an introduction to a book published twenty years ago, Harry S. Smith, Professor of Egyptology at University College London, translated this phrase correctly as 'the fallen one of Akhetaten'.[17]

When we look at both of the labels applied to Akhenaten, it is clear that they are not merely pejorative, but describe him as he was seen by the following generation, a rebel who fell from power. The meaning is here clear, the implication being that, as in the Talmud story of Moses becoming King of Ethiopia (see Chapter Two), he had to abdicate in favour of the queen's son, who can only be Tutankhamun, son of Nefertiti.

16

CORRIDORS OF POWER

A VARIETY of historical evidence also points to the fact that Akhenaten survived his fall from power.

Manetho's King List

Although the memory of Akhenaten and his three successors was suppressed completely and the official king lists excluded them, placing Horemheb's name immediately after that of Amenhotep III, in Manetho's king list of the Eighteenth Dynasty, as it has reached us through other authors, the four kings are mentioned. It seems that, despite the official hostility at the time, folklore tales, transmitted from generation to generation, kept alive the memory of the Amarna kings until, some time before the third century BC, the story of Egypt's history at this time was put down in writing. Of course, much confusion and distortion has affected the story in the process, and surviving Amarna monuments, such as its rock tombs and the quarry inscriptions, must have also been read and interpreted by the priests and scribes and helped in the rewriting of the story. In Manetho's king list we find four names inserted between Amenhotep III and Horemheb:

Achencheres
Rathosis
Achencheres
Achencheres

The German philologist Wolfgang Helck was able to show[1] that

Achencheres was a confused derivation of Akhenaten's name, while Rathosis is believed to be a confused form of Tutankhamun's nomen. Why would Egyptian memory give to three of these four Amarna kings one name, that of Akhenaten? The only possible conclusion is that this was the result of two contradictory pieces of evidence: a) four different kings ruled between Amenhotep III and Horemheb, b) Akhenaten lived during the reign of the four Amarna kings and this whole period was regarded in their memory as being his own rule.

The Power Struggle

At least two events early in Akhenaten's coregency with his father indicated strong opposition to his rule. The graffito of Amenhotep III's Year 30 from the pyramid temple of Meidum, which would be Year 3 of Akhenaten, pointed to a rejection by some powerful factions of the king's decision to cause 'the male to sit upon the seat of his father'. Again, the border stela inscription of Amarna shows that, before deciding to leave Thebes and build his new city, Akhenaten had encountered some strong opposition and been the subject of verbal criticism. Certainly, he would not have left the dynasty's capital without having been forced to do so.

A final confrontation between the throne and the priesthood was postponed simply because, after he departed from Thebes, he had nothing at all to do with the running of the country, which was left to his father, Amenhotep III. Another important factor was the complete reliance of Akhenaten on the armed forces for support. If we may take the reliefs from the tombs of the nobles at face value, then the city was virtually an armed camp. Everywhere we see processions and parades of soldiers, infantry and chariotry with their massed standards. Palaces, temples and the city borders seem to have been constantly guarded.

Akhenaten's man in the army, as we saw earlier, was Aye, his maternal uncle, the husband of Tiy, his and Nefertiti's nurse. As a result of this relationship, he could be regarded, according to ancient traditions, as a father figure. Aye was certainly the power behind Akhenaten's throne from the time of the death of Amenhotep III. Aye's origins, like those of Yuya, his father, were military. His extremely high ranks in both arms of the service, the infantry and the chariotry, show that he was in control of the army, without whose loyalty and support Akhenaten could have been overthrown in his first year as sole regent. After the beginning of the Eighteenth Dynasty, which was founded after the defeat and expulsion of the Hyksos invaders from the Eastern Delta, Egyptian Pharaohs had followed them into western Asia, forming the first empire of the ancient world that extended from the borders of Asia Minor and northern Iraq in the north up to a few miles north of Khartoum in the south. Egypt now had for the first time a regular army of full-time professional fighters, organized in local divisions. The victorious fighters shared war spoils as well as being rewarded by the king with gold, slaves and land. The army officers grew into a new aristocracy that, thanks to Akhenaten's policy, became deeply involved in politics towards the end of the dynasty, as a result of which the two last kings of the Eighteenth Dynasty, Aye and Horemheb, as well as the two first kings of the Nineteenth, Ramses I and Seti I, came from the army and had no relationship with either the original Tuthmosside house or the priesthood.

On the other hand, as the victorious kings of the Eighteenth Dynasty came from Thebes which in the sixteenth century BC had consisted of a few scattered small towns, it had by now grown into a vast cosmopolitan city, the capital of the empire. Abundant spoils of war came to Thebes and its gods, especially to Amun, the chief Theban deity, who now achieved great authority, particularly when he was associated with Re, the old Heliopolitan god, as Amun-Re, king of the gods. Many new temples were built and that at Karnak, main centre of Amun, grew into a gigantic construction, the largest temple ever built, with large areas of agricultural land and thousands of slaves allocated to it. The priests, and those of Amun in particular, became increasingly powerful from the time of Tuthmosis III. This king was not the son of the queen, although he was the king's son. So, in order to have him accepted as his heir, his father arranged a ceremony in Karnak where the image of Amun, carried by the god's priests, chose young Tuthmosis to be the son of Amun, a kind of adoption by the god which ensured his right to the throne. Tuthmosis III turned out to be the mightiest of all Egyptian Pharaohs, ruling for fifty-four years and fighting many wars in Asia to consolidate the empire.

In return for their co-operation in establishing his right to the throne, Tuthmosis III showed his gratitude to Amun's priests by giving them more power and wealth. As the king was the head of both the army and the temple, Egyptian Pharaohs exercised a balancing policy between the military and priestly powers. Although it is true that Pharaoh was regarded as a son of the god and, as such, had to be obeyed without question, he himself was also expected to abide by the country's old beliefs and traditions. Not only did Akhenaten reject this concept of kingship: he was no longer the son of any Egyptian god. The Aten was never worshipped as a god in Egypt before the Amarna religious revolution, which has to be regarded as having its origins in the time Yuya became associated with the royal family during the reign of Tuthmosis IV. Thus Akhenaten came to be regarded as a rebel, an outlaw, and without the support of Aye and his army he would have been disposed of as soon as his father, and protector, died.

But, as we saw earlier, unlimited loyalty from the army could not reasonably be expected. After all, the officers and soldiers themselves believed in the gods whose images the king ordered them to destroy, they worshipped in the temples which they were ordered to close. A conflict arose. Aye, still the strongest man in Egypt, realized the danger – the whole Amarna family and their followers, as well as the worship of the Aten, was under threat – and that compromise was the wisest course to follow. However, Akhenaten's belief in one God was too deep for him to accept a return to any of the former ways. Aye therefore advised him that, in his own interests, he should abdicate in favour of the young Tutankhamun and flee the country. After his departure, Aye, as Tutankhamun's adviser, allowed the old temples to be reopened and the ancient gods of Egypt to be worshipped again alongside worship of the Aten, a compromise that increased his own power, as it enabled him to pose as the saviour of both army and temple.

The climate of the country remained uneasy, but Aye's own position as the most powerful man in Egypt was sufficiently secure for him to appoint himself king after the death of Tutankhamun – which, as Harrison found a fracture in the bones at the back of his neck, could have been the result of assassination. In these circumstances, it is impossible to imagine, as some scholars have fancied, that Aye, Akhenaten's most potent supporter, would have permitted a *coup d'état* against the king, or, for that matter, that either the king or Tutankhamun would have survived such an event: rather the departure of Akhenaten should be seen as a political compromise that allowed Amarna rule to continue.

It was only on the death of Aye himself that Horemheb, another powerful military figure, emerged to take power on behalf of the dissident Establishment and to start the campaign of destruction designed to remove all trace of Amarna rule from Egyptian history.

17

THE FIRST MONOTHEIST

SINCE Freud first showed the similarity between the religions of Moses and Akhenaten fifty years ago in his book *Moses and Monotheism*, there has been endless argument about the identity of the first monotheist. As we saw in the introduction to this book, attempts have been made to place the Jewish Exodus long before the Amarna period, thus ensuring the honour for Moses. Then, when this approach failed and all the evidence pointed to the Exodus having taken place *after* the Amarna reigns, the focal points of attack became the discrediting of Akhenaten himself and efforts to demonstrate that the beliefs he introduced into Egypt were not monotheistic at all.

The holy books establish Moses as the first monotheist although, while the Hebrew patriarchs believed in one God, they accepted that other peoples had other gods to worship, as in the case of Laban (Genesis, 31:43–55). Yet, from historical sources, Akhenaten is the first person we know of to introduce worship of one God. An examination of their respective religious beliefs makes it clear that Moses and Akhenaten should not be looked upon, as has been largely the case, as rivals but as the same person.

Akhenaten's God

The early representations of Akhenaten's God showed the deity as of human shape with the head of a falcon, surmounted by a solar disc. Towards the end of his Year 2 or early in his Year 3 an important development took place in this representation. The human figure disappeared and in its place a golden disc was shown at the top of the scene with extended rays that came down over the members of the royal family as well as the temple, altar and palace. These rays ended in hands that held the symbols of 'life' and 'power'. To indicate the kingly status of Akhenaten's God, an uraeus (cobra) hung from the disc in the same way as an uraeus adorned the brow of the king. At the same time the name and epithet of the God was placed inside two cartouches, matching the manner in which the ruling king's name was written.

The God introduced by Moses to Israel is often spoken of and addressed as a 'king' (Isaiah, 41:21; 44:6; 52:7) and the so-called *Enthronement Psalms of Jehovah* (Psalms 47:93; 96–9) emphasize this kingly idea of the Lord. Yet the attribution of kingship to Jehovah was certainly foreign to Israelite thought at the time of the Exodus.

Akhenaten seems to have drawn on the traditional worship of the solar god of Heliopolis in many ways. The early name for Akhenaten's God was the same as the name of the Heliopolitan god Re-Harakhti (Horus of the horizon). Furthermore, the name given by the king to his early Karnak temple, *ben-ben* (obelisk), was the same as that of the Heliopolitan temples where the *ben-ben* (a small pyramid on a square base) was a characteristic of the solar temples. Meryre II, the high priest of Akhenaten's God, the Aten, was also given the same title – 'greatest of seers' – as the high priest of Heliopolis.

From the inscriptions both at the Karnak temple and at the rock tombs of Amarna, especially that of Aye, we can see how Akhenaten regarded his God:

'The living Aten, there is none other than He';

'Who Himself gave birth to Himself';

'He who decrees life, the Lord of sunbeams';

'The world came forth from Thy (Aten) hand';

'Thou createst the earth when Thou were afar, namely men, cattle, all flocks, and everything on earth which moves with legs, or which is up above flying with wings. The foreign countries of Syria (north) and Kush (south), and the land of Egypt, Thou placest every man in his place, and makest their food. Everyone has his food, and his lifetime is reckoned; and similarly their languages are wholly separate in form. For their colours are different, for Thou hast made foreign peoples different';

'Thou ... creator of months and maker of days, and reckoner of hours'.

We find echoes of these attributes in the God of Moses. He was:

a sole God

> Hear, O Israel: The Lord our God is one Lord. (Deuteronomy, 6:4)
>
> Thou shalt have no other gods before me. (Exodus, 20:3)

without a cult image

> Thou shalt not make unto thee any graven image, or any likeness of any thing that is in heaven above, or that is in the earth beneath, or that is in the water under the earth. (Exodus, 20:4)

the creator of the world

> In the beginning God created the heaven and the earth. (Genesis, 1:1)

the king of the world

> The Lord shall reign for ever and ever. (Exodus, 15:18)

the father

> And thou shalt say unto Pharaoh, Thus saith the Lord, Israel is my son, even my firstborn. (Exodus, 4:22)

Temple and Worship

The way the patriarchs who preceded Moses worshipped their God was by building an altar of stone at the spot where the Lord had spoken to them:

> And the Lord appeared unto Abram, and said, Unto thy seed will I give this land; and there builded he an altar unto the Lord, who appeared unto him. (Genesis, 12:7)
>
> And he erected there an altar, and called it El-elohe-Israel. (Genesis, 33:20)

They made offerings of drink and oil:

> And Jacob set up a pillar in the place where he talked with him, even a
> pillar of stone: and he poured a drink offering thereon, and oil
> thereon. (Genesis, 35:14)

And they also offered sacrifices:

> Then Jacob offered sacrifice upon the mount, and called his brethren
> to eat bread: and they did eat bread, and tarried all night in the mount.
> (Genesis, 31:54)

> And Israel took his journey with all that he had, and came to
> Beer-sheba, and offered sacrifices unto the God of his father Isaac.
> (Genesis, 46:1)

Moses was the first person to introduce a temple into Israelite
worship when he created the tabernacle in Sinai. It is true that the
Canaanites did build their own kind of stone temples in Palestine,
and even in some locations in the Eastern Delta during the Hyksos
period, but we have no evidence that the Israelites had, or made use
of, any such construction before the time of Moses. For his part,
Akhenaten adapted the Heliopolitan solar form of the Egyptian
temple – the same form used by Moses in the desert – to be used as
the place of worship for his new religion.

Accordingly, there was no Israelite priesthood before the time of
Moses. It was he who arranged the priesthood in two main levels,
the high priest and the ordinary priests, and instructed them on
what garments to wear, how to be purified and anointed and how to
go about fulfilling the duties of their office. Ritual and worship at
the newly-established Israelite tabernacle were similar to those
introduced by Akhenaten, who instructed his followers to sacrifice
the sacred Egyptian animals for his new God, again echoing an
incident that we find in the story of Moses:

> And Moses said, It is not meet so to do; for we shall sacrifice the
> abomination of the Egyptians to the Lord our God: lo, shall we
> sacrifice the abomination of the Egyptians before their eyes, and will
> they not stone us? (Exodus, 8:26)

Moses also introduced the ark, the receptacle in the temple in
which the Pentateuch scrolls were to be kept (Exodus, 25:10). The

ark is regarded as being the holiest part of the Jewish temple after the Pentateuch itself. This again was an Egyptian practice, as Akhenaten adopted the Egyptian holy boat, usually kept in the temple where it was used to carry the deity during processions.

Jehovah, Adonai and Aten

Before the time of Moses, the patriarchs identified their God in a variety of terms, all of which were names of ancient Canaanite deities, such as:

El: (Genesis, 33:20);

El 'Elyon (The Most High): (Psalms, 73:11);

El 'Olam (The Everlasting God): (Genesis, 21:33);

El Shaddai (God Almighty): (Genesis, 17:1);

El Ro-i (The God Who Sees Me, or The God Of Vision): (Exodus, 6:3);

Elohim: Elohim, the plural of Eloho, meaning 'a god' and thought to be a lengthened form of 'El', is used in the Bible more than two thousand times and is usually replaced in English by the word 'God', but it is also used for pagan gods and goddesses (Exodus, 12:12 and I Kings, 11:5).

Jehovah: This, the personal name of the God of Israel, is written in Hebrew with four consonants, YHWH, which is understood to mean 'I am' and is referred to as the 'Tetragrammaton'. Like Elohim, this name occurs frequently in the Bible and is usually replaced in English by the word 'Lord'.

Adonai (My Lord): The Hebrew word 'Adonai' is also usually rendered in English as 'Lord'. It is used in the Bible to refer to human beings ('The man, who is the lord of the land . . .', Genesis, 42:30') as well as God. We also find the combined form 'Adonai Jehovah' (My Lord Jehovah):

And Abram said, Lord God, what wilt thou give me . . .? (Genesis, 15:2)

And he said, Lord God, whereby shall I know that I shall inherit it? (Genesis, 15:8)

O Lord God, thou hast begun to shew thy servant thy greatness, and thy mighty hand . . . (Deuteronomy, 3:24)

The 'ai' can be removed from the word 'Adonai' as it is a Hebrew pronoun meaning 'my' or 'mine' and signifying possession. We are then left with 'Adon' (Lord) which, as correctly noted by Freud, is the Hebrew word for the Egyptian 'Aten' as the Egyptian 't' becomes 'd' in Hebrew and the vowel 'e' becomes an 'o'. The name of the God of Moses, Adon, is therefore in the above references the same as the name of the God of Akhenaten, Aten.

What of Jehovah? The Book of Exodus account of the argument that took place in Sinai between Moses and his God over the question of his return to Egypt to rescue the Israelites does not make any real sense unless Moses and Akhenaten were one and the same person. When his new religion was rejected, Akhenaten fled to Sinai, leaving the throne to his son, Tutankhamun, who was followed by Aye, then Horemheb. When Horemheb died, there was no Tuthmosside heir to the Eighteenth Dynasty apart from Akhenaten himself in desert exile. Pa-Ramses, Horemheb's vizier, commander of the army and mayor of Zarw in the Eastern Delta – where he resided and where the Israelites and Egyptian followers of Akhenaten had been imprisoned – prepared to proclaim himself the new King of Egypt as Ramses I.

Having been rejected by the majority of Egyptians, Akhenaten now decided to choose the Israelites as his own people. However, when the Lord urges him in the Book of Exodus story to challenge the new Pharaoh, it becomes clear that his main concern is not confrontation with Ramses I but how he is to succeed in obtaining the support of the Israelites. His first problem is that he does not speak their language sufficiently well:

> And Moses said unto the Lord, O my Lord, I am not eloquent . . . I am slow of speech and of a slow tongue. (Exodus, 4:10)

For this reason, Aaron, the Israelite feeding brother of his early childhood (see page 182), had to be enlisted as his spokesman:

> And the anger of the Lord was kindled against Moses, and he said, Is not Aaron the Levite thy brother? I know that he can speak well . . . (Exodus, 4:14)

The second problem facing Akhenaten in enlisting the support of the Israelites was to establish a relationship between his God and the

God of the Israelites' ancestors. Both Gods were the same in the sense that, unlike the ancient gods of Egypt, they had no image. The question of God's name, however, seems to have been a matter of compromise, giving rise to two strange passages in the Book of Exodus. The first arises when Moses asks which name he should use:

> And Moses said unto God, Behold when I come unto the children of Israel, and shall say unto them, The God of your fathers hath sent me unto you; and they shall say to me, What is his name? what shall I say unto them?
> And God said unto Moses, I AM THAT I AM: and he said, Thus shalt thou say unto the children of Israel, I AM (i.e. Jehovah) hath sent me unto you. (Exodus, 3:13–14)

The second passage, in which God informs Moses that he never appeared to the patriarchs under the name Jehovah, is even stranger in the light of the fact that we encounter this name in several chapters of the preceding Book of Genesis:

> And I appeared unto Abraham, and unto Isaac, and unto Jacob, by the name of God Almighty, but by my name JE-HO-VAH was I not known to them. (Exodus, 6:3)

It seems that Akhenaten would not reject the name of his God, the Aten, simply to secure the support of the Israelites. Therefore a compromise had to be reached. Its nature was that, while the Hebrew word 'YHWH' could be written, it could not be read aloud but had to be pronounced as 'Adonai'. Nobody knows when this Jewish practice started although I believe it dates from the time of Moses. Nor has any convincing explanation ever been put forward for the interdict. To say that a ban on uttering God's personal name was intended as a sign of respect is contradicted by the fact that all the other names given to the Israelite God before the time of Moses, as well as Adonai, are spoken aloud by the Jews. In fact, as Freud has noted, the God of Akhenaten is the same as the God of Moses, as can be clearly seen from the way the verse from Deuteronomy cited at the beginning of this chapter is written in Hebrew:

> *Shema Yisrael YaHWaH Elohina YaHWaH Ekhod.*

That is:

> *Hear, O Israel, Jehovah our God is the only God.*

However, according to this ancient tradition, when read aloud by Jewish believers, it becomes:

Shema Yisrael: Adonai Elohina Adonai Ekhod

This confirms that a compromise was reached in Sinai under which the old personal name of God, Jehovah, before the time of Moses would never be pronounced again and should in every case be replaced by Adonai, the name of the God of Akhenaten.

The Evidence of Sinai

We know from the biblical story that Moses fled to Sinai after killing the Egyptian – after falling from power according to the Talmud – and lived there until his return after the Pharaoh of the Oppression had died. What about Akhenaten? Although we do not have conclusive evidence that Akhenaten followed a similar course, there are many indications that point to this being the case.

In the early years of this century, Flinders Petrie led an expedition into Sinai where he recorded what he was able to find of ancient inscriptions. The resulting evidence showed that the Egyptians had sent expeditions to the mountains of Sinai since early dynastic times, mainly for the purpose of mining turquoise.

Sinai is in the form of a triangle with its apex to the south between the two arms of the Red Sea, the Gulf of Suez and the Gulf of Aqaba. At its northern base runs the road from Egypt to Asia, from Kantarah to Gaza along the Mediterranean coastline. To the south of this low northern land is a lofty limestone plateau, crossed by only a few narrow passes. The southern triangle, between the two arms of the Red Sea, is a mountain mass including Mount Sinai or Mount Horeb (modern name, Gebel Musa, which means the Mount of Moses). En route from the Eastern Delta through the valleys, before arriving at Mount Sinai we come to another important site, Sarabit el-Khadim, a mountain area with many turquoise mines.

On the high peak of Sarabit, 2600 feet above sea level, a shrine was constructed, originally in a cave, although by the time of the New Kingdom it had been extended outside and reached a total length of 230 feet. This temple was dedicated to Hathor, the local deity. Petrie found fragments of a limestone stela at Sarabit, made by Ramses I. Although the stela is not actually dated, this poses no problem as Ramses I ruled for little more than a year. What is surprising about the stela is that in its inscription Ramses I describes himself as 'the ruler of all that the Aten embraces'.[1] Of this unexpected reappearance of the fallen Aten, Petrie commented: 'To find the Aten mentioned thus after the ruthless Amunism of Horemheb is remarkable. Hitherto the latest mention of it was under King Aye.'[2]

The name of the Aten had been missing for thirteen years during the reign of Horemheb: now in the time of his successor, Ramses I, the hated God has reappeared, not in Egypt proper but in Sinai. The stela made more than a quarter of a century after Akhenaten's fall from power, also features the Amarna realistic style: 'The portion which is preserved of the figure [Ramses I's figure at the top of the stela] is carefully wrought, and in the dress resembles the work of Akhenaten.'[3]

This was not the only surprising discovery. At the temple Petrie found the dark green head, executed in the Amarna style, of a statuette of Queen Tiye, Akhenaten's mother. The complete statuette must have been about a foot high. Why should it be at Sarabit? 'It is strange that this remotest settlement of Egypt has preserved her portrait for us, unmistakably named by her cartouche in the midst of the crown,' Petrie remarked. 'The haughty dignity of the face is blended with a fascinating directness and personal appeal. The delicacy of the surfaces round the eye and over the cheek shows the greatest delicacy in handling. The curiously drawn-down lips with their fullness and yet delicacy, their disdain without malice, are evidently modelled in all truth from the life.'[4]

Petrie was also able to find evidence indicating that the rituals performed in the temple at Sarabit were of Semitic nature:

• The Offering of Burnt Sacrifices: He found a bed of clean white ash under a considerable portion of the temple, amounting to more than fifty tons, which he took to represent the remains of burnt sacrifices over a long period.[5] This practice is known from the Bible to have been Israelite.

• The Dedication of Conical Stones: Two cones of sandstone, alike in shape and size, were found in the temple. Stones of this type were used in certain forms of Syrian ritual and are not to be found in Egypt.

• An Elaborate Ceremony of Ablutions: At Sarabit there were three rectangular tanks and a circular basin, placed to be used at four different stages of entering the temple. This makes it clear that ablutions played a great role in the form of worship at Sarabit as they do in both Judaism and Islam.[6]

• The Practice of Visiting Sacred Places for the Purpose of Obtaining Oracular Dreams and the Setting Up of Memorial Stones at the Spot Where the Dream Occurred: Scattered over the area around the temple Petrie came across many slabs of sandstone, set upright. The slabs ranged in height from a few inches to a couple of feet, propped up by other stones if necessary to make them stand on end. Similar piled stones were found around Mount Sinai, indicating that both areas were regarded as sacred places. This archaeological find agrees with what we find in the Bible:

> And he (the Lord) said, Draw not nigh hither: put off thy shoes from off thy feet, for the place whereon thou standest is holy ground. (Exodus, 3:5)

Petrie noted that this piling of stones is part of a well-known system of sacred stones, set upright in adoration, that is not Egyptian, and for him the only explanation for this ritual would be the custom of sleeping at or near a sacred place in order to obtain some vision from the deity, which he compared with what the patriarch Jacob is said to have done:[7]

> And Jacob went out from Beersheba, and went toward Haran.
> And he lighted upon a certain place, and tarried there all night, because the sun was set; and he took of the stones of that place, and put them for his pillows, and lay down in that place to sleep.
> And he dreamed, and behold a ladder set up on the earth, and the top of it reached to heaven: and behold the angels of God ascending and descending on it. (Genesis, 28:10–12)

If Akhenaten lived at the Sarabit temple for twenty-five years, although he would not have changed any of his original beliefs it is easy to envisage his adopting some of the local Semitic rituals that did not conflict with them. But why Sinai – why would he choose Sinai for his place of refuge in exile?

Although Sinai was regarded as part of Egypt from the early days of Egyptian history, no army garrison was stationed there. Nor did it have a resident governor. Instead, during the Eighteenth and

Nineteenth Dynasties the area was placed under the control of two officials, the Royal Messenger in All Foreign Lands and the Royal Chancellor.

Neby, the Troop Commander and Mayor of Zarw, was also the Royal Messenger in All Foreign Lands. Zarw was Tiye's city, where the Israelites lived until their Exodus, and there are also indications that Zarw remained faithful to the Aten during the reigns of Tutankhamun and Aye. It was only when Horemheb appointed Pa-Ramses (later Ramses I) to the posts previously held by Neby that the climate changed. At least until that time, therefore, Akhenaten could count on being able to live in peace in his chosen refuge.

Nor was he under any threat from the Royal Chancellor, who was responsible for the mining expeditions sent to Sarabit. We know from inscriptions found in Sinai and other sources that, up to the time of Amenhotep III, the treasury was placed in the hands of one family, that of Pa-Nehas, for three generations. Akhenaten himself also appointed Panahesy, a descendant of Pa-Nehas, as his chancellor and Chief Servitor of the Aten in his temple at Amarna as well as the Servitor of the King in the temple. Thus the family of Pa-Nehas was not only involved in Akhenaten's government, but in his worship. It would therefore have been normal for them to suggest Sarabit as a place of exile where they would have been able to give him support.

Although there is as yet no complete proof, it is easy to see that, in the prevailing circumstances, Sarabit offered the best, if not the only, location for Akhenaten's exile – a holy place, close to another holy place, Mount Sinai, away from Egyptian control, where he could meditate and develop his religious ideas until, when Horemheb's death brought the Eighteenth Dynasty to an end, he came back to try to reclaim his throne.

The Ten Commandments

The Ten Commandments given by the Lord God of Moses to the Israelites in Sinai are clearly in an Egyptian tradition and would seem to have common roots with the Egyptian *Book of the Dead*.

Egyptians believed that, after their death, they faced a trial in the underworld before Osiris and his forty-two judges in the Hall of

Judgement. Spell 125 of the *Book of the Dead* contains a Negative Confession that the dead person has to recite on this occasion, containing such assurances as:

I have done no falsehood,

I have not robbed,

I have not stolen,

I have not killed men,

I have not told lies.

The Ten Commandments are a kind of positive form of this Egyptian Negative Confession:

Thou shalt not kill,

Thou shalt not steal,

Thou shalt not bear false witness against thy neighbour.

It therefore seems likely that Akhenaten, who did not believe in Osiris or his underworld, turned the moral code according to which the Egyptians believed their dead would be judged into an imperative code of behaviour for his followers in this life.

18

THE 'MAGIC' ROD OF MOSES

SOME of the most fascinating sections of the biblical story of Moses are those dealing with the magical power of his rod. When the Lord asked Moses to leave Sinai and return to Egypt in order to liberate the Israelites, Moses was not sure that they would either listen to him or believe in him:

> And Moses answered and said, But, behold, they will not believe me, nor hearken unto my voice: for they will say, The Lord hath not appeared unto thee. (Exodus, 4:1)

We are then told that the Lord gave Moses three magical signs that would confirm his identity as the messenger of God:

1   The rod he was carrying became a snake and was then restored to its former state (4:2–4);

2   His hand became leprous (white as snow) and then was healed again (4:6–7); and

3   He was promised that, if he poured the water of the Nile on the ground, it would turn to blood (4:9).

Magic implies the existence of a realm of power that transcends Nature and the deities. It is an attempt to influence events by occult means and is therefore in complete contrast with the monotheistic religion of both Moses and Akhenaten.

Ancient man believed that he was able to influence the mysterious forces surrounding him by means of magical rituals or utterances. This was true of Egyptians, who had special priests to practise these arts. They believed they could achieve their desired end by such means. Magic was employed particularly to protect the dead on their journey through the underworld, and to ensure their return for a second life.

The Bible, on the other hand, opposes all kinds of magic. Any belief in its efficacy is seen as contradicting the Israelite belief in the exclusive and supreme rule of one God, whose will cannot be influenced by human means. The subsequent confrontation between Moses and the Egyptian magicians and sorcerers, described in chapter seven of the Book of Exodus, explained as miracles in the case of Moses and magic in the case of the Egyptians, is not really convincing as both sides were said to have employed the same methods.

We know also that Akhenaten rejected all kinds of magic. Even the practices, dear to the Egyptians, relating to the spells of the *Book of the Dead*, that guaranteed a safe journey through the underworld, as well as the trial of the deceased before Osiris, the dead king of the dead, and his tribunal found no place in Akhenaten's religion. Osiris and other gods of the underworld were completely ignored by him and his followers. How, then, can we explain how Moses/Akhenaten, the first prophet of monotheism, turned to magic in order to confirm that he was the true messenger of the Lord?

When we examine the acts said to have been performed by Moses to establish his identity we find that they are largely related to some old Egyptian rituals that kings used to perform in their *sed* festivals for the purpose of rejuvenating their power. The biblical account reads as follows:

> And Moses and Aaron went in unto Pharaoh, and they did so as the Lord had commanded: and Aaron cast down his rod before Pharaoh, and before his servants, and it became a serpent.
>
> Then Pharaoh also called the wise men and the sorcerers: now the magicians of Egypt, they also did in like manner with their enchantments.
>
> For they cast down every man his rod, and they became serpents: but Aaron's rod swallowed up their rods.
>
> And he hardened Pharaoh's heart, that he hearkened not unto them; as the Lord had said. (Exodus, 7:10–13)

The first thing we notice here is that, whereas earlier in the Book of Exodus Moses was instructed to perform three different signs, here we have an account of only one – and that it was performed not by Moses, but by Aaron.

The Koran gives a slightly different account of this confrontation, an account which contains more significant details than are to be

found in the Bible and is in closer agreement with the earlier details
in the Book of Exodus:

Moses said: 'O Pharaoh!
I am an apostle from
The Lord of the Worlds, –

'One for whom it is right
To say nothing but truth
About Allah. Now have I
Come unto you (people), from
Your Lord with a clear (Sign)
So let the Children of Israel
Depart along with me.'

(Pharaoh) said: 'If indeed
Thou hast come with a Sign,
Show it forth, –
If thou tellest the truth.'

Then (Moses) threw his rod,
And behold! it was
A serpent, plain (for all to see)!

And he drew out his hand
And behold! it was white
To all beholders!

Said the Chiefs of the people
To Pharaoh: 'This is indeed
A sorcerer well-versed.

'His plan is to get you out
Of your land: then
What is it ye counsel?'

They said: 'Keep him
And his brother in suspense
(For a while); and send
To the cities men to collect –

'And bring up to thee
All (our) sorcerers well-versed.'

So there came
The sorcerers to Pharaoh:
They said, 'Of course
We shall have a (suitable)
Reward if we win!

He said: 'Yea, (and more), –
For ye shall in that case
Be (raised to posts)
Nearest (to my person).'

They said: 'O Moses
Wilt thou throw (first),
Or shall we have
The (first) throw?'

Said Moses: 'Throw ye (first).'
So when they threw,
They bewitched the eyes
Of the people, and struck
Terror into them: for they
Showed a great (feat of) magic.

He put it into Moses's mind
By inspiration: 'Throw (now)
Thy rod': and behold!
It swallows up straightaway
All the falsehoods
Which they fake.

Thus truth was confirmed,
And all that they did
Was made of no effect.

So the (great ones) were vanquished
There and then, and were
Made to look small.

But the sorcerers fell down
Prostrate in adoration,

Saying: 'We believe
In the Lord of the Worlds, –

'The Lord of Moses and Aaron.'

Said Pharaoh: 'Believe ye
In Him before I give
You permission? Surely
This is a trick which ye
Have planned in the City
To drive out its people:
But soon shall ye know
(The consequences).

'Be sure I will cut off
Your hands and your feet
On opposite sides, and I
Will cause you all
To die on the cross.' (Sura VII, 104–24)

This section of the Koran presents the confrontation in such a precise way that one wonders if some of the details were left out of the biblical account deliberately. Here Moses sounds less like a magician, more like someone who presents evidence of his authority that convinces the wise men of Egypt, who throw themselves at his feet and thus earn the punishment of Pharaoh. One can only suspect that the biblical editor exercised care to avoid any Egyptian involvement with the Israelite Exodus, even to the extent of replacing Moses by Aaron in the performance of the rituals.

The Koran also mentions the white hand ritual as having been performed by Moses in front of Pharaoh. As for the promise that the Nile would turn red, this should be seen as indicating the time of the year. During the season of Inundation, the Nile waters become reddish, and, if these events took place in the Eastern Delta, this would suggest the late days of summer, by which time this change of colour would have begun to affect the lower reaches of the river.

And what of the 'magic' rod of Moses? We know from Egyptian sources that kings used to have a collection of rods representing different aspects of their authority. One of the sceptres of the king's power was a rod in the shape of a serpent either made of, or covered with, brass. Now, the Hebrew word used in the Bible to indicate the rod of Moses is *nahash*, which has the meanings of both 'serpent' and 'brass'. The Haggadah, the legendary part of the Talmud, confirms the royal character of Moses's rod: 'The rod which Moses used ... was shaped and engraved in the image of a sceptre.'

During their *sed* festivals, celebrated by Egyptian kings, including Akhenaten, to rejuvenate their power, it was the custom to take part in rituals that included both the 'serpent rod' and 'hand' rituals performed by Moses. In the tomb of Kheruef, one of Queen Tiye's stewards, a throne scene shows the queen with her husband, Amenhotep III. Under the dais of the throne we see Kheruef and other officials, each holding something that he is about to hand to the king so that he can use it during the *sed* festival celebrations of his Year 30. In one scene, Kheruef is followed by eight palace officials, the first of whom is wearing an apron. He puts his right arm across his chest and his hand over his left shoulder while he holds his forearm with the left hand. The fourth of these officials holds a bundle of clothes in his right hand and a curved sceptre with serpent's head in his left.[1]

So, in the course of their *sed* festival celebrations, Egyptian kings performed rituals that corresponded to the 'serpent rod' and 'hand' rituals performed by Moses – and, in performing them, Moses was not using magic but seeking to establish his royal authority.

I think the correct interpretation of these accounts is that, when Akhenaten was forced to abdicate, he must have taken his royal sceptre to Sinai with him. On the death of Horemheb, the last king of the Eighteenth Dynasty, about a quarter of a century later, he must have seen an opportunity to restore himself to the throne. No heir to the Tuthmosside kings existed and it was Pa-Ramses, commander of Horemheb's army and governor of Zarw, who had laid claim to the throne. Akhenaten returned to Egypt and the wise men were gathered in order to decide between him and Pa-Ramses. Once they saw the sceptre of royal authority and Akhenaten had performed the *sed* festival rituals – secret from ordinary citizens – the wise men bowed the knee in front of him, confirming that his was the superior right to the throne, but Pa-Ramses used his army to crush the rebels. Moses was allowed to leave again for Sinai, however, accompanied by the Israelites, his mother's relatives, and the few Egyptians who had been converted to the new religion that he had attempted to force upon Egypt a quarter of a century earlier. In Sinai the followers of Akhenaten were joined subsequently by some bedouin tribes (the Shasu), who are to be identified as the Midianites of the Bible.

No magic was performed, or intended, by Moses. The true explanation of the biblical story could only be that it was relating the political challenge for power in a mythological way – and all the plagues of which we read were natural, seasonal events in Egypt in the course of every year.

19

WHO WAS WHO? – AND THE DEATH OF MOSES

I F Moses and Akhenaten were the same person, it must be possible to match some biblical characters with characters we know of in Egyptian history. We can best begin with Jochebed, the daughter of Levi, who is described in the Book of Exodus as Moses' nurse. She is, I think, to be identified as Tiy, the wife of Aye, last of the Amarna kings.

The American scholar Keith C. Seele has noted the special importance attached to Aye's wife at his Amarna tomb: 'The tomb of Aye and Tiy at Amarna is the only one in which both husband and wife are depicted with so nearly equal prominence. This exceptional treatment of the wife suggests the possibility that Aye owed his favour at court to her, or even that she was his superior in rank and family.'[1]

What strikes us first is that Tiy seems to have been named after Queen Tiye. We know from the Amarna tomb that she was 'nurse and tutress of the queen', Nefertiti. She was also, as Baikie noted: 'The great nurse, nourisher of the god (king), adorner of the king (Akhenaten).'[2]

Scholars have long debated the identity of Queen Nefertiti's parents. As we saw earlier, some have suggested that she was Tadukhipa, the daughter the Mitannian king Tushratta sent to Amenhotep III as a bride towards the end of his days, and that she could then have married his son, Akhenaten, instead: others that she was, in fact, Aye's daughter by an earlier wife who had died. Neither of these hypotheses has any grounds for support. Akhenaten, himself rejected on account of the non-royal origins of his mother, would not have married someone other than the heiress, the eldest daughter of Amenhotep III, and he had, in any case, married Nefertiti in his

Year 28, eight years before the arrival of Tadukhipa in Egypt. Nor can Nefertiti have been Queen Tiye's daughter, otherwise she would not have been the heiress.

Seele has argued that, as Nefertiti became 'Great Royal Wife of the King', it is probable that she was a princess of royal blood.[3] In addition, Ray Winfield Smith, reporting on the reconstruction work of the temple project of Akhenaten at Karnak, makes the point: 'An astonishing emphasis on Nefertiti is demonstrated by the frequency of her name in the cartouches on offering tables, as contrasted with the relatively few cartouches of Amenhotep IV. The queen's name alone occurs sixty-seven times, whereas only thirteen tables carry both names, and a mere three show only the king's name.'[4] He goes on to discuss the appearance of statues of the king and queen on offering tables that appear on the *talalat*, the small stones used in building Akhenaten's Karnak temple and later re-used by Horemheb after the temple's destruction: 'There are sixty-three Nefertiti statues and thirty-eight Amenhotep IV statues, with eleven unidentified. Significant is not only the preponderance of Nefertiti, but even more important the extraordinary domination of the larger offering tables by Nefertiti statues. It will be noticed that all of the five identified statues of the large size (72cm) are of Nefertiti.'[5]

The greater importance attached to Nefertiti than even the king himself in the first years of their marriage makes it more possible to agree with Seele's theory that she must have been a daughter of Amenhotep III, not by Tiye but by one of his other wives. As Horemheb later married Nefertiti's sister Mutnezmet, to strengthen his claim to the throne, this reinforces the view that Nefertiti's mother was Sitamun, Amenhotep III's sister and wife, who, from the traditional point of view, would have been regarded as the real Queen of Egypt, being the heiress daughter of Tuthmosis IV.

Tiy, then, was Nefertiti's nurse and also nursed her half-brother, Akhenaten, and Seele goes on to explain: 'It would be especially understandable if, as I have indicated, Nefertiti was the daughter of Amenhotep III. In that case, Nefertiti and her half-brother, Akhenaten, perhaps from childhood destined to be her husband, would have grown from infancy to maturity in close association with both Tiy and Aye. Egyptian history presents repeated precedents for the reward of royal nurses and their families at the hands of Pharaoh.'[6] Seele also indicates that the nurse of Nefertiti and Akhenaten must have had another child of her own: 'The Egyptian word for "nurse" employed in her title almost certainly means that Tiy was the actual nurse – the wet-nurse – of Nefertiti during her babyhood. If this interpretation be correct, it is evident that Tiy had been the mother of a child – presumably the child also of Aye – and thus became available as the nurse of the princess, Nefertiti.'[7]

Even today, bedouin children thus nursed by a woman call her 'mother', the same name that they use for their real mother. The naming of Akhenaten's nurse after his real mother, Tiye, confirms the relationship, and at the Amarna tomb of Aye and Tiy the king is seen bestowing honour on his nurse as well as on her husband.

If Nefertiti were the eldest daughter, she could have been a few years older than Akhenaten, which would explain why she is more prominent in the scenes of the king's Karnak temple. Although we do not know for certain whether the child Tiy nursed at the same time as Nefertiti was a boy or a girl, if the other elements of the biblical story can be identified from Egyptian evidence, then it must have been Aaron, about three years before the birth of Akhenaten. Thus Nefertiti would stand for the biblical character of Miriam, while the nurse's real son, Aaron, was simply what the bedouin call 'a feeding brother' to Moses.

Such a relationship would explain the strange way he is introduced in the Book of Exodus, for, after the birth of Moses is reported in the second chapter, a long time elapses before we hear of Aaron. He makes his appearance in the story only after Moses had grown to manhood, fled to Sinai and is resisting the Lord's orders to return to Egypt to rescue the Israelites, pleading that he is 'slow of speech, and of a slow tongue'. It is only then that we learn of Aaron, and in a very strange way, when the Lord asks: 'Is not Aaron the Levite thy brother? I know that he can speak well.' (Exodus, 4:10, 14)[8]

The Koran also confirms that Moses and Aaron were related only through the feeding-mother relationship. When Moses comes back from the Mount to find the Israelites worshipping a golden calf, he becomes very angry, so he:

> Seized his brother by (the hair
> Of) his head and dragged him
> to him. Aaron said
> "Son of my mother!" . . . (Sura VII:150)

In Manetho's account, it was Amenhotep III who fled to Ethiopia (Nubia): in the Talmud it was Moses. The strange name given to Moses' queen, Aten-it, relates her to Akhenaten's God. No doubt what is meant by the Talmud reference to Ethiopia, which is described as being a city, is the Amarna location, and the queen's desire to place her son on the throne instead of Moses could represent Tutankhamun replacing his father, Akhenaten, whose policies had placed the whole dynasty in the possible danger of being overthrown.

One can even see the character of Aye as the man who, according to the Koran, advised the king to leave the city as the chiefs (nobles) were plotting to kill him.

> And there came a man,
>   Running, from the furthest end
>   Of the City. He said:
>   'O Moses! the Chiefs
>   Are taking counsel together
>   About thee to slay thee:
>   So get thee away, for I
>   Do give thee sincere advice.' (Sura XXVIII, 20)

The only clue to the historical source of the account of how Moses slew an Egyptian would appear to lie in the Amarna Tablets, the foreign archives of the Eighteenth Dynasty, which were found by a peasant woman in the ruins of Akhenaten's capital in 1887 and, unfortunately, suffered considerable damage before they reached a dealer in antiquities and their importance was realized.

Among them is a letter, sent to Akhenaten by Abd-Khiba, King of Jerusalem, in which the king accuses him of allowing the Hebrews in Egypt to kill two Egyptian officials without being punished for their crime: '... the Khabiru (Hebrews) are seizing the towns of the king ... Turbazu has been slain in the very gate of Zilu (Zarw), yet the king holds back ... Yaptih-Hadad has been slain in the very gate of Zilu, yet the king holds back.'[9]

Much argument has surrounded the question of whether the word *Khabiru*, used in the Amarna letter, is to be equated with the biblical word for 'Hebrew'. The various points of view can be found summarized in a useful research by the biblical scholar H. H.

Rowley.[10] (For my own conclusions – that the term indicated a social class rather than a people – see Appendix G.)

Part of Josephus' account of events in Egypt makes two points: 'This king, he [Manetho] states, wishing to be granted . . . a vision of the gods, communicated his desire to his namesake, Amenophis, son of Paapis [son of Habu], whose wisdom and knowledge of the future were regarded as marks of divinity. This namesake replied that he would be able to see the gods if he purged the entire country of lepers and other polluted persons, and sent them to work on the stone quarries to the east of the Nile, segregated from the rest of the Egyptians. They included, he adds, some of the learned priests, who were afflicted with leprosy.'

The points in question may have their historical inspiration in the fact that:

1   Moses/Akhenaten preached about a God who, unlike the ancient gods of Egypt, had no visible image;

2   When Akhenaten was persuaded to leave Thebes for his new capital at Amarna, those of his followers who stayed behind were sent to work in the stone quarries.

Manetho's account also describes how Amenophis (Amenhotep III) subsequently advanced from Ethiopia with a large army and his son, Rampses, at the head of another, and that the two attacked and defeated the shepherds and their polluted allies, killing many of them and pursuing the remainder to the frontiers of Syria.

This is an allusion to Ramses I, during whose brief reign the Exodus took place.

Analysis of the origins of the tribe of Israel and of the Levites would need a book in itself. Here it is worth making a few points briefly.

Contrary to the general view, the name Amarna does not derive from a Muslim Arab tribe which settled in the area later. No evidence of such an event exists. The name derives from the name in the second cartouche of Akhenaten's god – *Im-r-n*. Amram, or Imran, was the name given in the Bible to Moses' father and it is the name Akhenaten gave to his 'father', the Aten.

Across the river from Amarna there is the modern city of Mal-lawi (Mallevi), which means literally 'The City of the Levites'.

This could be explained by the fact that the Levites, who held priestly positions with Moses, held the same positions with Akhenaten at Amarna. For example, Meryre II was the High Priest of the Aten at his Amarna temple:[11] the Hebrew equivalent of this name is Merari, who is described (Genesis, 46:11) as one of the sons of Levi. Similarly, Panehesy was the Chief Servitor of the Aten at Akhenaten's temple:[12] the Hebrew equivalent of this name is Phinehas, the son of Eleazar and grandson of Aaron (Exodus, 6:25) in whose family the priesthood was to remain:

> Wherefore say, Behold, I give unto him (Phinehas) my covenant of peace.
>
> And he shall have it, and his seed after him, even the covenant of an everlasting priesthood; because he was zealous for his God, and made an atonement for the children of Israel. (Numbers, 25:12–13)

It is therefore a possibility that we are dealing here with the same people who served Akhenaten at Amarna and then followed him to Sinai after his fall from power.

Discovery late in 1989 of the tomb, almost intact, of Aper-el, the hitherto unknown vizier to Akhenaten, also provides a semantic link between the Israelites and the Amarna regime.

Similar names are known to have existed in Egypt at this time, but never in the case of high officials. The name 'Aper' corresponds to the Egyptian word for 'Hebrew', which meant to ancient Egyptians a nomad, and the final 'el' is the short form of 'Elohim', one of the words used in the Bible as the name of 'the Lord'.

The fact that Akhenaten's vizier was a Hebrew worshipper of El confirms the link between the king and the Israelites living in Egypt at the time. Furthermore, the fact that Queen Tiye was associated with her husband, Amenhotep III, in donating a box to the funerary furniture of Aper-el (see Chapter 8) indicates the possibility that the vizier was a relation of the queen's, most probably through her Israelite father, Yuya (Joseph).

The Death of Moses

The account in the Old Testament of the failure of Moses to reach the Promised Land, his death and his burial in an unmarked grave is another curious episode.

We are told initially, as we saw earlier, that, when his followers complained of thirst, Moses used his rod to smite a rock and bring forth water. It was called 'the water of Meribah' – a location in the north-centre of Sinai, south of Canaan – and it was for this action, although there is no indication that Moses had done anything forbidden to him, that he was denied his reward. When the Israelites were camped on the banks of the Jordan, near Jericho and opposite Canaan, he learned, according to the Book of Deuteronomy, that he was to be denied the opportunity to cross the river, no matter how hard he pleaded:

> I pray thee, let me go over, and see the good land that is beyond Jordan, that goodly mountain, and Lebanon.
> ... the Lord said ... speak no more unto me of this matter ...
> ... thou shalt not go over this Jordan. (Deuteronomy, 3:25–7)

Later in the Book of Deuteronomy we have an account of the actual death of Moses. The Lord said to him: 'Get thee up into this mountain Abarim, unto Mount Nebo, which is in the land of Moab' – the borders between Sinai and eastern Jordan – 'that is over against Jericho; and behold the land of Canaan, which I give unto the children of Israel for a possession: And die in the mount ... Because ye trespassed against me among the children of Israel at the waters of Meribah-Kadesh, in the wilderness of Zin ... thou shalt not go thither unto the land which I give the children of Israel.' (32:49–52)

After admonishing and blessing his people, Moses left them with Joshua and climbed the mountain. There, after viewing the Promised Land, he met his death – and was buried by the Lord in an unmarked grave in the plains of Moab below.

In contrast to this straightforward story, Talmudic sources have a rich collection of contradictory accounts of the manner of Moses' death. A reference to a confrontation between him and the 'Angel of Death' on the Mount before he died, with an indication of a struggle between the two, has persuaded some biblical scholars that Moses was killed. Sigmund Freud interpreted this suspicion in his book *Moses and Monotheism* to mean that Moses had been killed by his own followers for being too rigid in his views. I do not think this is an accurate interpretation of what happened.

The key, it seems to me, lies in the reason given why Moses was not allowed to enter Canaan, the Promised Land. According to the Book of Exodus, the reason is that Moses struck a rock with his rod to obtain water for his thirsty followers. This is not really convincing. Why should this practical action be the cause of punishment? It is not as if there is any suggestion that he had been forbidden to indulge in such conduct.

However, when we look back at the wars of Seti I, the second king of the Nineteenth Dynasty, against the Shasu we find that the first confrontation took place in the vicinity of one of the Egyptian fortresses on the route between Zarw and Gaza. Such fortresses were built in areas that had wells. It would therefore seem to be a more likely explanation – even if it can be only supposition – that Moses, under pressure from his thirsty followers, entered one or more of these fortresses and obtained water by using his royal sceptre. Intrusions of this type would have been reported by the Egyptian guards to their superiors at Zarw, resulting in Seti I sallying forth to put a stop to the unrest that the Shasu were causing among the Sinai settlements. After the initial battle, Seti I, as we saw earlier, chased the Shasu, identified as the Israelites, into northern Sinai – and, if these Talmudic references to the death of Moses are correct, it must have been there that Moses died, out of sight of his followers, most probably at the hand of Seti I.

This would explain how a new version of the Osiris-Horus myth came into existence from the time of the Nineteenth Dynasty. Osiris, the King of Egypt, was said to have had to leave the country for a long time. On his eventual return he was assassinated by Set, who had usurped the throne, but Horus, the son of Osiris, confronted Set at Zarw and slew him. According to my interpretation of events, it was in fact 'Set' who slew 'Horus'; but their roles were later reversed by those who wished to believe in an eternal life for Horus. This new myth developed to the point where Osiris/Horus became the principal god worshipped in Egypt in later times while Set was looked upon as the evil one.

This myth could have been a popular reflection of a real historical event – a confrontation between Moses and Seti I on top of the mountain in Moab.

EPILOGUE

LACK of historical evidence to support the stories we find in the Old Testament has resulted broadly in three schools of thought.

Some people accept these accounts of miracles and abnormal happenings unquestioningly, although they demand rational or scientific explanations for the events they encounter in their everyday lives; some dismiss the Old Testament as a work of imagination, purely mythological, with no historical value; some have tried to marry these two schools of thought by setting a number of the better-known biblical tales against a historical background, although this must be regarded simply as story-telling, not serious historical research.

My own view has long been that the Old Testament is a historical work whose stories, recounted in language that frequently strikes our sophisticated ears as extravagant, became distorted and exaggerated during the many centuries when they were transmitted by word of mouth, and suffered further at the hands of various editors. It is difficult to imagine how all these biblical tales became etched so deeply in human memory if they did not have a basis in reality.

This is not to say that there are not genuine miracles in the Old Testament. There is no need to question the fact that, if he had a message for Moses, the Lord attracted his attention by means of a bush that appeared to be burning (radiant light is a recurrent feature in accounts of Marian apparitions in our own age, such as those at Lourdes). Yet to many modern minds the popular image of Moses as some kind of super-magician with a rod that could turn into a snake and part the waters of the Red Sea is an impediment to belief.

I hope that my work, in providing a link between biblical and known historical events and putting forward rational explanations

for many of the seemingly mystifying events we find described in
the Old Testament, will serve to overcome such doubts and objections. In the case of this particular book, it will enable Moses, the
great law-giver who delivered the Ten Commandments, to be
studied from two sources – the Bible and Egyptian history. In
addition, it points the way to the identification of other biblical
figures and, by fixing the date of the Exodus, makes it possible to
establish when and how the Israelite entry into Canaan took place, as
well as other events that have long been the subject of debate and
argument.

APPENDICES

APPENDIX A

(i) The Shasu Wars

ON the east side of the northern wall of the great Hypostyle Hall in Amun's temple at Karnak we find two series of scenes distributed symmetrically on either side of the entrance to the temple. The action of the scenes converges towards the door at the centre, near which the god Amun stands to welcome the victorious Seti I. At the two extreme ends, far from the doorway, we find depicted the battles that took place in distant lands, and as we move towards the door we are shown the capture of war prisoners, followed by the arrival back in Egypt, the presentation of captives and spoils to Amun, culminating in the slaying of prisoners as sacrifices to the god. The scenes are arranged in three horizontal rows, each showing a different war.

The first chronologically, the bottom row of the east wall, is a representation of the war against the Shasu. After setting out on the route from Zarw to Gaza – known in the Bible as 'the way of the land of the Philistines' (Exodus, 13:17) – and passing the fortified water stations, 'pushing along this road in the Negeb the king scatters the Shasu, who from time to time gather in sufficient numbers to meet him. One of these actions is depicted in this relief as taking place on the desert road.[1] ... Over the battle scene stands the inscription: "The Good God, Sun of Egypt, Moon of all land, Montu (the Theban god of war) in the foreign countries: irresistible, mighty-hearted like Baal (an Asiatic god, the counterpart of the Egyptian Seth), there is none that approaches him on the day of drawing up the battle-line ... The rebels, they know not how they shall (flee); the vanquished of the Shasu (becoming like) that which

exist not." '² In his campaign it seems that Seti I pursued the Shasu
into the northern Sinai area and Edom, which includes 'the waters of
Meribah', as well as Moab – the borders between Sinai and Canaan/
Jordan – before returning to continue his march along the northern
Sinai road between Zarw and Gaza until he reached Canaan itself.
Just across the Egyptian border he arrived at a fortified town whose
name is given as Pe-Kanan (the Canaan), which, according to
Gardiner, is the city of Gaza.³

In another scene we find the following inscription over the
defeated Shasu: 'Year 1. King of Upper and Lower Egypt, Menmare
(Seti I). The destruction which the mighty sword of Pharaoh ...
made among the vanquished of the Shasu from the fortress of Tharu
(Zarw) to Pe-kanan, when His Majesty marched against them like a
fierce-eyed lion, making them carcasses in their valleys, overturned
in their blood like those that exist not. Everyone that escapes his
fingers says: "His might towards distant countries is the might of his
father, Amun, who hath assigned to him victorious valour in the
countries." '⁴

In addition to those Shasu he had already slaughtered in battle,
Seti brought many bedouin prisoners back to Egypt, tied to his
chariot, to be sacrificed. The scene showing the king being welcomed back on his arrival at Zarw has an inscription that provides
the reason for Pharaoh's campaign against the Shasu: 'One came to
say to His Majesty: "The foe belonging to the Shasu are plotting
rebellion. Their tribal chiefs are gathered in one place, waiting on the
mountain ranges of Kharu."⁵ ... Now as the good god (Pharaoh),
he exults at undertaking combat; he delights at an attack on him; his
heart is satisfied at the sight of blood. He cuts off the heads of the
perverse of heart. He loves an instant of trampling more than a day
of jubilation. His Majesty kills them at one time, and leaves no heirs
among them. He who is spared by his hand is a living prisoner,
carried off to Egypt.'⁶

The king, as can be seen from the following scenes, then proceeded with his Shasu prisoners to the temple of Amun at
Karnak. Over them we find: 'Captives which His Majesty carried
off from the Shasu, whom His Majesty himself overthrew, in
Year 1.'⁷ Then comes the depiction of the final act – the sacrifice
by Seti I personally of his Shasu captives at the feet of the Theban
god Amun.

(ii) The Hattusili Peace Treaty

Year 21, first month of Winter, day 21, under the majesty of the King of Upper and Lower Egypt Usimare Setpenre, son of Re, Ramses-mi-Amun, granted life eternally and forever, beloved of Amun-Re, Harakhti, Ptah South-of-His-Wall, lord of Onkhtowe, Mut lady of Ishru and Khns-Neferhotpe, being arisen upon the Horus-throne of the Living like his father Harakhti eternally and evermore.

On this day, when His Majesty was at the town of Pi-Ramses-mi-Amun doing the pleasure of his father Amun-Re, Harakhti, Atum lord-of-the-two-lands-of-Heliopolis, Amun-of-Ramses-mi-Amun, Ptah of Ramses-mi-Amun and Setekh great-of-valour, son of Nut, according as they give to him an infinity of *sed* festivals and an eternity of peaceful years, all lands and all hill countries being prostrate under his sandals; there came the king's messenger ... the messenger of Hatti (the land of the Hittites) ... carrying [the tablet of silver which?] the great chief of Hatti, Hattusili [caused] to be brought to Pharaoh in order to beg pe[ace from the Majesty of Usimare] Setpenre ...

The treaty which the great prince of Hatti, Hattusili, the strong, son of Mursili, the great chief of Hatti, the strong, the son of Suppi[luliuma, the great chief of Hatti, the str]ong, made upon a tablet of silver for Usimare ...: the good treaty of peace and brotherhood, giving peace ... forever. But hereafter, beginning from this day, the great chief of Hatti, is [in?] a treaty for making permanent the policy which ... so as not to permit hostilities to be made between them forever. And the children of the children [of] the great chief of Hatti shall be [?] in brotherhood and at peace with the children of Ramses-mi-Amun, the great ruler of Egypt; they being in our policy of brotherhood and our policy [of peace]. [And the land of Egypt?] with the land Hatti [shall be?] at peace and in brotherhood like us forever; and hostilities shall not be made between them forever.[1]

(iii) A Dissenting Voice

In discussing where the battles of Ramses II against the Shasu took place Dr Kenneth A. Kitchen of Liverpool University says: 'The area in question is indicated by two or three other sources ... One is Obelisk I at Tanis: "Terrible and raging lion who despoils the Shasu-land, who plunders the mountain of Seir with his valiant arm." Here, Shasu is by parallelism equated with Mount Seir, "which is Edom" (cf. Genesis, 36:8,9). The second source is a topographical list of Ramses II at Amara West in which the words *t ŠSW* Shasu-land, are qualified by each one in turn of the six names *S'r, Rbn, Pysps, Yhw, Šm't* and *Wrbr*. Thus Seir is classed as being at least part of the Shasu-land along with the rest. Of the other names, Bernard Grdseloff, the Polish Egyptologist, has aptly compared *Rbn* with the Laban of Deuteronomy, 1:1 (and Libnah of Numbers, 33:20,21) and *Šm't* with the Shimeathites of I Chronicles, 2:55, all in the area of Seir/Edom, the Negeb, or the Araba rift valley between them. Thirdly one may cite a stela of Ramses II from Gebel Shaluf.

'On the right edge (among other things) Anath says to the king: "[I] give to thee [the] Shasu-land ... " while line two on the front of the stela surely must be read: "*ḥk dw [n] s['r ...]*, i.e. who plundered the mountain [of] Se['ir]." Again, Shasu and Seir go together. This evidence clearly suggests that Ramses or troops of his raided the Negeb, the uplands of Seir or Edom, and perhaps part of the intervening Araba rift valley ... Thus we have evidence for the activity of Ramses II (or at least of his forces) in both Edom and Moab.'[1]

After dealing with possible dates for the confrontation between Ramses II and the Shasu, Dr Kitchen makes the following comment on the latter's sudden appearance on the scene with the beginning of the Nineteenth Dynasty: 'It is significant that, after the mentions of Shutu in the nineteenth century BC (six centuries earlier), no more clear Egyptian reference to southern Transjordan occurs before the reign of Seti I.'[2]

We therefore have the situation, as we saw earlier, that, in the first year of Seti I, the Shasu were emerging from Sinai and posing a threat to Canaan, Edom and Moab. Then, at the time of Ramses II, about two decades later, they have left Sinai and are to be found in Edom and Moab. If we compare the sudden appearance of the Shasu bedouin and their movements with the Israelite Exodus from Sinai we find that they followed the very same route. Dr Kitchen, too, was struck by this fact: 'For Old Testament studies, the new information has some bearing on the date of the Hebrew conquest of central Transjordan and their entry into W. Palestine, not to mention the date of the Exodus.'[3]

Nevertheless, after showing that both movements were similar, Dr Kitchen rejected the possibility that they might be identical: 'Now it would be highly unrealistic to have Ramses's forces invading the region of Dibon, north of the Arnon [in the land of Moab], once the Hebrews under Moses and Joshua had taken over this area.' What made Dr Kitchen believe that this would be unrealistic? 'Otherwise, one might expect a mention of "Israel" in the same class of records of Ramses II that mention "Seir" and "Moab" before its known occurrence on Merenptah's famous Israel stela.'[4]

Although he saw the close similarity between Shasu movements and the emigration of the Israelite tribes from Sinai to Palestine as recorded in the Bible, Dr Kitchen failed to recognize that these were the very same people. This was a consequence of his preconceptions about when and how the Exodus took place. His acceptance of 430 years as the length of the Sojourn, as well as the idea that the Israelites should have their separate geographical land of Israel once they had crossed the border, prevented him from grasping the historical reality to which his own translations pointed.

APPENDIX B

(i) The Amarna Rock Tombs of Huya and Meryre II

PROFESSOR Redford, who does not agree that a scene and inscription in the tomb of Huya, steward to Queen Tiye, at Amarna is evidence that Amenhotep III was alive and in Amarna after the second half of Akhenaten's Year 8, quotes Norman de Garis Davies, whose book *The Rock Tombs of El Amarna* was published by the Egypt Exploration Society of London in 1905, as having also rejected this scene as evidence of a coregency. This is not strictly accurate. Davies preferred not to accept the idea for three reasons – the fact that Tiye and Baketaten are shown separated from Amenhotep III; the fact that the uplifted hands of Tiye and Baketaten imply an unusual measure of reverence, suggesting that the king was dead; and the fact that Akhenaten's name precedes that of his father in the accompanying inscription on the jamb of the door. Davies commented: 'But for this and the difficulty of reconciling the situation with other records, this equipoise of the two royal households would have suggested a coregency of the two kings even at this late date in Akhenaten's reign.'[1]

The points raised by Davies are not, in fact, serious objections to a coregency. There are two explanations for the form the scenes take, one historical, the other artistic. Huya was Queen Tiye's steward, appointed to his position by her son, Akhenaten, and had no direct relationship with her husband, Amenhotep III. If Tiye was shown sitting by her husband she would have been a minor character, in his shadow, as Nefertiti is shown in the shadow of Akhenaten: by separating her from her husband, Huya gave his mistress enhanced importance. The artistic explanation is that in Egyptian tombs and temples we usually find two similar scenes or inscriptions, coming from left and right to meet in the jamb or centre of the door. In the Huya scenes, three female attendants have been added to the Amenhotep III scene to make up for the fact that there is only one princess depicted, not four, and the uplifted hands of Tiye and Baketaten balance the gestures of Akhenaten's two elder daughters in the opposite scene, where they are shown waving their fans towards their parents. There is nothing in the scene depicting Amenhotep III, who sits under the rays of the Aten, waving a hand to his family, to suggest that he was dead at the time.

As for the inscription, although he was ill in his latter years, Amenhotep III remained the senior partner in the coregency until the day he died. In the normal course of events, one would expect his name to precede that of his coregent son – but not at Akhetaten. Here, in the domain of the Aten, the name of the Aten's only son and prophet, Akhenaten, had to come first.

Redford goes on to argue, as we saw earlier, that, as Tiye is shown alone on the outer wall of the hall in question, Amenhotep III must have already been dead when construction of the tomb began: 'Presumably, if the decoration of the tomb kept pace with its excavation, the scenes in the first hall showing Tiye alone would have been carved before the lintel jambs.'[2] A detailed analysis of the whole hall of Huya's tomb, as well as the neighbouring tomb of Meryre II, makes it clear, however, that the walls were not decorated in the order that Redford assumes, and, in addition, that their decoration provides further evidence pointing to a coregency of twelve years.

South Wall: This is the wall near the entrance to the first hall. On the right of the door is a banquet scene featuring Tiye, entitled 'King's mother, Great King's Wife'; Akhenaten, Nefertiti and two of their daughters (only the name of the eldest, Merytaten is found); and Tiye's daughter, Baketaten, identified by the inscription 'the King's daugher, begotten and beloved by him, Baketaten'. This is the first time the princess was depicted. The rays of the Aten extend from the top centre of the scene. To the left of the doorway we find a scene of an evening entertainment which has the same shape and includes the same characters except in the case of Nefertiti's two daughters, who seem here to be a younger couple. The rays of the Aten are missing from this evening scene and have been replaced by cartouches of the God and the king.

East Wall: Here there is a picture of Tiye visiting an Aten temple called 'the Sunshade', which can either be part of the main temple of the Aten or a separate temple built specially for her visit. Inside the temple, Akhenaten is seen holding his mother's hand and leading her affectionately towards an interior building. Aten shines on the royal pair as well as on the building towards which they are proceeding. They are preceded by Huya and followed by the young princess, Baketaten, who holds three gifts for the altar and has two nurses to watch over her.

West Wall: This features a unique scene bearing the following inscription: 'Year 12, the second month of Winter, day 8. Life to the Father, the double Ruler, Re-Aten, who gives life for ever and ever! The King of South and North Neferkheprure and the Queen Nefertiti, living for ever and ever, made a public appearance on the great palanquin of gold to receive the tribute of Kharu (Palestine/ Syria) and Kush (Nubia), the West and the East; all the countries collected (gathered) at one time, and the islands in the heart of the sea, bringing offerings to the King (when he was) on the great throne of Akhenaten for receiving the imposts of every land, granting them the breath of life.'[3]

Akhenaten and Nefertiti are depicted, borne in the State palanquin on the shoulders of a dozen carriers. At least four of their daughters follow behind the chair. At its side walk officials, servants and military personnel. Davies noted that in Huya's tomb and a later version of the same day's events in the neighbouring tomb of Meryre II some of the troops carried a hooked staff and commented: 'As the curved staff is a Bedawi weapon, according to Wilson (Sir J. Gardiner Wilson, an early British Egyptologist of the last century), we probably have here the troops who have escorted the embassies into Egypt.'[4] What Davies meant was that these bedouin troops, whom Akhenaten had entrusted with the task of guarding his guests and him personally, could have come from the desert borders of the Eastern Delta and Sinai – that is, the Shasu.

While Huya's tomb shows only the procession on the occasion of the Tribute of the Nations, the next stage of the celebrations, after the royal family, including all six princesses, had arrived at the open pavilion, is depicted on the East Wall of Meryre II's tomb – with an inscription that suggests a different reason for the gathering. The inscription reads: 'Year [12, second month of the winter season, day 8] of the King of Upper and Lower Egypt . . . Akhenaten, great in his duration, and the great wife of the King, his beloved, Nefertiti, living for ever and ever. His Majesty appeared on the throne of the Divine and Sovereign Father, the Aten, who lives on Truth, and the chiefs of all lands brought the tribute.'[5] The implication of the Meryre II inscription, which has a bearing on whether or not there was a coregency, is that the chiefs of all the lands brought their tribute because Akhenaten had inherited the throne as sole ruler. But to return to the tomb of Huya . . .

North Wall: On either side of the lintel scenes described earlier are two almost identical scenes, representing Huya's appointment to his offices. To the left of the hall doorway, which leads to the inner tomb, we see Akhenaten and Nefertiti leaning from the decorated loggia of the palace to present collars of gold to Huya, who stands below them. Behind the royal pair are two of their younger daughters and nurses, watching the event. To the right of the doorway we have the king and queen again with their two elder daughters. Thus, as in the case of the opposite wall, near the entrance, we have four princesses represented, the younger two to the left, the elder two on the right. As in the former scene, Huya stands below the king and is shown with his neck laden with gold collars and both arms covered to the elbow with gold armbands. A further scene below contains a tiny picture showing a sculptor – 'the overseer of sculptors of the great royal wife Tiye, Auta' – at work in his studio, putting the final touches to a statue of Baketaten, the daughter of his mistress, who is represented as a young girl.

The only dated scene is on the West Wall, depicting the celebrations of Year 12, although the appearance in this tomb of only the late form of the Aten's name suggests that the tomb should be dated after the second half of Year 8. However, there are other means by which we can arrive at approximate dates. Four daughters are shown on the South and North Walls of the hall to Huya's tomb: six daughters are shown in the Year 12 celebrations depicted on the East Wall of Meryre II's neighbouring tomb. It is therefore safe to say that, because of the presence of the two additional princesses in the latter tomb, the West Wall of Huya's hall, showing the same scenes of celebration, must have been decorated at least two years after the South and North Walls, which would date them to about Year 10. The East Wall does not show any of Akhenaten's daughters, but Baketaten, the daughter of Amenhotep III and Queen Tiye, is depicted, looking the same age as on the South and North Walls. It is therefore reasonable to deduce that this wall, too, was decorated around Year 10 of Akhenaten with the celebratory scenes on the West Wall following two years or so later.

(ii) The Tomb of Kheruef

Three main points can be made about the tomb of Kheruef:

• Much of it is unfinished.

• It has suffered damage in three stages. Initially, as Kheruef seems to have fallen from grace while still working on his tomb, scenes and inscriptions were erased by his enemies, 'who chiselled out his figures and the figures of the high officials (or perhaps members of his family) who were accompanying him. They chiselled out also the texts referring to his activities or biography and in most cases his names and titles ... intending to wipe out all memory of him.

'The second mutilation is more important for us because it was made by the agents of Amenhotep IV, in all probability at the beginning of his movement before it became extreme. The walls of the tomb are covered with prayers to the different deities, but none of these has been touched except Amun. The cartouches of Amenhotep III and Amenhotep IV both contained the word "Amun", but it was never removed, although the agents chiselled out carefully the name of the same deity in an adjacent line. Another word was chiselled out carefully wherever it occurred ... the word "gods", which for the worshippers of the Aten was a symbol for polytheism.'[1]

A third type of destruction is evident, as noted by Labib Habachi,[2] where the figures of Amenhotep IV were also erased, which in this case has to be the work of his enemies from Horemheb to the Ramesside kings of the Nineteenth Dynasty. The fact that the tomb was not completed and that the first mutilation did not come from Akhenaten's followers indicates that Kheruef fell from favour while the old king was still alive and then, at a later stage, came Akhenaten's followers to erase Amun's name.

• The tomb provides us with two dates. One scene in the first court depicts Kheruef offering gifts to Amenhotep III and Queen Tiye on the occasion of the Pharaoh's first jubilee in Year 30: another shows him performing a similar task in Year 36 on the occasion of the king's third and last jubilee. The work in the first court is, however, unfinished.

Who was Kheruef? The main source of information about his titles and positions is the tomb, in which we find him described as 'Hereditary Prince and Governor', 'Royal Scribe' and 'Steward of the great royal wife Tiye'. Nothing in the tomb relates him directly or indirectly to Akhenaten: he is the Steward of Tiye, appointed to this position by her husband, Amenhotep III. The fact that Akhenaten is shown in this tomb with his father therefore has to be explained away by those who do not accept a coregency. The course they have chosen, without the slightest shred of evidence, is to claim that, after the death of Amenhotep III, Kheruef was appointed by the new king to continue for a while in his post.

As we have seen, the only two dates we have in this tomb are Year 30 and Year 36. Thus we can safely assume that decoration of the tomb started some time after Year 30. But when did it cease? Redford himself has noted: 'This enormous hypogeum (underground chamber) displays decoration on only a few walls, and there is good evidence that the work had halted abruptly, perhaps on the fall from favour or the death of Kheruef.'[3] It is clear that the façade area – the corridor with the libation scene and the lintel of the doorway, where there is a further cartouche of Akhenaten, who is also depicted in scenes with his mother, Queen Tiye – is virtually complete, the exception being the North Wall which has red lines intended to guide the artist in his work. If, as Redford and other opponents of the coregency claim, work on the tomb stopped after Amenhotep III's death, during the sole rule of his son, how does one explain that it is the son's scenes that are virtually complete while those belonging to his father were still unfinished?

The only reasonable conclusion is that Amenhotep IV was shown in Kheruef's tomb, adoring his father on the occasion of the old

king's first jubilee in Year 30. Kheruef continued to work for Queen
Tiye until just after Year 36 when he fell from favour and was
dismissed from office. His enemies then tried to wipe out all traces of
him and, not much later, the Atenists also destroyed the name of the
god Amun. What confirms this as the correct sequence of events is
the fact that, as we saw earlier, Akhenaten did appoint another
official, Huya, to take the place of Kheruef. If the coregency between
the two kings lasted for twelve years, then Year 37 of Amenhotep III,
when Kheruef fell from favour, coincided with Year 10 of Akhenaten, in which year, as we saw from Huya's tomb, Akhenaten
appointed this official to the post of steward to Queen Tiye.

(iii) The Year of Tribute

Aldred has argued that the celebrations of Akhenaten's Year 12,
represented in the Amarna tombs of Huya and Meryre II, show the
king receiving gifts on his accession to sole rule.[1] This seems likely.
There was no war campaign in foreign countries that would account
for such tribute and, if it were simply the regular yearly tribute, it is
difficult to imagine all the foreign nations involved gathering in
Amarna at the same time. Furthermore, this is the only time such an
event is to be found depicted in the Amarna tombs. Redford is
justified, however, in rejecting Aldred's attempt to generalize the
conclusion so as to imply that all such tribute scenes in Eighteenth
Dynasty tombs must be taken to represent a coronation celebration,
or that this event in Amarna coincided with the appointing of new
officials or their reappointment.

(iv) The Tomb of Ramose

Here Amenhotep IV appears in a tomb that belongs to the reign of
his father, Amenhotep III, whose name is found in the tomb.
Ramose was mayor of Thebes and a vizier of Upper Egypt. Aldred
accepted the Ramose tomb as evidence of a coregency: Redford
does not. In other cases where the two kings are represented together

in tombs, he has argued that Amenhotep III should be regarded as
already dead: here he accepts that he is mentioned as alive, but takes
the view that Amenhotep IV was not represented in the tomb until
after the old king's death. Redford makes the point that one of
Ramose's relatives and a Minister of Recruitment for Amenhotep
III – the son of Habu whose name was also Amenhotep – is shown
among the dead in a scene on the East Wall of the transverse hall. As
he and some of the others depicted in this necropolis scene are known
to have died before and around Year 34 of Amenhotep III, Redford
rightly says the scene cannot be dated earlier than that year, but he
goes on to argue that decoration of the whole tomb did not start
before that date: 'Ramose must have survived the thirty-fourth year
of his sovereign, and in all probability a decade more ... the tomb
presents a strong case against any coregency of Amenhotep III with
Akhenaten.' This view cannot, however, be supported by the
evidence.

Ramose's positions as mayor and vizier are known from his tomb.
In addition, he had his name inscribed on the rocks of Sehel and
Bigeh in the region of the First Cataract in Upper Egypt, the
southern limit of his jurisdiction. There he paid reverence to the
cartouches of Amenhotep III and the local gods. This, then, estab-
lishes that he had been appointed to his position by Amenhotep III.
The inscription is not dated, which means we do not know when he
was appointed, but Aldred has pointed out that dockets found at the
remains of the Malkata palace complex of Amenhotep III at Western
Thebes showed that the vizier Ramose donated four jars of ale for
the first jubilee of the king in his Year 30.[1] It must therefore have
been around Year 30 that Ramose's tomb was started because it was
mainly the king's high officials who donated gifts on these occasions.

Both sides of the entrance to the tomb are decorated with the
usual scenes of sacrifice to the solar deities and gods of burial. In one
scene on the East Wall, in which Ramose is accompanied by officials,
the text reads: 'The making of an oblation of all things good and
pure [to] Amun-Re, king of the gods, [to] Re-Harakhti, [to] Atum,
to Khepera ... [Ramose ... says "I give praise to Re-Harakhti]
when he dawns, that he may cause me to be among his followers and
that my soul may rest in the evening boat day by day."' In a
sub-scene three men singers are chanting: 'The two lands of Horus
acclaim Amun on the great throne when he shines forth as

Amun-Re ... May he prolong the years of Neb-Maat-Re (Amen-hotep III), to whom life is given ... O mayor-vizier Ramose. Thy lord, Amun-Re rewards thee in thy abode of the living. All the gods of the west rejoice because of thee, in that thou makest a ritual offering to Amun-Re-Harakhti; to Atum, lord of On (Heliopolis) ... to Osiris-Khentiamenti; to Hat-Hor, regent of the necropolis; to Anubis ... and to all the gods of the underworld.' As we can see, the name of Amenhotep III is mentioned in this section, Amun is still king of the gods, many of whose names occur, but at the same time special importance is given to Re-Harakhti, the name Akhenaten bestowed on his God in the very early days.

The East Wall also bears the necropolis scene, featuring son of Habu. Although Amenhotep III is not mentioned specifically, it is evident that he was still the king as all the other figures depicted in the scene are royal officials who died before him, but the inscriptions introduce a new, and strange, expression in a quotation attributed to Ramose: 'I had a serviceable spirit, doing justice *for the king of my time*. I was rewarded for it by my god (the king).' Another scene on this wall represents the meal-of-the-dead rites, as well as the cere-mony of using sacred oils and ointments, and Osiris – one of the gods abolished by Akhenaten – and the Osiris Ramose (the dead Ramose) are the subject of the inscriptions.

The upper half of the South Wall is taken up by funeral scenes, in which Ramose is shown as already dead. On the West Wall, following the Theban custom of showing the reigning king on both sides of the inner doorway, we have a king shown. The cartouche on one side, bearing the nomen of the king, is erased, but his praenomen (or coronation name), Amenhotep, is well preserved. It is followed by Akhenaten's epithet, 'great in his duration', confirming that it is Amenhotep IV who is here represented as the reigning king. The young king is shown in the old artistic style and looks exactly like his father in face and form.

There are, in addition, two figures of Ramose. The first shows him carrying a stout staff, terminating in the crowned ram's head of Amun, and the text reads: 'Said by the mayor-vizier Ramose: "For thy *ka* (soul), a bouquet of thy father [Amun Re, Lord] of the Thrones of Egypt, President of Karnak. May he praise thee ... May he overthrow thy enemies ... while thou art firmly established on the throne of Horus." ' The king's enemies mentioned here would normally have been foreigners who attacked the borders of the country, but Akhenaten is known not to have fought a war, especially in his early years. As the reference here is followed by the wish that the king should be established on the throne, the enemies in this case could only have been those who opposed his appointment as king.

The text of Ramose's speech accompanying the second figure reads: 'For thy *ka*, a bouquet of thy father, the living Re-Harakhti, who rejoices on the horizon . . . the brightness of which is Aten.' The style of the work as well as the representation of the new God, 'Re-Harakhti . . . the brightness of which is Aten', indicates a very early period in Akhenaten's reign. The disc of the sun is shown in its early form while Amun is still represented as the king's father, 'Lord of the Thrones of Egypt'. The early period is also confirmed by the absence of Queen Nefertiti, who is always seen later accompanying her husband.

Davies describes, however, the dramatic change in style when Amenhotep IV is depicted on the opposite side of the doorway: 'The contrast which this wall presents to that on the other side of the doorway is an epitome of the most striking episode in Egyptian history, when the seemingly indissoluble continuity of Egyptian traditions was broken through with a suddenness which better knowledge of the movements of thought and political outlook might discount, but which none the less gives a fully revolutionary character to the change. Three or four years seem to have sufficed to bring into outward being that for which one would have proposed a century of preparation at least.'

The author goes on to describe the scene: 'Physiognomies, pose, royal dress, palace, architecture, foreigners, wear unfamiliar modes; even the sun-disk with its guardian cobra has a different angle of appearance. Nor is the change superficial. The attitude of the king to supernatural powers has altered; the sun reaches down to earth and temple insignia have disappeared. His relations to his people, too, are more intimate; he no longer sits on the throne like an imposing automaton. The place and manner of his appearance are different, and every figure and group in front of him has acquired greater vitality. Dignity and decorative symbolism may be diminished, but they have been broken down by a new sensitiveness and warmth of feeling . . . Egypt had awaked one morning, it would seem, to find the gods in full retreat, the sun shining, the king at the palace window, and the populace dancing in the streets ... The Aten had been "found".'²

Amenhotep IV and Queen Nefertiti are shown, for the first time, in what later became known as the Amarna style of art, appearing in the window of the palace that seems to have been the young king's building in his father's Malkata complex. The sun disc, with extended rays ending in hands, the new symbol of the Aten, shines from the top centre of the picture, presenting the key of life to the nostrils of the royal pair. The Aten names, like those of a king, are placed within two cartouches and, added to the God's cartouches, is a royal salute: 'May Aten live, rich in festival periods, lord of heaven and earth, within Gem-pa-aten in the temple of Aten.' This indicates that the Aten temple at Luxor had already been built and the king's *sed* festival celebrated. All the cartouches of the king, queen and the Aten, except that including the name Amenhotep, have been largely defaced in the aftermath of the fall of Amarna, and the faces of the royal pair have been chipped off. The text gives the king's speech to Ramose, who stands beneath the window: '[Said by] the king of Upper Egypt, living on truth ... Amenhotep ... to ... the mayor-vizier Ramose: "... the matters I put in thy charge ... which I have commanded. All that existed ... the kings since the time of the God." '

To which Ramose replies: 'May [the] Aten [do] according to that which thou hast commanded ... thy monuments shall be as lasting as heaven and thy life as long as (that of) Aten in it. May thy monuments increase like the increase of heaven. Thou art unique ... The mountains present to thee what they have kept hidden; for thy loud voice gains on their hearts even as thy loud voice gains on the hearts of men; they obey thee even as men obey.'³

The upper half of the wall depicts Ramose being honoured by the king in a series of scenes, one of which shows him loaded with so many collars of gold beads that his neck cannot accommodate all of them. Other than in the name of Amenhotep, the word 'Amun' does not appear on this wall.

Nothing remains of the tomb façade except a scrap of Ramose's figure at the foot of the left jamb. However, on the thickness of the rock frontage of the tomb Ramose is shown 'entering (the tomb) with the favours of the good god (the king, Amenhotep III or

Amenhotep IV?) to rest in . . .' and small fragments have been found bearing the inscriptions '. . . appearing as truth' . . . and again the curious expression 'the king of my time'.[4]

The burial section of the tomb is not inscribed, but the internal side of the door is decorated in fine relief. On one side Ramose offers separate prayers, one to the king and the second to the gods of the underworld. The prayer to the king reads: 'I come in peace to my tomb with the favour of the good god (the king, Amenhotep III or Amenhotep IV?). I did what was approved by the king of my time (?), for I neither minimized the substance of what he enjoined, nor did I commit any offence against the people in order that I might rest in my sepulchre on the great right-hand (the western part) of Thebes.'

Although the Ramose tomb is not dated, the available evidence enables us to arrive at four dates, two for Amenhotep III and two for his son, Amenhotep IV. As Ramose had already been appointed to his posts as mayor and vizier before Year 30 of this king, we should expect work to have started on his tomb around that time, and as son of Habu is shown, already dead, in one of the scenes, and he died around Year 34, this scene has to be dated not long after that year of the old king.

In the case of Amenhotep IV, the scenes on either side of the doorway leading to the inner burial section are distinctly different in style and can be dated to different periods of his reign.

The first scene represents the king in the old style. Early in his reign Akhenaten was shown, in the sandstone quarry at Gebel Silsilah in Nubia, worshipping Amun-Re. The inscription below records his quarrying of sandstone for the 'great ben-ben (temple) of Harakhti at Karnak'. The king describes himself as 'first prophet of Re-Harakhti'. It is clear that this inscription at Silsilah refers to the Re-Harakhti temple at Karnak and, as the panel also shows Amenhotep IV worshipping Amun, it can hardly be dated to later than his first or second year because the Re-Harakhti temple was begun very early in his reign.

The second scene, on the opposite side of the doorway, is in the new Amarna art style, the first time we find it in a tomb before the Amarna rock tombs, dated to Year 8 or Year 9 of Akhenaten. The new symbol of the Aten has already appeared; the God is now named Aten instead of Re-Harakhti, and he is placed in two cartouches. No mention is made in this scene of Amun. Akhenaten's temple at Karnak is referred to. There is also a reference to Akhenaten's jubilee, celebrated in his Year 4.

Such a presentation would not have been possible before Amenhotep IV's very last days at Thebes, a short time before, in the eighth month of Year 6, he notified his change of name from Amenhotep IV to Akhenaten on a boundary stela at Amarna. This scene should therefore be assigned to his late Year 5 or early Year 6.

Some further light on the dating of the Ramose's tomb can be derived from considering who donated it. Although it is true that Amenhotep III appointed Ramose to his posts as mayor and vizier, it seems to me for several reasons to have been Amenhotep IV who gave Ramose his tomb:

• Amenhotep III's name appears only once, near the entrance of the tomb, using his praenomen, Neb-Maat-Re, in a prayer of Ramose to Amun-Re that he 'may prolong the years of Neb-Maat-Re'. This suggests that this king was already suffering from some illness which, from a letter by Tushratta and Ushter's arrival in Egypt, could be dated about Year 36 (see Chapter Eight);

• In contrast, it is Amenhotep IV who is shown in the special position on either side of the inner doorway that was used during the Eighteenth Dynasty for scenes of the ruling king: had the old king been the donor of the tomb, Ramose would have shown him on at least one side of the doorway;

• The strange – and, as far as I know, unique – reference to a sovereign by an official as 'the king of my time' can possibly be better understood if interpreted as meaning 'my master', who gave me my tomb and ordered me to carry out some work for him, and does seem to mean Akhenaten rather than his father. Although it was Amenhotep III who appointed him to the posts of mayor and vizier, Ramose was responsible for some construction work on Akhenaten's temples at Karnak and Luxor;

• The fact that Ramose apologizes for carrying out the orders of 'the king of my time' suggests something unusual about both the king and the nature of the orders, which can only be a reference to Akhenaten. Ramose tries to deny that he obeyed the king's orders simply in order to obtain his tomb at Western Thebes. This protest would not have been necessary had Amenhotep III been the donor of the tomb;

• The fragment found at the façade bore the text '... appearing as (in) truth', which is an epithet of Akhenaten's.

It was Akhenaten, then, who gave Ramose his tomb and that is why he is represented in it, as well as his father. In fact we see the young king rewarding the vizier with too much gold for fulfilling his orders, which appear to relate to the construction of his new temples for Re-Harakhti at Karnak and for the Aten at Luxor.

The association of Amun-Re with Re-Harakhti in this tomb represents a very early stage of Akhenaten's inscriptions as Re-Harakhti was the name he gave his God initially. In almost every scene, whether near the entrance or inside, Re-Harakhti is associated with Amun whenever the latter god appears. This is true of what Redford chooses to describe as the early scenes – those near the entrance, followed by the funeral scenes – as well as the last ones. The association of Amun and Harakhti, in fact, represents the association of Amenhotep III and his son in a coregency.

Ramose, contrary to common belief among scholars, was never converted to Atenism. He is never shown worshipping Akhenaten's God. All the usual gods are represented in his tomb, even in the very last scene on the reverse of the doorway into the inner burial section. This has to be regarded as later than the Amarna-style scenes as it is always the most remote scene, sometimes including the latest information about the dead man, added after his death. Yet here he still has the same loyalty to the other gods and sticks to the old style, indicating that the tomb was completed after Akhenaten had already left Thebes. Ramose himself did not follow Akhenaten to Amarna, but remained in Thebes as Amenhotep III's mayor and vizier until the time of his own or the old king's death.

(v) The Tushratta Letters

Tushratta first appeared on the scene before the dispatch of the four letters that form part of the coregency debate. He sent a letter to Amenhotep III telling him that, despite an internal power struggle, he had succeeded in securing the throne after the death of his father, Shutarna. He reminded Pharaoh of the friendly relations between him and Shutarna and also took the opportunity to make the point that his sister, Gilukhipa, was one of Pharaoh's wives. In addition, he mentioned an attack on his country by the Hittites, whom he had destroyed completely. Out of the resulting bounty, he enclosed a present for Amenhotep III. This letter is not dated, but it is thought to have arrived about Year 30 of Amenhotep III.

The second letter we have from him indicates that Amenhotep III wished to increase the relationship between the two families by also marrying Tushratta's daughter, Tadukhipa. Tushratta then sent a messenger to Egypt with a third letter, demanding gold in return for his daughter's hand in marriage. This matter appears to have been resolved amicably as a fourth letter seems to have arrived at the same time as the bride-to-be, Tadukhipa. Finally, before Amenhotep III's death, came a fifth letter, dated by an Egyptian docket to 'Year 36, fourth month of Winter', which was accompanied by an image of the Mitannian goddess Ishtar. The implication is that Amenhotep III was already ill and it was hoped that Ishtar might cure him. However, Mitannian magic does not appear to have worked and the king became less and less active until his eventual death early in his Year 39.

After that date came the four letters – one addressed to Queen Tiye, the other three to Akhenaten – which form part of the coregency debate. A fuller account of their contents follows in the order in which I believe they arrived.

No. EA27 (addressed to Akhenaten): This first letter to Akhenaten dwells upon the gold issue. The Mitannian king complains: 'Your father ... wrote ... in his letter, at the time when Mani (the Egyptian messenger) brought the price for a wife ...: These implements, which I now send you, are (still) nothing ... when my brother gives the wife, whom I desire, and they bring her to me, so that I see her, then I will send you ten times more than these. And golden images ... an image for me and a second one as image for Tadukhipa, my daughter, I desired from your father ...

'Your father said: "... I will give you also lapis lazuli, and very much other gold besides (and) implements without number, I will give you together with the images." And the gold for the images, my messengers ... have seen with their own eyes. Your father also had the images cast in the presence of my messengers and made them complete, and full weight ... And he showed very much other gold, without measure, which he was about to send me, and spoke to my messenger saying: "Behold the images and behold very much gold and implements without number, which I am about to send to my brother, and look upon it with your own eyes." And my messengers saw it with their own eyes. And now, my brother, you did not send (these) ... images ... but you have sent some that were made of wood with Mani.'[1]

The letter makes the point that, if Akhenaten has any doubts about the truth concerning the promised gold, he should 'ask his mother'.

No. EA26 (addressed to the queen): The text begins: 'To Tiye, the Queen of Egypt ... Tushratta, King of Mitanni. May it be well with you; may it be well with your son; may it be well with Tadukhipa [my daughter], your bride.'[2] Subsequently, Tushratta goes on to complain: 'The present, which your husband commanded to be brought, you have not sent me; and gold statues ... Now, however, Napkhuriya (Akhenaten), your [son] ... has made (them) of wood.'[3]

No. EA29 (addressed to Akhenaten): After delving even more deeply into the history of the friendly relations between the two royal families in order to persuade the new king to continue them and to send the promised gold, the letter invites him again to seek confirmation from his mother that Tushratta is speaking the truth: 'From the days of my youth, Nimmuriya (Amenhotep III), your father, wrote to me of friendship ... Tiye, the distinguished wife of Nimmuriya, the loved one, your mother, she knows them all. Ask Tiye, your mother ... And when Nimmuriya, your father, sent to me and wanted my daughter, I would not consent to give her ... And I sent Khamashshi, my brother's messenger, to Nimmuriya, to pay the dowry, inside three months ... And finally, I gave my daughter. And when he brought her and Nimmuriya, your father, saw her ... he rejoiced very greatly ... Tiye, your mother, knows what I said, and Tiye, your mother, ask her if among the words which I said there was one that was not true ... therefore I made request for images ... and Nimmuriya said to my messenger: "Behold, the golden images altogether, which my brother requests."

... And when my brother Nimmuriya died ... I wept on that day (when the messenger came with the news); I remained sitting, food and drink I did not enjoy that day, and I mourned ...

'When Napkhuriya (Akhenaten), the distinguished son of Nimmuriya by his distinguished wife Tiye, entered upon his reign I spoke saying: "Nimmuriya is not dead." ... [Now my brother] when he formerly wrote to me, at the time when he sent Giliya back (with the news of Amenhotep III's death and a letter from Tiye) ... he sent Mani, my brother sent only wooden (statues), but gold [he did not send] ... Pirizzi and Puipri I sent to express sympathy (they brought the letter dated Year 2 or Year 12: see Chapter Eight) ... Now the word, which your mother had said to Giliya, [I heard and therefore] ... and the images [of gold] ... for which I made request you have not given me ... my messengers for four years ...

'The images which I requested from your father, give; and now [when I have sent] my messengers for the second time [if he] does not prepare and give [them], he will grieve my heart ... Your mother Tiye knows all about these things, and (therefore) ask your mother Tiye ... [Now my brother said:] "Giliya ought to return to him. Because I should otherwise grieve my brother's heart, I will send Giliya back." [However, I said]: "Inasmuch as I have sent back quickly my brother's messengers, so let my brother always my messengers [send back quickly] ... gives me word and sends Mani to me, then I will ... Giliya, with friendly intentions, to my brother.'[4]

From this letter it is clear that the messenger Mani is in Egypt because Tushratta is asking for him to be despatched with the gold. In Letter No. EA28, however, we learn that he is not only in Mitanni, but being held hostage against the return of two of Tushratta's messengers. After the usual initial friendly formalities, Tushratta comes straight to the point: 'Pirizzi and Puipri, my messengers, I sent them to my brother at the beginning of his reign, and ordered them to express sorrow very strongly. And then I sent them again. And this message, on the former occasion, I gave to my brother:' – this letter is now missing – 'Mani, the messenger of my brother, I will retain until my brother sends my messenger, and until he arrives ... Now, however, my brother has in general not allowed them to go and has retained them very much indeed.'[5]

APPENDIX C
The *Mos* Case

To start at the very beginning of the *Mos* action, the tomb inscriptions begin: 'Copy of the examination [made by] the priest of the [litter] Aniy who was an officer of the court, of the Hunpet of the shipmaster Neshi [which was in the] village of Neshi, as follows:

'"I arrived at the village of Neshi, the place where the lands are and of which the citizeness Ur[nero] and the citizeness Takharu spoke. They assembled the heirs of [Neshi] together with the notables of the town ..."'[1]

It was, as we saw in Chapter Nine, the mother of Khayri who began legal proceedings in Year 14-plus – the number of months is missing – of Ramses II to establish her son's ownership of the land, arguing that he was the descendant of Neshi through his grandmother, Urnero. In the tomb account of the events that followed Khayri is referred to by name only once and is elsewhere called *mos* (the son and heir), to indicate his claim as the rightful inheritor: 'Then Nubnofret, my (*Mos*'s) mother, came to cultivate the share of Neshi, my father.[2] [But] one prevented the cultivation of it. She complained against the trustee Khay (the defendant). One [caused them to appear before] the [vizier] (in) Heliopolis in Year 14-plus of king [Usermre-Setepenre] Ramses Meiamun, given life.'[3]

In the latter stages of the action the word *mos* is again used, but in this case to establish that Huy, the father of the plaintiff, was the rightful heir of Neshi, the original owner of the land. After the goatherd Mesman came:

Papa, priest of the temple of Ptah: 'I knew ... [the scribe Huy], the child (*mos*) of Urnero [who] cultivated this land [year] by year. He having been engaged in cultivating it while saying: "I am the child (*mos*) of Urnero, daughter of Neshi."'

[Hori], bee-keeper of the Treasury of Pharaoh: '[As to the scribe Huy], (he was the) child (*mos*) of Urnero, and as to Urnero (she was the) daughter of Neshi.'

Nebnufer, chief of the stable: 'As to the scribe Huy, he used [to cultivate his lands year] by year. He acted according to all his desire(s). They carried in for him the crops of the fields year by year. He used to dispute with the citizeness Takharu (his mother's sister), mother of the soldier Sementawi, and then he disputed with Sementawi her son so that [the land] should be given [to] Huy and they were confirmed.'

Citizeness Tentpaihay: 'As Amun endures, and as the ruler endures, if I speak falsely, let me be (banished) to the back of the house. As to [the scribe Huy] (he is) the child [*mos*] of Urnero, and as to Urnero, (she is) the daughter of Neshi.'

APPENDIX D

Pi-Ramses and Zarw

THE recent archaeological discoveries at Kantarah (see Chapter Eleven) have made it unnecessary to argue in as much detail as I had earlier envisaged that this was the area where Pi-Ramses, the city of the Exodus, was to be found on the site of the Hyksos capital Avaris, and the fortified city of Zarw. However, some further evidence that led me to this conclusion may be of interest to the reader.

(i) The City of Pi-Ramses

Pi-Ramses was the Eastern Delta residence and capital of kings of the Nineteenth, Twentieth and early Twenty-first Dynasties until, during the Twenty-first Dynasty, a new capital was established at Tanis, south of Lake Menzalah in the northern part of the Delta. One reason why the precise location of Pi-Ramses has been the subject of considerable debate and disagreement is that it appears to have been constructed at an existing site: another that Ramses II, the third king of the Nineteenth Dynasty who gave the city its name, ruled for sixty-seven years and left many constructions all over the Eastern Delta.

Texts of the Ramesside period speak frequently of a location called *Pi-Ramses myr Amun*, House of Ramses, Beloved of Amun. We learn, for example, from his triumphal poem known as the *Poem of Pe-natour*, mentioned briefly in Chapter Eleven, that when, in the summer of his Year 5, Ramses II set out on his first Asiatic campaign he 'passed the fortress of Zarw' and it seems that he remained for some time in a location beyond the fortress. The text then proceeds to say that 'His Majesty being in [the town of] Ramses, Beloved of Amun' started his march on Palestine from this point. This text indicates that the Ramses residence not only lay beyond the fortress of Zarw, but at the start of the 'road of Horus' that leads to Gaza.[1] What confirms this location is the fact that, on his return from this campaign, the first place mentioned was the 'House of Ramses, Beloved of Amun Great of Victories'. It was only when proceeding from Egypt to Palestine that he had to pass the fortress of Zarw before reaching his Eastern Delta residence.

Dr Kitchen of Liverpool University is one of a number of scholars who does not accept this interpretation. Instead he regards the 'town of Ramses, Beloved of Amun' as being a different city that Ramses II built in Phoenicia, to the south of Syria. This view is based upon the fact that in the text there are five missing squares, followed by the Egyptian word for 'cedar'. The text then goes on to tell us that the king 'proceeded northward and arrived at the upland of Kadesh (in Syria)'. It is this juxtaposition of 'cedar' and Kadesh that has led such scholars to believe that the reference is to a city in Phoenicia.

Gardiner rejected this view, however, as there is no evidence from any other source that points to the existence of such a Ramses city in Phoenicia.[2] Then, as the extant text mentions only two points – the starting point, 'the town of Ramses', and the arrival point, Kadesh – it seems curious that he jumped from the fortress of Zarw to a city in Phoenicia without any explanatory reason.

In fact, the mention of 'cedar' cannot be taken as evidence of a Phoenician location for the Ramses city. In the Kamose Stela, the king, after arriving at the Hyksos capital, Avaris, on his war of liberation, talks of 'ships of fresh cedar' as well as 'all the good products of Retenu (Palestine)' which he captured in war from the Avaris (Zarw) area.[3]

A further point is that mention in the text of *passing* the fortress of Zarw may have contributed to misunderstanding of its precise location. It is clear from the positions held by all the known mayors of Zarw that it consisted of two entities – a fortress and a city. Their relationship is made clear in Seti I's reliefs at Karnak. The fortress was situated on either side of the canal linking the Waters of Horus with the Sea of Reeds; the city lay beyond it to the east, at the start of the 'road of Horus' leading to Palestine. Anyone coming from Egypt and wishing to reach Sinai had therefore to enter the western part of the fortress, cross to the eastern part – where Pi-Ramses was built – by the bridge (*kantarah*) that linked the two sections, and then pass through the city of Zarw.

Another text found in a papyrus known as *Anastasi V* mentions a letter, also touched on briefly in Chapter Eleven, sent by two army officers to the Royal Butler in which they describe how they were despatched from the palace where Pharaoh was in residence – Memphis, perhaps – to deliver three stelae to Pi-Ramses. They report how they reached Zarw by boat and are about to unload their vessels at 'The Dwelling of Ramses, Beloved of Amun', from which point they will have to drag the stelae to their final destination.[4] This text appears to agree with the *Poem of Pe-natour* in placing Pi-Ramses in the vicinity of Zarw, but beyond it from the Egyptian side.

It was also at Zarw that Seti I, the second king of the Nineteenth Dynasty, was welcomed – as can be seen from his Karnak records – by high priests and officials on his return from his first-year campaign against the Shasu in Sinai and Southern Palestine. This indicates that the royal family must have had a residence in this area from the early days of the Nineteenth Dynasty. The implication, as they had no means of knowing precisely when Seti I would return from his campaign, is that the high priests and officials who greeted him were residing in Zarw at the time of his arrival. As for Seti himself, both he and his father had been Mayors of Zarw and Commanders of its Troops during the reign of Horemheb and it is a logical deduction that he had had a residence there since that time.

This is by no means the end of the evidence linking Zarw with Pi-Ramses. In 1886, Francis Griffith, the English Egyptologist, found part of an obelisk at Kantarah bearing the names of Ramses I, Seti I and Ramses II. Clédat later discovered the missing portion of the obelisk and recognized correctly that it came from Zarw. Griffith also found at this location a base for an image, dedicated by Ramses I. Both the obelisk and the image base mentioned the god 'Horus of Mesen' (Seth), often referred to as the god of the Eastern Delta's fourteenth nome.

Although from an early time in Egyptian history Seth was regarded as a god of Upper Egypt, he was also associated with the area of the Eastern Delta at the frontier, near the start of the Sinai desert and the road to Asia. It is even thought the whole of the fourteenth nome, the north-eastern area of the Delta between Kantarah and the ancient Pelusiac branch of the Nile, was named Sethroite after him.

From the end of the Sixth Dynasty, during the twenty-second century BC, Seth, as mentioned earlier, became discredited as a result of the development of the myth that he had been responsible for the assassination of the good god Osiris: he became associated with Evil and is the source of the later name Satan. However, after another four centuries, as we saw in Chapter Eleven, Nehesy, a king of the weak Thirteenth Dynasty, re-established the worship of 'Seth, Lord of Avaris' as the chief deity of the fourteenth nome. According to Manfred Bietak, the Austrian Egyptologist: 'Nehesy (c. 1715 BC) is known from several monuments as the first king with the title: Beloved of Seth, Lord of Avaris. This Seth later became the principal god of the Hyksos, but was clearly established in Avaris by the local dynasty before the rise of the Hyksos rule.'[5]

An obelisk of this Nehesy was found in Tanis, but must have been brought there from its original location as it was not *in situ*. John van Seters, the American Egyptologist who researched the origins of the Hyksos, tried to identify the obelisk's origin from its text: 'On one fragment ... were traces of a dedication by the "eldest royal son, Nehesy, beloved of Seth, Lord of Rakhit" and on another fragment the inscription "beloved of Hershef (Arsaphes)". There is a degree of uncertainty about the location of the place name Rakhit, which means "gateway of the cultivated fields". The gateway referred to would then be the region of Sile (Zarw), where the cultivated area meets the desert.'[6]

It is clear that Nehesy established Seth, Lord of Avaris, in the same location as that of Zarw. Further confirmation of this is provided by the 400-year stela, the most important evidence regarding the continuity of worship of the god Seth at Avaris and Pi-Ramses for four centuries. Although the stela was actually found at Tanis, which became the new capital towards the end of the Twenty-first Dynasty and is one of the other sites suggested as the location of Pi-Ramses, it was not *in situ*, and Jean Clédat, the French Egyptologist, believed that it must have been moved there from Zarw because, although it was made during the reign of Ramses II, it includes a commemoration of an event – the four centuries of worship of Seth – that took place at Zarw during the reign of Horemheb when his grandfather, Ramses I, and father, Seti I, were both Mayors of Zarw and Commanders of the fortress: 'Now there came the Hereditary Prince; Mayor of the City and Vizier; Fan-Bearer on the Right Hand of the King, Troop Commander; Overseer of Foreign Countries; Overseer of the Fortress of Sile (Zarw); ... Seti, the triumphant, the son of the Hereditary Prince; Mayor of the City and Vizier; Troop Commander; Overseer of Foreign Countries; Overseer of the Fortress of Sile; Royal Scribe; and Master of Horse ...'[7]

The celebration of Seth's worship at Zarw is a further pointer to the fortified city having occupied the same site as Pi-Ramses and Avaris, and the fact that both these high officials of Horemheb, who became the first two kings of the Nineteenth Dynasty, had all their titles relating them to Zarw, and to nowhere else, is a further implication that they must have had a residence at Zarw during their vizierates. It is this residence that is most likely to have been rebuilt to become what was later called Pi-Ramses.

(ii) The Fortified City of Zarw

The first mention we find of Zarw dates from the campaign by Ahmosis I that resulted in the defeat of the Hyksos and the establishing of the Eighteenth Dynasty: 'The war against the Hyksos may have lasted longer than is usually reckoned ... The fall of Avaris is usually put early in the reign of Ahmosis I. Yet the neglected colophon (written section) on the *Rhind Mathematical Papyrus* tells of fighting in the eleventh year of an un-named king. Since the main text on the papyrus is dated to the thirty-third year of Apophis, whom Kamose (the brother and predecessor of Ahmosis I) opposed, this can only be ... a successor ... On the twentieth of the first month (of Year 11) "the Southerner" invested the frontier fortress of Zarw, near modern Kantarah, and entered it a few days later ...'[1]

This account makes it clear that Zarw and Avaris occupied the same site. From this point, however, the name Avaris disappears from the scene and the next mention is of Zarw, which occurs more than a century later, during the reign of Tuthmosis III and at the time of the first Asiatic campaign that followed the death of Queen

Hatshepsut: 'Year 22, month four in Peret, day 25 . . . Zarw, the first victorious expedition . . .'

Then we have the evidence of the Tuthmosis IV stela, found at Serabet El-Khadim in Sinai, which makes it clear that Neby, his Mayor of Zarw, was also 'Royal Messenger in all countries, Steward of the Harem of the Royal Wife', indicating that Tuthmosis IV's queen, Mutimuya, the mother of Amenhotep III, must have had an estate or residence at Zarw. Björkman, commenting on Neby's titles, wrote: ' . . . the constellation of titles . . . might be interpreted as a vague indication of the existence of a harem of the Queen in Zarw, supervised by the local mayor, Neby.'[2] There is reference to another 'Mayor of Zarw' on jar seals found in the Malkata complex at Thebes in the reign of Amenhotep III, who ultimately made a present of the city to his wife, Queen Tiye. We still have the name as late as the Greek Ptolemaic period, when it was called Sile.

(iii) The Case Against Qantir/Tell el-Dab'a

Manfred Bietak, the Austrian archaeologist in charge of the excavations at Tell el-Dab'a and Qantir, which are just over a mile apart, gave an interim report in 1979 on the expedition's findings.[1]

To the north of Tell el-Dab'a there is a natural lake basin while old survey maps, partly confirmed by the ground survey, show traces of a feeder-channel from the direction of the former Pelusiac branch of the Nile and a drain-channel flowing from the lake towards the larger Bahr el-Baqar drainage system. North and east of the lake remains were found of the Middle Kingdom (the Eleventh and Twelfth Dynasties, c. 1991–1785 BC) and the Second Intermediate Period that followed, including the weak Thirteenth and Seventeenth Dynasties (c. 1785–1575 BC), at which time the Asiatics infiltrated the Eastern Delta and began the era of Hyksos rule there that lasted just over a century until they were vanquished in battle by Ahmosis, founder of the Eighteenth Dynasty (c. 1575 BC). Among other finds in this new area were the lintel of a house belonging to vizier Paser of Ramses II and, almost two miles to the east of Tell el-Dab'a, an old well bearing the same king's name.

In all, eleven strata were found. The remains at the very bottom belonged to the earliest settlement, starting some time before 1750 BC, and the latest an early Ptolemaic settlement of a limited area, dated to the third century BC. The strata covering the Hyksos period (E3–1 and D3–2) are characterized by increasing density of occupation. The remains of two Canaanite temples were found, dating from *c.* 1690–1660 BC and 1660–1630 BC respectively, and there was evidence that from about 1630–1610 BC to 1610–1590 BC the settlement began to develop its own Asiatic cultural line, distinct from Syria and Palestine. The site was largely abandoned after the Hyksos period, but occupied again towards the end of the Eighteenth Dynasty, the time of Horemheb. Remains of a temple were found, including a lintel of a sanctuary dedicated to 'Seth, great of might' and bearing the name of Horemheb.

Bietak encapsulated the expedition's conclusions in the following words: 'To summarise briefly, apart from the later remains there is evidence, extending through a series of strata, of a huge town site of an Asiatic (Canaanite) community of the Syro-Palestinian Middle Bronze Age Culture IIA and B in the north-eastern Nile Delta from the time of the Thirteenth Dynasty until the beginning of the Eighteenth Dynasty. Although several other sites of this culture have been discovered and identified since the beginning of our excavations, Tell el-Dab'a is the largest and most impressive of all the sites, and, by its fine stratigraphic series and abundant excavated material, the most representative.'[2]

He went on to say: 'The temples of stratum E3–2 are Canaanite, and the size of the main sacred area excavated thus far shows that we have here, at the beginning of the Second Intermediate Period, the most important city-state of the Syro-Palestinian Middle Bronze Age Culture in the eastern Nile delta. It is not difficult to deduce, therefore, that this Asiatic community, after it had had time to establish itself in the eastern Nile delta, must have been responsible for the Hyksos rule in Egypt . . .

'After a break in occupation we have evidence of a pre-planned town of the Ramesside Period covering four to five square kilometres (some 250 acres).'

In this final statement, Bietak is not commenting on the results of the excavations at Tell el-Dab'a, but has introduced the remains at Qantir, just over a mile to the north, without any justification beyond the proximity of the two locations. And what conclusion did he come to about the implications of the expedition's findings? 'All the evidence taken together – the cultural and the stratigraphic – would fit well with the identification of the site on the one hand with the capital of the Hyksos, Avaris, and on the other with the delta residence of the Ramessides, Pi-Ramses, as already maintained by M. Hamza, W. C. Hayes, L. Habachi and John van Seters.'[3]

In fact, in the light of what is known about Pi-Ramses, rather than confirming the Tell el-Dab'a site as that of Pi-Ramses/Avaris, the results obtained by the Austrian expedition make such a conclusion impossible:

• Pi-Ramses/Avaris, according to the Nineteenth Dynasty texts we examined earlier, lay in the vicinity of, and beyond, Zarw. Zarw was a frontier fortress, the forefront of every foreign land, the end of Egypt, located between Palestine and Egypt. This description cannot be applied to Tell el-Dab'a which, while beside the Nile and in the Eastern Delta, was situated some thirty miles inland from the 'end of Egypt';

• Pi-Ramses lay in the centre of a great vineyard. There is nothing in the evidence found at Tell el-Dab'a to confirm, or even indicate, that it was a wine-producing area. The five ostraca of wine jars found at nearby Qantir were said to have come from the west of Pi-Ramses. This location was not identified, however, and could therefore well have been in another area. Moreover, the stela of Kamose, brother of Ahmosis, who drove out the Hyksos, makes it clear that Avaris, their capital, was in a wine-producing area because one of the threats contained in the stela is that, when Avaris has been taken, 'I shall drink of the wine of your vineyard, which the Asiatics I captured press out for me.'

The existence of vineyards at Pi-Ramses is also confirmed by the *Papyrus Anastasi*, and remains of wine jars, originating from Zarw, that were found in the Malkata palace as well as in Tutankhamun's tomb, confirm that Zarw was also a wine-producing area. We know from other sources that, in addition, the area west of Alexandria as well as Memphis and Fayyum were wine-producing areas, but there is none to indicate that either Qantir or Tell el-Dab'a were;

• Pi-Ramses could be reached by water from Memphis. This is equally true of Tell el-Dab'a. However, we have the story about the

three stele sent from the place where Pharaoh was in residence –
Memphis, probably – that had to be unloaded at the 'Dwelling of
Ramses, Beloved of Amun' after passing through the fortress of
Zarw. Bietak suggests[4] that, after arriving at Zarw, the stele were
taken by water to Pi-Ramses, which is for him Qantir/Tell el-Dab'a.
This does not make sense. In the first place, the letter to the Royal
Butler speaks of the stele being unloaded *after* the vessel had passed
Zarw and then being dragged into position; secondly, if they had been
en route from Memphis to Qantir/Tell el-Dab'a, why would they
first be transported to Zarw on the frontier, some thirty miles to the
east, and then brought back? Any vessel proceeding from Memphis to
Zarw along the former Pelusiac branch of the Nile would have had to
pass Qantir/Tell el-Dab'a. Why continue the voyage to Zarw when,
if Qantir/Tell el-Dab'a was the ultimate destination, it would have
been simpler to leave the river and use the canal that connected it with
the harbour lake to the north of Tell el-Dab'a?;

• Pi-Ramses was connected by water with the fortress of Zarw and
with the Waters of Shi-hor (north and north-west of Zarw) and the
Waters of Pa-Twfy, that supplied it with papyrus and has been
identified as Lake Ballah, to the south of Zarw, and as the pleasure
lake mentioned in Amenhotep III's scarab. In the sense that Qantir/
Tell el-Dab'a had a harbour linked by canal to the Nile, it is possible
to say that it was also linked by water with the Waters of Shi-hor
and the Waters of Pa-Twfy. This link is a tenuous one, however: one
might equally well argue that Qantir/Tell el-Dab'a was linked by
water with Thebes, some 400 miles away, or any other locality on
the eight branches of the Nile at that time. The logical inference
from the mention of the two places being linked by water is that
they were close together, as one might say that the Isle of Wight is
linked by water with the coast of Hampshire, the nearest point on
the British mainland.

All three locations – the fortress of Zarw, the Waters of Shi-hor
(described in the Bible as marking the frontier of Egypt) and the
Waters of Pa-Twfy – may be said therefore to be linked with other
places in Egypt by water, but they do form part of the Zarw area
itself;

• Seth was the main god of Pi-Ramses/Avaris. Although temples of
Seth were found at Tell el-Dab'a in the areas dating from the Middle

Kingdom and the time of Horemheb, no mention of him has been found in the areas dating from either the Hyksos or Ramesside periods. As for Qantir, although Seth was one of the gods worshipped there, the main deity was certainly Amun, according to the discoveries of the Egyptian archaeologist Muhammad Hamza. In 1928 Hamza unearthed a large number of faience tiles that came from a Ramesside palace in the Qantir area. The palace had been built by Seti I and enlarged by Ramses II. Hamza also found at a little distance to the north a faience factory, including around 800 moulds with different names and titles. The palace remains, including the workshop area, are in excess of 300 square yards. Two statues of Ramses II were found at Qantir. The temple area, which might have included more than one temple, is roughly 600 square yards, and a number of doors of private houses were also discovered.

Yet neither the name of Pi-Ramses nor any of the main deities we know to have been worshipped there were found at Qantir, even on the 800 different moulds. In fact a completely different epithet was found on some of them, 'in the land of Amun', on which Hamza commented: 'Qantir was considered indeed the land of Amun. Under Ramses III, this god was worshipped at Qantir with the peculiar title "He who hears the one who is far away".'[5] It is true to say that Amun, in addition to Seth, was included among the main gods in the Ramses city, but there he had a different epithet – 'Amun of Ramses, Beloved of Amun' – that has never been found in the Qantir area.

We have no archaeological evidence as yet about the identity of the main god worshipped at Zarw and shall have to await the results of the current excavation by the Egyptian Organization of Antiquity;

• Pi-Ramses/Avaris were situated in the fourteenth Egyptian nome. This is also true of Qantir/Tell el-Dab'a and Zarw. It is now accepted by all scholars that Zarw was the capital of that nome. Yet, if Pi-Ramses was the capital of the entire Empire, how could it be less important than Zarw in its own nome?

• One essential point about Pi-Ramses/Avaris is that they were both military fortified areas. Each had a fortress that was rebuilt at least three times – by the kings of the Middle Kingdom, rebuilt by the

Hyksos and later refortified by the kings of the Eighteenth Dynasty. Although we know from Manetho's writings; the stela of Kamose, brother of Ahmosis I, who defeated the Hyksos, and the auto-biography of Ahmose, one of the king's naval officers in the campaign, that Avaris was mainly a fortified area, no remains of fortifications of any kind were found in the Hyksos section of the excavations at Tell el-Dab'a. Nor do we find any real remains of Ramesside fortifications at Qantir;

• Pi-Ramses/Avaris were also called the 'Dwelling of the Lion'. As no textual evidence has been obtained from either Qantir or Tell el-Dab'a we have no indication from there about this matter, but we know from the very way Zarw was written that a seated lion formed part of its name. Furthermore, according to the mythological account of the struggle between Horus of Edfu, the son of Osiris, and Seth, the brother of Osiris who murdered him and took his throne, which appeared in writing during the Ramesside period, it took place at Zarw where Horus took the form of a lion.

As for the suggestion that two neighbouring locations – Tell el-Dab'a, which Bietak takes as Avaris, and Qantir, just over a mile distant, which he takes to represent the Ramesside residence – formed part of the same site, we have no archaeological evidence to support this assumption, no ancient connecting road, no walls enclosing both locations or, as in the case of Akhenaten's pre-planned new capital at Amarna, no boundary stelae. We are asked to take Bietak's word for it. The area that separates the two locations has yielded nothing to suggest that they formed one ancient site. In addition, we know that the Ramessides built their residence on the existing site of Avaris, whereas the site of Qantir had not previously been used.

We also know that the siege of Avaris conducted by Ahmosis lasted for many months. The reason was that he could not assault it on foot, but had to approach by water. In the case of Zarw, the Waters of Shi-hor covered the approaches to the north and west, the Waters of Pa-Twfy protected the south, and a canal, crossed by a guarded bridge, connected the two waters, closing off the west side completely. To the east lay the Sinai desert. That is why Ahmosis' siege lasted so long. In the case of Qantir and Tell el-Dab'a, however, both locations were easily accessible by land from almost any direction, as well as lacking the heavy fortifications to resist an attack.

Furthermore, the Tell el-Dab'a excavations have revealed no settlement in the area from the end of the Hyksos rule to the time of Horemheb. If Pi-Ramses is to be regarded as the Ramses of the Old Testament, the city rebuilt by the Israelites – who arrived in Egypt in the reign of Amenhotep III and settled in the very Pi-Ramses area – the lack of any trace of their existence at Tell el-Dab'a is yet another indication that this cannot have been the site of Pi-Ramses. In any case, as I believe the Israelites had already left Egypt proper for Sinai during the second year of Ramses I, the city of Ramses must have started before that date.

(iv) A Theban Site for Tiye's City

One scholar who has championed a site for Zarw-kha, Tiye's city, distant from the Eastern Delta is Georg Steindorff, the German Egyptologist, who suggested that the pleasure lake referred to in the scarab was actually the lake known today as Birket Hapu, which was dug to the south-east of Amenhotep III's Malkata royal compound at Western Thebes, where it served as a palace harbour connected to the Nile. Steindorff was led to this view because the Malkata complex was known as 'The House of Neb-Maat-Re Aten Gleams', which repeats the name of the vessel in the pleasure lake scarab. However, scholars have not been happy with this theory for a variety of reasons:

1   None of the many inscriptions found that bear the name Malkata mentions Zarw-kha or relates Malkata to Queen Tiye;

2   The dimensions of Birket Hapu are 2750 by 1080 yards, about four times the size of the pleasure lake, and there is no evidence that Birket Hapu was enlarged after its original construction;

3   While the Malkata remains prove that the king was there from his early years – Year 8 has been found – the majority of the buildings in the Malkata compound, which would have been accompanied by the construction of the lake, do not seem to have been built before the beginning of Amenhotep's third decade, contradicting the scarab date of Year 11;

4   As the scarab lake covers an area of about 720,000 square yards, it would not have been possible to complete it in fifteen days unless it involved digging a short canal to fill an existing depression with the waters of the Nile: a much bigger, artificial lake like Birket Hapu must have taken far longer to create.

(v) A Middle-Egypt Site for Tiye's City

More recently, the fact that a similar name to Zarw-kha – Darwha – has been found on two papyri of the Twentieth Dynasty led Yoyotte to suggest[1] the possibility of identifying Tiye's city with the location mentioned in these Ramesside texts – the vicinity of the city of Akhmim in Middle Egypt. As some of the titles held by Yuya and Tuya, the parents of Queen Tiye, indicate that they held positions in Akhmim, it has been thought by many scholars that this must have been their city of origin. On the other hand, while it is possible that Tuya could have come from Akhmim, Yuya has been suspected of being of non-Egyptian origin (and I have argued that he was actually Joseph, the Israelite Patriarch).

But even if, as Yoyotte suggests, Tiye was born in Akhmim, this does not make it her city in the sense that she owned it, which is the implication of the scarab text. Furthermore, Yoyotte places Tiye's city as being in the *vicinity* of Akhmim, in which case, on the basis of Yoyotte's own argument, 'her city' cannot have even been the city of her birth, but another city which she acquired later, and the scarab reference cannot relate to Akhmim. Nor is Akhmim called Zarw-kha in any text. Finally, as the location suggested by Yoyotte comes from a Twentieth Dynasty text, this could have been a new place that did not exist at the time of the Eighteenth Dynasty two centuries earlier.

Yoyotte has put forward this alternative siting for Tiye's city because he objects to the identification of the border city of Zarw on mainly philological grounds, his reason being that the name Zarw-kha is spelt in the scarab with different hieroglyphic signs from those we find in other texts:

Scarab   Other Texts

If we take away the two final signs, as they are not to be regarded as letters but determinatives indicating a city, we are left with five letters. And if we take off the final letter 'kha', as it is not to be regarded as part of the name but merely as indicating that the name belongs to a city, we are left with four signs on the scarab. Henri Naville, the Swiss Egyptologist, has been able to show that the first sign in Zarw, is the equivalent of the Hebrew letter *sadhê*, the Arabic *çade*, the same as the other hieroglyphic first letter appearing in the other texts .[2] (The fact that there is no matching letter either in Greek or Western languages explains why different readings – Thel, Sile and Djarw as well as Zarw – occur.) In a private discussion Yoyotte agreed that Naville's interpretation of the first sign on the scarab was correct. He also has no quarrel with the final hieroglyph, which can be interpreted as either 'w' or 'u'. It is the symbols in between which persuaded him that we are dealing with two different cities, not one.

On the scarab we have – that is, the Hebrew and Arabic *'ayin*, plus 'r' – while in other texts we simply have a seated lion . However, the distinction is more apparent than real. Naville was also able to show that it was the practice sometimes to use the seated lion, for which the Ancient Egyptian word was "'r', as an alternative method of expressing the two consonants, *'ayin*, plus 'r': 'The reading of the lion is *'r*; we have a considerable number of examples of it.' He went on to cite various words sometimes spelt one way, sometimes the other: 'Therefore in the name , Zarw, we find according to the usual transcription of Egyptian into Hebrew, צ, ץ, = ç' and ר, = r.'[3]
This would read Ça'rw. In addition, Naville noted that 'ayin' in Egyptian is not always used as a consonant and cannot consequently be noted as an essential part of the name.[4] There is therefore no philological justification for suggesting that because the name Zarw is written one way on the scarab and with simply the seated lion in other texts, we are dealing with two different cities.

APPENDIX E
The Body In Tomb No. 55

THE rather confused evidence about the identity of the body in
Tomb No. 55 suggests that the last days of the joint reigns of
Akhenaten and Semenkhkare coincided with a time of internal
turbulence in the affairs of Egypt.

Contents of the Tomb

Inside the tomb the remains of a large wooden gilded shrine were
found, with inscriptions indicating that it was dedicated by Akhenaten to the burial of his mother, Queen Tiye. In addition, the names
of Tiye and her husband, Amenhotep III, occurred on various small
objects. Another part of the chamber yielded a coffin, with inscriptions including the titles and cartouches of Akhenaten. Inside the
coffin was a mummy and, nearby, there were four canopic jars. Four
magic bricks, to protect the deceased in the underworld, were also
found in situ, inscribed with the name of Akhenaten.

According to Weigall,[1] the entrance of the tomb showed the
remains of at least two closures. There was part of an original wall of
rough limestone blocks, cemented on the outside, and above the
ruins of this there was a second, more loosely constructed, wall. The
second wall had been partly pulled down and had not been built
again. On fragments of the cement, impressions of the necropolis
seal, a jackal crouching over nine captives, were found, and fragments of small clay sealings, inscribed with the name 'Neb-
kheprw-re' (Tutankhamun), were also discovered, scattered in the
rubbish. All the antiquities recovered from this tomb are now in the

Cairo Museum except a few objects, including one of the four canopic jars, which were given to Davis, the American sponsor of the excavation, and are now in the Metropolitan Museum of Art in New York.

The Mummy

As a result of Queen Tiye's name being found on the shrine as well as on other funerary objects, Davis concluded that the tomb and the mummy it contained were hers. The coffin had originally lain upon a bier, but, when the wood rotted away because of the damp, the coffin collapsed and the mummy partly projected from under the lid. The flesh of the mummy had consequently also rotted away, leaving the skeleton as the only bodily remains.

When he had opened the tomb, Davis called two medical men (a Dr Pollock of Luxor and 'a prominent American obstetrician') to examine the skeleton. They agreed with him that it belonged to a woman, thus reinforcing his belief that the remains were those of Queen Tiye. Later, Davis was disappointed, and even personally upset, when the remains were examined by Grafton Elliot Smith, at the time Professor of Anatomy in Cairo Medical School, who concluded that the skeleton was that of a man and, influenced by the other opinions at the time regarding the ownership of the mummy, announced that he did not think 'there can be any serious doubt that these are really the remains of Khouniatonou (Akhenaten)'.[2]

Smith also concluded that the remains belonged to a man who was about twenty-five or twenty-six years of age at the time of his death. Akhenaten is known to have ruled for at least seventeen years, had been married either on coming to the throne or shortly before, with his first daughter Merytaten being born either late in his first year or during his second year. Consequently, Egyptologists believed that he could not have been less than thirty (thirty-three according to our conclusions) at the time of his assumed death. Nevertheless, even this did not seem to cause Smith to change his mind: 'If, with such clear archaeological evidence to indicate that these are the remains of Khouniatonou, the historian can produce irrefutable facts showing that the heretic king must have been twenty-seven, or even thirty, years of age, I would be prepared to admit that the weight of the anatomical evidence in opposition to the admission of that fact is too slight to be considered absolutely prohibitive.'[3] This view was held for a long time and supported by some Egyptologists, especially Weigall and Aldred.

In his report Smith also indicated that the skeletal remains from Tomb No. 55 had some features similar to those of two of Akhenaten's ancestors. He found that 'the configuration of the upper part of the face, including the forehead, was identical with that of Yuya, Akhenaten's maternal grandfather', while 'a curious and unusual bony ridge passing from the nasal spine to the alveolar point in his skull occurs also as a peculiarity of the skull of Amenhotep III (Akhenaten's father), also in the molar teeth.' In addition he noted: 'The general structure of the face, and especially the jaw, is exactly that portrayed in the statues of Akhenaten. These physical features prove pretty conclusively that the mummy is that of a male member of the royal family who had in his veins the blood of both Yuya and Amenhotep III.'[4]

More than a decade passed. Then Smith, seemingly still convinced that the remains found in Tomb No. 55 were those of Akhenaten, tried to overcome Egyptologists' objections regarding the contradiction between the anatomical evidence relating to the mummy's age with their demand for an age of at least thirty years for Akhenaten when he fell from power in his Year 17. He wrote: 'In considering this difficult problem I naturally turned to consider those pathological conditions which might cause delay in the union of the epiphyses (the growing ends of shafts of long bones). Of these, the most likely seemed to be the syndrome described by Fröhlich in 1900, now known as dystrophia adiposogenitalis. In patients presenting this condition cases have been recorded in which the bones at thirty-six years of age revealed the condition which in the normal individual they show at twenty-two or twenty-three, so this suggested the possibility of bringing the anatomical evidence into harmony with the historical data. In support of this solution there are the very peculiar anatomical features of Akhenaten when alive, which have been made familiar to us by a large series of contemporary portraits. Forty years ago archaeologists were puzzled by the pictures of this Pharaoh, and it was suggested that he was a woman masquerading as a man. In the light of our present knowledge, however, they seem to be quite distinctive of Fröhlich's Syndrome and afford valuable support to the suggestion that this was the real cause for the delay in the fusion of the epiphyses. In addition to this, the skull – both the brain case and the face – reveals certain important peculiarities. There is a slight degree of hydrocephalus (water on the brain) such as is often associated with Fröhlich's Syndrome and also an overgrowth of the mandible, such as may result from interference with pituitary.'[5]

One wonders what anatomists three thousand years from now might identify as the abnormality suffered by some of the models who posed for Picasso's paintings? Smith may have been misled by the fact that the Amarna revolution produced two distinct kinds of art: while one was naturalistic, representing an image as near to its original as possible, as for instance the limestone dyad of Akhenaten and Nefertiti in the Louvre; the second school was romantic, giving an exaggerated form of its models, the best example of this being the four Osirian colossi of Akhenaten found at Karnak. To take this representation, which is almost a caricature, as representing the form of the original is not fair, particularly when Smith had the skeleton, although damaged, at his laboratory to examine at leisure. No doubt his complete pre-conviction that these bones belong to Akhenaten helped to make him err in his judgement.

Shortly afterwards, another examination of the remains was carried out by D. E. Derry, Professor of Anatomy in the Faculty of Medicine at Cairo University. Derry, whose examination included restoring the skull, rejected Smith's conclusions: 'A complete re-examination of the question of the age of the bones was then instituted. In the first place it was found that the conformation of the skull does not support the statement that the person to whom it belonged suffered from hydrocephalus. The skull is undoubtedly of an unusual shape, but the type was not uncommon in the Old Empire, particularly in members of the royal families ... It appears, as will be shown later, in the head of King Tutankhamun. It belongs to a type known to anthropologists as platycephalic, in which the skull is flattened from above downwards and correspondingly widened. It is indeed the very reverse of the shape produced by hydrocephalus.'[6] Derry's final conclusion was that the remains were those of a man no more than twenty-three, or at the most, twenty-four years of age when he died.

Derry also made the point: 'During the unwrapping of the mummy of Tutankhamun the writer noticed that the head of the king resembled that of the so-called Akhenaten skeleton. When the head was measured, in so far as that was possible under the circumstances, it was found that the diameters of the two skulls approximated closely. This is all the more remarkable when we remember that the shape of the so-called Akhenaten skull is unusual and that in width it exceeded any skull ever measured by the writer in Egypt. Such a likeness to his supposed father-in-law in the man who had married Akhenaten's daughter could only mean some blood relationship and therefore it was concluded that Tutankhamun must have been a son of Akhenaten, probably by another wife.'[7]

The age of the skeleton at the time of death, plus the facts that the tomb of Tutankhamun had already been found and that Reginald Engelbach, one of Derry's early students, had been trying to argue that the coffin found in Tomb No. 55 belonged to Semenkhkare, persuaded Derry to accept this viewpoint and he concluded: 'We are compelled to accept the remarkable likeness of the two skulls as indicating a common origin and that in all probability Semenkhkare and Tutankhamun were brothers. It is hardly necessary to point out that the similarity in the heads of the two men, who married sisters, renders the theory of hydrocephalus even more untenable, and particularly so unless we accept the suggestion that they themselves were brothers or at least closely related.'[8]

Nevertheless, this conclusion was not accepted by Aldred: 'We may here limit comment upon Derry's report to two observations. Firstly, his definition of the hydrocephalus as causing only a ballooning of the skull requires some qualification. Secondly, it is not wholly unexpected that two contemporary male members of the royal house such as Tutankhamun and the occupant of the coffin, who would almost certainly have had several progenitors in common, could have had similar skull measurements. But if the profiles of the two heads are superimposed upon each other and orientated in the same plane, it will be seen how sharply they also differ. The skull is a distortion of the mummy-head with its prognathous profile, over-grown mandible and prominent supraorbital (above the eye socket) ridges.

'However, let us approach the problem from another direction. In the early years of his reign, probably in Year 2, Amenhotep IV (Akhenaten) built the Aten temple at Karnak from which have come the remarkable colossi figures now in the Cairo Museum, (J.E. Nos. 49528–9 and 55938). The last of these, which has been aptly described by Pendlebury as "a wonderful pathological study", shows the young king apparently entirely naked without any signs of genitalia ...

'In the past, one of the difficulties in the way of a more precise identification of Akhenaten's pathology both from the bones believed to be his [by Aldred, of course] and from the extravagant representations at Karnak and el-Amarna, has been the impossibility of his being an endocrinopath [a sufferer from disorder of the endocrine glands, which secrete into the blood hormones that have a particular effect on other organs or parts of the body] and also the father of at least six daughters. This is, however, a contradiction that will have to be faced unflinchingly, and, if it should ever be proved conclusively that he suffered from a chronic endocrine disorder, some other candidate will have to be sought as the father of Nefertiti's children. The full significance of Akhenaten's ostentatious parade of his domestic life will also have to be properly assessed. All such speculation, however, had better be left until a more thorough examination of the bones has been fully reported.'[9]

In order to challenge Derry's conclusions, Aldred 'referred the whole question of the pathology of Akhenaten as represented in these and other sculptures to Dr A. T. Sandison, Senior Lecturer in Pathology in the University of Glasgow and Honorary Consultant Pathologist to the Western Infirmary, Glasgow', and was 'greatly indebted to him for his expert comments'. Sandison was asked:
a) If the monuments, especially the Karnak Colossi, show that Akhenaten was abnormal, and, if so, what was the probable nature of his disease;
b) If the skeletal remains, as examined and described by Elliot Smith and Derry, show that the subject was likely to be abnormal, and, if so, what was the probable nature of the disease; and
c) If the answers to questions (a) and (b) could be 'reconciled'.

Sandison did not disappoint Aldred: 'The evidence of the monuments strongly suggests that Akhenaten suffered from an endocrine abnormality presenting hypogonadism [deficiency of one of the sexual glands] and adiposity, and with residual evidence of an earlier phase of hyperpituitarism [over-function of the pituitary gland in the brain, resulting in gigantism] manifested by cranial and facial changes. The skeletal remains found in Valley Tomb No. 55 have not been described or illustrated as fully as is desirable. Nevertheless, the pelvic abnormality and facial and cranial structure support a diagnosis of hypogonadism and pituitary cranial dysplasia [abnormal development or growth]. Pending fuller publication, the two groups of phenomena those derived from study of the monuments and those derived from study of the remains seem to be reconcilable. This gives considerable support to the view, long held, that the alleged remains of Akhenaten from Valley Tomb No. 55 are indeed those of that Pharaoh. One consequence which must receive consideration, however, is the virtual certainty that Akhenaten was incapable of procreation at the time of death and for many years previously. It is, however not inconceivable that during an earlier period of hyperpituitarism, e.g. shortly after puberty, his potency and fertility might not have been grossly impaired.'

Fairman reacted with an article in the same issue of the *Journal of Egyptian Archaeology*: 'In view of the amount of prejudice and contradictory statements provoked by the skeleton found in the coffin it would be the height of folly for one like myself, who has no medical competence, to argue on anatomical matters. It is useless even for a medical man, in the present circumstances, to argue on the sole evidence of the published descriptions, measurements and photographs of the body, and there is a most pressing need for a new and exhaustive anatomical and pathological examination of the body, using anthropometric and radiographic techniques.'[10]

The latest examination, which started in 1963 under the supervision of R. G. Harrison, the late Derby Professor of Anatomy at the University of Liverpool, confirmed Derry's conclusion that the remains were those of Semenkhkare. He further decided that the skeleton belonged to a man about 5ft 7in in height whose death occurred in his twentieth year.[11] Harrison also confirmed Derry's conclusions regarding the similarity in facial appearance with Tutankhamun.[12]

Not only did the result of Harrison's re-examination disappoint Aldred's expectations by proving that the remains could not have belonged to Akhenaten: Harrison also concluded: 'It is possible to be certain that there is no evidence of hydrocephalus in the skull of these remains ... The presence of a pituitary tumour may also be excluded ... The bodily physique and proportions are also within normal limits and unlike those which occur in established endocrinopathies.'

Regarding Aldred's above-mentioned statement that 'if the profiles of the two heads [that of the skeleton and Tutankhamun's] are superimposed upon each other ... it will be seen how sharply they also differ', Harrison stated: 'When photographs of the vertex of the two skulls are compared, there is a similarity in their shape, both skulls being brachycephalic. Not only are the measurements of the skull vaults similar, but there is also a close correspondence in the width between the angles of the mandibles.'[13]

As for the attempts by Aldred and Sandison to diagnose Akhenaten's anatomical physique from his portraits, Harrison said: 'In a scholarly but purely theoretical treatise, they make extensive conclusions in trying to see in the strange artistic Amarna representation of Akhenaten a representation of a case of Fröhlich's Syndrome (dystropia adiposogenitalis). They make extensive conclusions based only on already published opinions, theories and dates, and an examination of the Akhenaten monuments. These monuments depict a king with an elongated face, prominent and pointed chin, large full lips, coarse nose, wide pelvis, prominent abdomen, buttocks, thighs and breasts. The thighs are large, but the lower legs and arms are slim, and the hands and fingers not excessively large.

'Aldred and Sandison regard these changes in the trunk and limbs as feminisation, occasioned by a disorder of the pituitary gland. They hypothesise a transitory phase of pituitary hyperfunction going on to hypofunction: in the hyperfunctional phase acromegaloid changes were manifested in the skull (found in Tomb No. 55) and soft tissues in the face. They do not imply that Akhenaten was a true acromegalic (sufferer from gigantism), however, since there is no enlargement of the extremities or gigantism. They also consider that the changes in the trunk and limbs of the Akhenaten monuments are consistent with those occurring in dystrophia adiposogenitalis. From the published evidence of the remains (found in Tomb No. 55), they concluded that the findings go some way to sustain a provisional diagnosis of pituitary cranial dysplasia, and that they are reconcilable with the evidence they have deduced from the monuments of Akhenaten.'[14]

While agreeing with Aldred and Sandison that the monuments display an interesting physique, and that certain interpretations may be made from it, Harrison pointed out; 'It is important to ascertain whether his monuments depict a true likeness. Even if this is so, only limited and qualified clinical interpretations are admissable.'[15]

Nor does the archaeological evidence agree with Aldred's assumption regarding Akhenaten's representation. His argument has focused on one of the four Osiride statues of Akhenaten, made during the early years of his reign when he was still at Thebes, to be placed at the entrance of the temple he was building at Karnak for his new God. Although in three of these statues the king is wearing a kind of kilt, the fourth, which has larger lower parts, has no kilt. Aldred has argued that the king is shown here in the nude, without genitalia, indicating a true physical state. However, Julia Samson of University College London, found evidence to contradict Aldred's explanation in 'the actual method used for carving the kilt, which settles the long controversy as to how it could have been added to the king's nude statue from Karnak. The belt is made by cutting back the surface of the abdomen to leave a ridge, and the linen folds of the kilt are then carved over the hips, curving up to the belt buckle. On the one unfinished colossal statue of Akhenaten found in Karnak, the only one that is nude, his kilt would have been added in this way, because the stone is already recessed around the Aten plaques at the waist and would have been further cut back, as on the finished colossi, to make the ridge for the belt.

'There would have been (then) no necessity for further delineation of the king's figure, about which there has been so much conjecture ... This underlines the fallibility of theories about his physical build and condition being based on unfinished statues. Rather than the son of the sun choosing to be represented as unable to father his children, the probability is that the one nude, unfinished statue was never raised to a standing position. It is unlikely that the Amun priests left in Thebes after the royal removal to Akhetaten (Amarna) would have exerted every effort to finish the Aten temple and, if Nefertiti's daughters were the children of someone else and not Akhenaten, it is inexplicable why a son was not introduced into the royal household as an heir.'[16]

APPENDIX F
Some Further Evidence Of Survival

(i) The Shrine

A LARGE wooden shrine of gesso (gypsum) and gilt, like those surrounding the sarcophagus of Tutankhamun, was discovered, dismantled, in Tomb No. 55. The sides, one of which was found in the corridor, had been taken to pieces as if an attempt had been made, then abandoned, to move the shrine out of the tomb. The shrine is decorated with reliefs showing Queen Tiye and her son, Akhenaten, making offerings to the Aten. The engraved copper tangs (handles) give the names and titles of the queen and the inscription states that the shrine was made for Queen Tiye by her son, whose own cartouche and figure have been carefully erased. There is no doubt or disagreement that this shrine belonged to Queen Tiye.

(ii) The Small Objects

A number of small objects, mostly toilet articles and the like, were found among the Tomb No. 55 debris. Some of these objects are inscribed with the name of Queen Tiye or her husband, Amenhotep III, making it likely that most, if not all, of these small objects belonged originally to the queen.

(iii) The Coffin

The coffin in Tomb No. 55 was made of wood, covered completely with gold leaf and inlaid with semi-precious stones. It resembles closely the second of the three coffins of Tutankhamun. However, instead of the head of the coffin wearing the usual royal head-dress, this one has a Nubian wig. Originally the coffin had been laid over a bier, but, as this had rotted away, the coffin collapsed and the mummy jerked partly out of the lid. The coffin is inscribed with a now damaged text that includes titles and cartouches of Akhenaten, which have been erased.

Much of the speculation and disagreement about the identity of the original owner of the coffin has arisen from the excised cartouches and titles of Akhenaten, evidence that the text on the coffin has been adapted to suit the present occupant, Semenkhkare, and a possibility that the royal emblem, the uraeus, was placed later on the coffin's forehead. The differing views on the matter are:

• Georges Daressy, the French Egyptologist, concluded that the coffin had been made originally for a woman whom he believed to be Queen Tiye;

• Weigall thought, because of Akhenaten's cartouches, that the coffin belonged to him;

• Engelbach, about a quarter of a century later, tried to prove that the coffin belonged originally to Semenkhkare, dated from a time before he became coregent and was then changed to indicate his royal status;

• Gardiner argued in 1957 on philological grounds that the original owner of the tomb was Akhenaten himself;

• Aldred and Fairman put forward the view in the 1960s that the coffin had been made originally for Akhenaten's eldest daughter, Merytaten, then adapted for her husband, Semenkhkare.

Inside the coffin, sheets of gold, which had apparently formed the lining, lay over the mummy. A pectoral sheet of gold had been placed on the mummy's head, similar to the one discovered on the body of Tutankhamun. A necklace and a piece of gold, each inscribed with the early name of the Aten, used before Year 9 of Akhenaten's reign, were found among the debris. According to both Weigall and Smith, the mummy was also enclosed in bandages inscribed with Akhenaten's name, but these were later lost in Smith's laboratory.

Although the Aldred-Fairman suggestion regarding the original owner of the coffin seems on balance to be more probable, there is no certain evidence to support any of the above-mentioned conclusions.

(iv) Canopic Jars

Four canopic jars were found near the coffin. They contained black material consisting of a hard, compact, pitch-like mass surrounding a well-defined central zone of different material, brown in colour and of a friable nature. This core was made up of nitrogenous material containing a small proportion of fatty matter, thus being the remains of viscera.

The lids of these jars were carved with heads wearing a wig. As the heads did not have beards it was thought that the jars had been made originally for a woman. It was also thought that the uraeus coils, the royal sign, were cut into the striations of the wigs later, indicating that this woman was not royal. As the texts that had been incised on the body of the jars have been ground away, this confirms that the original owner was different from the one who eventually used them. A. Lucas, a chemist, was able to prove that the inside of the jars indicates that the jars were used only once.[1]

Although some scholars have suggested that the jars belonged originally to Akhenaten, this seems unlikely as his name did not figure on the jars, which had been used only once, plus the fact that, had they been his, only his cartouches would have been erased from the text, as in the case of the shrine and coffin. Furthermore, the fact that the pattern of the wig used for these jars is very similar to that appearing on the coffin found in the same tomb suggests that both the jars and the coffin were made originally for the same woman, in this case Merytaten, Akhenaten's eldest daughter, before she was married to Semenkhkare and became a queen.

(v) Magical Bricks

Four bricks of dried, gritty mud were found *in situ*, distributed around the tomb. Although they have suffered, like everything else in the tomb, from the effects of damp, Akhenaten's name could be read on at least two of the bricks, whose function was to protect the dead person from intruders. The four bricks form a complete set, each having to be placed in a certain position in relation to the mummy in order to fulfil its protective function.

That these magical bricks belonged originally to Akhenaten is not the subject of dispute, and the fact that they were found *in situ* in Tomb No. 55 was one of the strong points that led Aldred and others to believe that the remains in the coffin were his. However, the skeletal remains have since been shown to be those of Semenkhkare. Why, then, was no attempt made either to erase Akhenaten's name or adapt the text to suit Semenkhkare? It is now agreed that Akhenaten's reign ended a few months, if not a few days, before the death of Semenkhkare. In this case, had Akhenaten's reign ended with his death, his funerary arrangements, which would have taken seventy days, might not even have ended when the arrangements for Semenkhkare's burial began. How then does one explain that Akhenaten's original magical bricks, which formed an essential part of the funerary rituals, were found *in situ* in Semenkhkare's tomb? The only possible conclusion is that they were not needed by Akhenaten who, although he had fallen from power before Semenkhkare's death, was himself still alive.

Fairman was opposed to using the evidence of Akhenaten's magical bricks to prove that the remains found in Tomb No. 55 were those of the king. He therefore tried to weaken this conclusion by suggesting that, although they had been made originally for Akhenaten early in his reign, the king could have changed his mind later and rejected this traditional practice as a result of the development of his religious ideas: 'For the testimony of the magical bricks to be incontrovertible two things are necessary: it must first be proved that the use of such magical bricks was still retained in the funerary practices of the end of the Amarna Period; and it must also be proved that the texts themselves are such as could reasonably be expected to have been employed when the Aten cult was fully developed.'[2]

Fairman is not justified in these objections. First of all, Semenkhkare's burial *was* an 'end of the Amarna period' burial, the only one we have. If Akhenaten had died when he fell from power in his Year 17, it would have been Tutankhaten's responsibility to bury him, just as it was his responsibility to bury Semenkhkare. This is confirmed by the remains of the young king's seal found in Tomb No. 55. At the time, and up to his Year 4, he was still called Tutankhaten and his capital and residence were at Amarna. There is no evidence that the old Egyptian gods, especially those usually associated with the underworld, were represented in Tomb No. 55. At this early stage of his rule Tutankhamun would have followed the same burial procedure with Akhenaten as he did with Semenkhkare.

Then again, if Akhenaten, having originally ordered the magical bricks to be made, later changed his mind, he would not have left the bricks forgotten in the stores. He would either have ordered any changes he thought necessary to be made or even have ordered their destruction if his developed religious beliefs caused him to reject their use. This was the course he followed in changing his own name from Amenhotep IV to Akhenaten and erasing the name of Amun in his father's name. He would not have left his name on objects that offended his monotheistic belief, for it was the Egyptian creed that, as long as an inscription existed in the wrong form, the wrong beliefs lived.

(vi) Tutankhamun's Tomb

Some funerary objects – small items, such as statuettes and bracelets – made originally for Akhenaten, but evidently never used for any burial of his, were found in the tomb of Tutankhamun, who was not buried until nine years after the end of Akhenaten's rule. A list of these objects was given by Martin.[3] The numbers cited referred to objects as they appear in *A Handlist to Howard Carter's Catalogue of*

Objects in Tutankhamun's Tomb, compiled by Helen Murray and Mary Nuttall of the Griffith Institute, Oxford, and published in 1963: 'Those connected with Akhenaten appear to be nos. 54ee, 54ff, 54vv, 256 4t, 261a, 281a, 291a, 300a, 596a, 620(40) and an un-numbered sealing. Cf. also objects of Akhenaten, Semenkhkare or Merytaten nos. 1k, 46gg, 48h, 79 + 147, 101s, 256a, 256b(4), 261(1), 262, 405, 448, 620(13), 620(41), 620(42) and un-numbered gold sequins.'

Thus not only does the evidence from the royal tomb at Amarna prove that Akhenaten was never buried there: at Thebes, where it was thought that he was either buried originally in Tomb No. 55 or that his mummy was moved there from Amarna, it is now accepted that the skeleton in Tomb No. 55 is that of Semenkhkare, not Akhenaten. Then, as some original, essential parts of the funerary equipment of Akhenaten were found *in situ* in Tomb No. 55 they could not have been used for Akhenaten, reinforcing the belief that he was still alive at the time of Semenkhkare's burial.

APPENDIX G
The Hebrews

T H E word for Hebrew in the Hebrew language of the Bible is *'Ibri*. Scholars have differed about its specific meaning, but the most common view is that the word is related to the Hebrew preposition *'ibr* meaning 'across' and that it was modified to describe Abraham, the founder of the tribe of Israel, and his descendants because of their migration from Ur in Mesopotamia across the river Euphrates to the land of Palestine-Jordan.

The expression 'Hebrew' is used in the Pentateuch (the first five books of the Old Testament) as a name for the Israelites to differentiate between them and Egyptians and Philistines. Therefore, as the word *Khabiru*, which occurs frequently in Amarna letters, has been shown by many scholars to be similar to the word for 'Hebrew' (*'Ibri*), there has been an attempt to identify the people referred to in these letters with the Israelites. A number of factors have served to confuse the issue, however:

• Many Amarna letters sent from the Palestinian city States to Amenhotep III, Akhenaten and Tutankhamun indicate that they had encountered a great deal of trouble in their territories as a result of people sometimes called *Khabiru* and sometimes referred to as *Sa-Gaz*. (There is considerable evidence to support the belief that both peoples were associated);

• It is clear from the letters that these people were composed of small groups, acting simultaneously in different parts of Palestine, north as well as south, and not a united group under one leadership;

• At the time these letters were sent to Amenhotep III, Akhenaten and Tutankhamun, in the fifteenth and fourteenth centuries BC, the

Israelites were still in Egypt, according to most scholars, whether we believe in an Exodus during the reign of Ramses I or Ramses II;

• There are references to 'Peru (the way Egyptian texts represent the word 'Hebrew') being in Egypt from the time of Amenhotep III during the second half of the fifteenth century BC, right through the Amarna period and as late as the time of Ramses IV, a little before the middle of the twelfth century BC, long after the Exodus, whichever date we accept for it;

• From Egyptian sources we find the word 'Peru used to indicate labourers working for the State at heavy manual labour in connection with building operations of the kings, especially the quarrying and transportation of stone;

• The Babylonian texts, known as the Nuzu Texts, use the word Khabiru to indicate a class of slaves and, as with the Egyptian word 'Peru, the word appears to indicate a social class of hard labourers rather than an ethnic group;

• The Bible does not refer to the Israelites as 'Hebrews' after the Exodus and during the entry into Canaan with Joshua.

The conclusion is obvious. The word 'Hebrew' was used to designate a particular social class – either disorganized groups of wandering slaves or labourers in the Palestine city States, who were quite distinct from the Hebrews in Egypt, or the Israelites in Egypt, who were known as Hebrews while they were engaged in harsh labour. However, this term was no longer applied to them once they had been freed by Moses and were looked upon as a nation. Thus, as the term 'Hebrew' denoted a social class rather than a people, not all Hebrews can be regarded as Israelites although the Israelites were classed as Hebrews while they laboured at building the treasure cities of Pithom and Raamses.

The implication of the King of Jerusalem's letter (see Chapter 19) is that the two Egyptian officials murdered by the Hebrews at Zarw may have been among the supervisors of their work, and it is possible that these very incidents – or something similar – could have been responsible for bringing to a head the anti-Akhenaten movement in the army that eventually caused his downfall and flight to Sinai.

NOTES

BIBLICAL quotations are from either the Authorized Version or the New English Bible. Further details of works cited below will be found in the Bibliography, pp. 253–5.

INTRODUCTION

1   Breasted, *A History of Egypt*, p. 355.
2   Breasted, *The Dawn of Conscience*, p. 296.
3   Weigall, *The Life and Times of Akhenaten*, p. 2.
4   Baikie, *The Amarna Age*, p. 234.
5   Gardiner, *Egypt of the Pharaohs*, p. 214.
6   Pendlebury, *Tell el-Amarna*, p. 15.
7   Aldred, *Akhenaten*, pp. 101–4.
8   Redford, *Akhenaten, the Heretic King*, pp. 232–5.

1   BRICKS WITHOUT STRAW

1   Osman, *Stranger in the Valley of the Kings*.

2   WAS MOSES A KING?

1   Polano, *Selections from the Talmud*, p. 132.
2   *Ibid.*, p. 126
3   Waddell, *Manetho*.
4   Josephus, *Against Apion*.
5   *Against Apion III*, p. 295.
6   *Against Apion I*, p. 281.
7   *Ibid.*, p. 287.
8   Osman, *Stranger in the Valley of the Kings*.
9   Redford, *Pharaonic King-Lists*, p. 293.

3   THE ISRAEL STELA

1   Aldred, *Akhenaten and Nefertiti*, p. 8. Gardiner, who unlike Aldred does not believe in a coregency during the Amarna period, here gives a figure of 267 years.
2   *Ibid.* Aldred also disagrees with Gardiner about the length of the reign of Seti I.
3   Pritchard, *Ancient Near Eastern Texts*, pp. 377–8.

4   REBELLION IN SINAI

1   Murnane, *The Road to Kadesh*, p. 144.
2   Schmidt, *Ramses II*, p. 180.
3   Kitchen, 'Asiatic Wars of Ramses II', p. 66.
4   *Ibid.*
5   *Ibid.*, p. 68.
6   *Ibid.*, p. 70.
7   Posener, *A Dictionary of Egyptian Civilisation*, p. 83.
8   *Ibid.*, pp. 82, 83.
9   This has been interpreted as meaning that the king's body was recovered and buried.
10   Ali, *The Meaning of the Glorious Qu'ran*.

5 SOJOURN – AND THE MOTHER OF MOSES

1 Cassuto, *A Commentary on the Book of Exodus*, p. 86.
2 *The Illustrated Bible Dictionary*, Part 2, p. 1016.
3 Pritchard, *Ancient Near Eastern Texts*, p. 320.
4 Brown, *Hebrew and English Lexicon*, p. 108.
5 Cassuto, *Commentary*, p. 54.

6 THE RIGHTFUL SON AND HEIR

1 *Exodus Rabbah I*, p. 24.
2 Ranke, *Die ägyptischen Personennamen*, p. 164.

7 THE COREGENCY DEBATE (I)

1 Redford, *History and Chronology*, pp. 86–169.
2 Redford, *Akhenaten, the Heretic King*, p. 79.
3 Carter, *The Tomb of Tutankhamen*, p. 5.
4 Redford, *History and Chronology*, p. 109.
5 Davies, *The Rock Tombs of el-Amarna*, Part III, p. 21.
6 *Ibid.*, p. 23.
7 Redford, *History and Chronology*, p. 107.
8 *Ibid.*
9 *Ibid.*, p. 108.
10 Carter, *The Tomb of Tutankhamen*, p. 14.
11 *Ibid.*, p. 6.
12 Redford, *History and Chronology*, pp. 111–12.

8 THE COREGENCY DEBATE (II)

1 Redford, *History and Chronology*, p. 115.
2 Carter, *The Tomb of Tutankhamen*, vol. III, p. 3.
3 Redford, *History and Chronology*, p. 119.
4 *Ibid.*, p. 144.
5 *Ibid.*, p. 145.
6 *Ibid.*, p. 168.

7 *Ibid.*, p. 69.
8 *Ibid.*, pp. 71–2.
9 *Ibid.*, p. 51.
10 *Ibid.*, p. 79.
11 Hayes, 'Inscriptions from the Palace of Amenhotep III', pp. 36–7.

9 THE REIGN OF HOREMHEB

1 Harris, 'How Long Was the Reign of Horemheb', p. 95.
2 Martin, 'Excavations at the Memphite Tomb of Horemheb', p. 15.
3 Redford, 'Chronology of the Egyptian Eighteenth Dynasty', p. 123.
4 Peet, *The City of Akhenaten*, Vol. III, pp. 157–8.
5 Harris, 'How Long Was the Reign of Horemheb', p. 96.
6 Gardiner, 'A Later Allusion to Akhenaten', p. 124.
7 Gaballa, *The Memphite Tomb Chapel of Mose*, p. 25.
8 *Ibid.*, p. 23.
9 *Ibid.*, pp. 23, 24.
10 *Ibid.*, p. 23.
11 *Ibid.*, pp. 24–5.
12 Björkman, 'Neby, the Mayor of Tjaru', pp. 43–51.
13 Bietak, 'Avaris and Piramses', p. 270.

10 A CHRONOLOGY OF KINGS

1 Maspero, *The Struggle of the Nations*, p. 387.
2 Breasted, *Ancient Records of Egypt*, pp. 59–60.
3 *Ibid.*, p. 60.
4 Maspero, *The Struggle of the Nations*, p. 386.
5 *Ibid.*, p. 380.
6 *Ibid.*, p. 379.
7 Reisner, 'The Viceroys of Ethiopia', p. 28.

11 THE BIRTHPLACE OF AKHENATEN

1 Breasted, *Ancient Records of Egypt*, vol. 3, p. 349; also Yoyotte, *Le Bassin de Djârouka, Kêmi*, vol. 15, p. 23.

2   Osman, *Stranger in the Valley of the Kings*, p. 107.
3   Hayes, 'Inscriptions', p. 101.
4   *Papyrus Anastasi* III.
5   *Ibid.*, IV.
6   Gardiner, 'The Delta Residence of the Ramessides', p. 136.
7   Waddell, *Manetho*, p. 83.
8   Gunn & Gardiner, 'New Renderings of Egyptian Texts', p. 49.
9   Gardiner, 'Delta Residence', p. 185.
10   Naville, 'The Geography of the Exodus', p. 22.
11   Clédat, 'Le Site d'Avaris', pp. 185–201.
12   Although the cross inside the circle is not found in all cases, this may be the result of weathering or error by the scribe.
13   Clédat, 'Notes sur l'Isthme de Suez', p. 58.

12   AKHENATEN: THE EARLY YEARS
1   Harris & Weeks, *X-Raying the Pharaohs*, p. 144.
2   Hayes, 'Inscriptions', p. 159.
3   Björkman, 'Neby, the Mayor of Tjaru', p. 51.
4   Černý, *Hieratic Inscriptions from the Tomb of Tutankhamun*, p. 2.

13   HORIZON OF THE ATEN
1   Davies, *The Rock Tombs of el-Amarna*, Part V, p. 30.
2   *Ibid.*, p. 29.
3   Schulman, 'Military Background of the Amarna Period', p. 52.
4   *Ibid.*, p. 66.
5   This will be the subject of a separate work, but the similarity of the names of the Aten priests and those of the followers of Moses is dealt with briefly in Chapter Nineteen.
6   Schulman, 'Military Background', p. 67.
7   Pritchard, *Ancient Near Eastern Texts*, p. 251.

14   THE TOMB OF AKHENATEN
1   Martin, *The Royal Tomb at el-Amarna*, Part 1.
2   *Ibid.*, p. 104.
3   *Ibid.*, p. 30.
4   *Ibid.*, p. 105.
5   *Ibid.*, p. 106.
6   Pendlebury, 'Clearance of the Royal Tomb at el-Amarna', pp. 123–4.
7   Hamza, 'The Alabaster Canopic Box of Akhenaten', p. 537.
8   Martin, *The Royal Tomb*, p. 105.
9   *Ibid.*, p. 106.
10   *Ibid.*, pp. 31–2.
11   Gardiner, 'The So-Called Tomb of Queen Tiye', p. 19.
12   Martin, *The Royal Tomb*, pp. 105–6.
13   *Ibid.*, pp. 30–1.
14   Edwards, *Tutankhamun*, p. 153.

15   THE FALLEN ONE OF AMARNA
1   Gunn, *The City of Akhenaten*, Part III, vol. 1, p. 159.
2   *Ibid.*, p. 152.
3   *Ibid.*, I, pl. lxiii.
4   Seele, 'King Aye and the Close of the Amarna Age', p. 175.
5   *Ibid.*
6   Fairman, 'The Supposed Year 21 of Akhenaten', p. 108.
7   *Ibid.*
8   Gunn, *The City of Akhenaten*, Part I, p. 165.
9   Fairman, 'Supposed Year 21', p. 108.
10   Fairman, 'The Chronology of the Eighteenth Dynasty', p. 121.
11   Frankfort & Pendlebury, *The City of Akhenaten*, Part II, p. 103.
12   Derry, 'Skeleton Hitherto Believed to be that of King Akhenaten', p. 115.
13   Gardiner, 'Graffito from the Tomb of Pere', p. 10.
14   Redford, 'Chronology of the Eighteenth Dynasty', p. 177.
15   Gardiner, 'A Later Allusion to Akhenaten', p. 124.
16   Gaballa, *The Memphite Tomb of Mose*, pl. lxiii.

17   Samson, *Amarna, City of Akhenaten*
      and Nefertiti, p. 1.

16   CORRIDORS OF POWER
1   Helck, *Untersuchungen zu Manetho und*
      den ägyptischen Königslisten, p. 41.

17   THE FIRST MONOTHEIST
1   Kitchen, *Ramesside Inscriptions*, Part I,
      p. 1.
2   Petrie, *Researches in Sinai*, p. 127.
3   *Ibid.*
4   *Ibid.*, p. 126.
5   Černý, *The Inscriptions of Sinai*, Part
      II, p. 45.
6   *Ibid.*, p. 47.
7   Petrie, *Researches in Sinai*, p. 68.

18   THE 'MAGIC' ROD OF
      MOSES
1   Fakhry, 'The Tomb of Kheruef at
      Thebes', p. 485.

19   WHO WAS WHO? – AND
      THE DEATH OF MOSES
1   Seele, 'King Aye', p. 70.
2   Baikie, *The Amarna Age*, p. 241.
3   Seele, 'King Aye', pp. 168–80.
4   Smith, *The Akhenaten Temple Project*,
      p. 22.
5   *Ibid.*, p. 27.
6   Seele, 'King Aye', pp. 168–80.
7   *Ibid.*, p. 170.
8   According to the Elohistic source of
      the Pentateuch, Moses and Aaron
      were of the tribe of Joseph.
      However, this source uses 'Levite'
      to indicate not a member of a clan,
      but a man specially eligible for the
      priesthood (*The Jewish*
      Encyclopaedia, New York and
      London, 1904, p. 20).
9   Albright, 'The Town of Sell',
      pp. 6–8.
10   Rowley, *From Joseph to Joshua*.
11   Davies, *The Rock Tombs of el-Amarna*,
      vol. I.
12   *Ibid.*

APPENDIX A
(i)   *The Shasu Wars*
1   Breasted, *Ancient Records of Egypt*,
      vol. III, p. 45.
2   *Ibid.*, p. 46.
3   Gardiner, *Egypt of the Pharaohs*,
      p. 253.
4   Breasted, *Ancient Records*, vol. III,
      p. 47.
5   Kharu can mean either the people of
      Palestine/Syria or the land of the
      Horites, south of the Dead Sea:
      here it indicates the territory of
      Canaan.
6   Pritchard, *Ancient Near Eastern Texts*,
      p. 254.
7   *Ibid.*

(ii) *The Hattusili Peace Treaty*
1   Langdon & Gardiner, 'Treaty ...
      Between ... Hattusili ... and ...
      Ramses II', pp. 185–7.

(iii) *A Dissenting Voice*
1   Kitchen, 'Asiatic Wars of Ramses II',
      p. 66.
2   *Ibid.*, p. 69.
3   *Ibid.*, p. 70.
4   *Ibid.*

APPENDIX B
(i)   *The Amarna Rock Tombs of Huya and*
      Meryre II
1   Davies, *The Rock Tombs of el-Amarna*,
      Part III, p. 16.
2   Redford, *History and Chronology*,
      p. 109.
3   Davies, *Rock Tombs*, Part III, p. 9.
4   *Ibid.*, Part II, p. 42.
5   *Ibid.*, p. 38.

(ii) *The Tomb of Kheruef*
1   Fakhry, 'Tomb of Kheruef at
      Thebes', p. 457.
2   Habachi, 'Clearance of the Tomb of
      Kheruef', p. 348.
3   Redford, *History and Chronology*,
      p. 117.

(iii) *The Year of Tribute*
1   Aldred, 'Year Twelve at el-Amarna', p. 114.

(iv) *The Tomb of Ramose*
1   Aldred, 'Two Theban Notables', p. 117.
2   Davies, *The Tomb of the Vizier Ramose*, pp. 30–1.
3   *Ibid.*, p. 33.
4   *Ibid.*, p. 37.

(v) *The Tushratta Letters*
1   Redford, *History and Chronology*, pp. 71–2.
2   Winckler, *Tell el-Amarna Letters*, p. 67.
3   Redford, *History and Chronology*, p. 69.
4   *Ibid.*, p. 52.
5   *Ibid.*, p. 79.

APPENDIX C *The Mos Case*
1   Gaballa, *The Memphite Tomb Chapel of Mose*, p. 25.
2   'Father' is used here in the sense of 'forefather'.
3   Gaballa, p. 23.

APPENDIX D *Pi-Ramses and Zarw*

(i) *The City of Pi-Ramses*
1   Gardiner, 'Delta Residence', p. 178.
2   *Ibid.*, p. 180.
3   Habachi, 'Preliminary Report', p. 201.
4   Gardiner, 'Delta Residence', p. 132.
5   Bietak, 'Avaris and Piramses', p. 255.
6   van Seters, *The Hyksos*, p. 101.
7   Pritchard, *Ancient Near Eastern Texts*, p. 253.

(ii) *The Fortified City of Zarw*
1   Nims, *Thebes of the Pharaohs*, p. 199.
2   Björkman, 'Neby, the Mayor of Zarw', p. 50.

(iii) *The Case Against Qantir/Tell el-Dab'a*
1   Bietak, 'Avaris and Piramses, pp. 225–90.

2   *Ibid.*, p. 271.
3   *Ibid.*, p. 273.
4   *Ibid.*, p. 289.
5   Hamza, 'Ramses's Palace at Qantir', p. 59.

(v) *A Middle-Egypt Site for Tiye's City*
1   Yoyotte, *La Bassin de Djârouka, Kêmi*, pp. 23–33.
2   Naville, 'The Geography of the Exodus', p. 22.
3   *Ibid.*, p. 24.
4   *Ibid.*, p. 23.

APPENDIX E *The Body in Tomb No. 55*
1   Weigall, 'The Mummy of Akhenaten', p. 197.
2   Smith, *The Royal Mummies*, p. 52.
3   *Ibid.*
4   *Ibid.*
5   *Cambridge University Medical Society Magazine*, Issue No. 4, 1926, pp. 34–9.
6   Derry, 'Skeleton hitherto Believed to be that of King Akhenaten', pp. 115–19.
7   *Ibid.*
8   *Ibid.*
9   Aldred, 'The Tomb of Akhenaten at Thebes', p. 51.
10   Fairman, 'Once Again the so-called Coffin of Akhenaten', p. 39.
11   Harrison, 'Anatomical Examination of the Remains Purported to be Akhenaten', p. 111.
12   *Ibid.*, p. 114.
13   *Ibid.*
14   *Ibid.*, p. 97.
15   *Ibid.*
16   Samson, *Armana, City of Akhenaten and Nefertiti*, pp. 23–4.

APPENDIX F *Some Further Evidence of Survival*
1   Lucas, 'The Canopic Vases from the Tomb of Queen Tiye', pp. 120–2.
2   Fairman, 'Once Again . . .', p. 37.
3   Martin, *The Royal Tomb at el-Amarna*, p. 1.

BIBLIOGRAPHY

Albright, W. F., 'The Town of Sell
(Zarw) in the Amarna Tablets', *Journal
of Egyptian Archaeology*, vol. 10, 1924
Aldred, Cyril, *Akhenaten*, Abacus, London,
1968
Akhenaten and Nefertiti, Thames &
Hudson, London, 1973
'The Tomb of Akhenaten at Thebes',
Journal of Egyptian Archaeology, vol. 47,
1961
'Two Theban Notables during the Later
Reign of Amenophis III', *Journal of
Near Eastern Studies*, vol. 18, 1959
'Year Twelve at el-Amarna', *Journal of
Egyptian Archaeology*, vol. 43, 1957
Ali, Abdullah Yusuf, *The Meaning of the
Glorious Qu'ran*, Nadim, London, 1975
Baikie, James, *The Amarna Age*, A. & C.
Black, London, 1926
Bietak, Manfred, 'Avaris and Piramses
Archaeological Exploration in the
Eastern Delta', *Proceedings of the British
Academy*, vol. 65, 1979
Björkman, Gun, 'Neby, the Mayor of
Tjaru (Zarw) in the Reign of
Tuthmose IV', *Journal of the American
Research Center in Egypt*, vol. 10, 1974
Breasted, James Henry, *Ancient Records of
Egypt*, Chicago, 1906
The Dawn of Conscience, Charles
Scribner's Sons, New York, 1933
A History of Egypt, Charles Scribner's
Sons, New York, 1905, 1909; Hodder
& Stoughton, London, 1924
Brown, Francis, *Hebrew and English Lexicon
of the Old Testament*, based on the

lexicon of William Gesenius (tr.
Edward Robinson), Clarendon Press,
Oxford, 1906
Carter, Howard, *The Tomb of
Tutankhamen*, Cassell, London, 1933
Cassuto, U., *A Commentary on the Book of
Exodus* (tr. Israel Abrahams), Hebrew
University, Jerusalem, 1961
Černý, Jaroslav, *Hieratic Inscriptions from
the Tomb of Tutankhamun*, Griffith
Institute, Oxford, 1965
(ed.) *The Inscriptions of Sinai*, Egypt
Exploration Society, London, 1955
Clédat, Jean, 'Notes sur l'isthme de Suez',
*Bulletin de l'Institut Français
d'Archéologie Orientale*, vol. 23, 1924
'Le Site d'Avaris', *Recueil d'études
égyptologiques dédiées à la mémoire de
Jean-François Champollion*, Champion,
Paris, 1922
David, N. de G., *The Rock Tombs of
el-Amarna*, Egypt Exploration Society,
London, Part I 1903, Part III 1905,
Part V 1908
The Tomb of the Vizier Ramose, Egypt
Exploration Society, London, 1941
Derry, D. E., 'Note on the Skeleton
hitherto Believed to be that of King
Akhenaten', *Annales du Service des
Antiquités de l'Égypte*, vol. 31, 1931
Edwards, L. E. S., *Tutankhamun*, Victor
Gollancz, London, 1979
Fairman, H. W., 'The Chronology of the
Eighteenth Dynasty', *Journal of Near
Eastern Studies*, vol. 25, 1966
'Once Again the so-called Coffin of

Akhenaten', *Journal of Egyptian Archaeology*, vol. 47, 1961

'The Supposed Year 21 of Akhenaten', *Journal of Egyptian Archaeology*, vol. 46, 1960

Fakhry, Ahmed, 'A Note on the Tomb of Kheruef at Thebes', *Annales du Service des Antiquités d'Égypte*, vol. 42, 1943

Frankfort, H., and John Pendlebury, *The City of Akhenaten*, London, 1933

Freud, Sigmund, *Moses and Monotheism*, London, 1939

Gaballa, G. A., *The Memphite Tomb Chapel of Mose*, Aris & Phillips, Warminster, 1977

Gardiner, Alan H., 'The Delta Residence of the Ramessides', *Journal of Egyptian Archaeology*, vol. 5, 1918

Egypt of the Pharaohs, Clarendon Press, Oxford, 1961

'The Graffito from the Tomb of Pere', *Journal of Egyptian Archaeology*, vol. 14, 1928

'A Later Allusion to Akhenaten', *Journal of Egyptian Archaeology*, vol. 24, 1938

'The So-Called Tomb of Queen Tiye', *Journal of Egyptian Archaeology*, vol. 43, 1957

Gunn, Battiscombe, *The City of Akhenaten*, Egypt Exploration Society, London, 1923

Gunn, Battiscombe, and Gardiner, Alan H., 'New Renderings of Egyptian Texts', *Journal of Egyptian Archaeology*, vol. 5, 1918

Habachi, Labib, 'Clearance of the Tomb of Kheruef at Thebes', *Annales du Service des Antiquités de l'Égypte*, vol. 55, 1956

'Preliminary Report on the Kamose Stele', *Annales du Service des Antiquités de l'Égypte*, vol. 53, 1956

Hamza, Muhammad, 'The Alabaster Canopic Box of Akhenaten', *Annales du Service des Antiquités de l'Égypte*, vol. 40, 1940

'Ramses's Palace at Qantir', *Annales du Service des Antiquités de l'Égypte*, vol. 30, 1930

Harris, James E., and Weeks, R., *X-Raying the Pharaohs*, Charles Scribner's Sons, New York, 1973

Harris, J. R., 'How Long Was the Reign of Horemheb', *Journal of Egyptian Archaeology*, vol. 54, p. 95

Harrison, R. G., 'An Anatomical Examination of the Pharaonic Remains Purported to be Akhenaten', *Journal of Egyptian Archaeology*, vol. 52, 1966

Hayes, William C., 'Inscriptions from the Palace of Amenhotep III, *Journal of Near Eastern Studies*, vol. 10, 1951

Helck, Wolfgang, *Untersuchungen zu Manetho und den ägyptischen Königslisten*, Berlin, 1956

The Illustrated Bible Dictionary, Inter-Varsity Press, Sydney and Auckland, 1980

Josephus, Flavius, *Against Apion* (tr. H. St J. Thackeray), Heinemann, London, 1926

Kitchen, K. A., 'Asiatic Wars of Ramses II', *Journal of Egyptian Archaeology*, vol. 50, 1964

Ramesside Inscriptions, B. H. Blackwell, Oxford, 1975

Langdon, S. (with Alan H. Gardiner), 'The Treaty of Alliance Between Hattusili, King of the Hittites, and the Pharaoh Ramses II of Egypt', *Journal of Egyptian Archaeology*, vol. 6, 1920

Lucas, A., 'The Canopic Vases from the Tomb of Queen Tiye', *Annales du Service des Antiquités de l'Égypt*, vol. 31, 1931

Martin, Geoffrey T., 'Excavations at the Memphite Tomb of Horemheb', *Journal of Egyptian Archaeology*, vol. 65, 1979

The Royal Tomb at el-Amarna, Egypt Exploration Society, London, 1974

Maspero, Gaston, *The Struggle of the Nations*, SPCK, London, 1896

Murnane, William J., *The Road to Kadesh*, The Oriental Institute of the University of Chicago, Chicago, 1985

Naville, Henri, 'The Geography of the Exodus', *Journal of Egyptian Archaeology*, vol. 10, 1924

Nims, Charles F., *Thebes of the Pharaohs*, Elek, London, 1965

Osman, Ahmed, *Stranger in the Valley of the Kings*, Souvenir Press, London, 1987

Peet, T. E., *The City of Akhenaten*, Egypt Exploration Society, London, vol. III, 1951

Pendlebury, John, 'Report on the Clearance of the Royal Tomb at el-Amarna', *Annales du Service des Antiquités de l'Égypte*, vol. 3, 1931
Tell el-Amarna, Lovat, Dickson & Thompson, London, 1935

Petrie, W. M. Flinders, *Researches in Sinai*, John Murray, London, 1906

Polano, H., *Selections from the Talmud*, Frederick Warne, London, 1894

Posener, George (with Serge Sauneron and Jean Yoyotte), *A Dictionary of Egyptian Civilisation*, Methuen, London, 1962

Pritchard, James B. (ed.), *Ancient Near Eastern Texts* (tr. John A. Wilson), Princeton University Press, Princeton, NJ, 3rd edn, 1969

Ranke, Hermann, *Die ägyptischen Personennamen*, Münster, 1902

Redford, Donald B., *Akhenaten, the Heretic King*, Princeton University Press, Princeton, NJ, 1984
History and Chronology of the Eighteenth Dynasty of Egypt, University of Toronto Press, Toronto, 1977
'On the Chronology of the Egyptian Eighteenth Dynasty', *Journal of Near Eastern Studies*, vol. 25, 1966
Pharaonic King-Lists, Annals and Day-Books, Benben Publications, Mississanga, Ontario, 1986

Reisner, George A., 'The Viceroys of Ethiopia', *Journal of Egyptian Archaeology*, vol. 6, 1920

Rowley, H. H., *From Joseph to Joshua*, British Academy, London, 1950

Samson, Julia, *Amarna, City of Akhenaten and Nefertiti*, Aris & Phillips, Warminster, 1978

Scharf, Alexander, *Archiv für Orientforschung*, Vienna, 1935

Schmidt, John D., *Ramses II*, Johns Hopkins University Press, Baltimore and London, 1973

Schulman, Alan R., 'Military Background of the Amarna Period', *Journal of the American Research Center in Egypt*, vol. 3, 1964

Seele, Keith C., 'King Aye and the Close of the Amarna Age', *Journal of Near Eastern Studies*, vol. 14, 1955

Smith, E. G., *The Royal Mummies*, Cairo, 1912

Smith, Ray W., *The Akhenaten Temple Project*, University Museum, University of Pennsylvania, 1976

van Seters, John, *The Hyksos*, Yale University Press, New Haven and London, 1966

Waddell, W. G., *Manetho*, Harvard University Press, 1940

Weigall, Arthur, *The Life and Times of Akhenaten*, Thornton Butterworth, London, 1910, 1923
'The Mummy of Akhenaten', *Journal of Egyptian Archaeology*, vol. 43, 1957/8

Winckler, Hugh, *Tell el-Amarna Letters*, Reuther & Reichard, Berlin; Luzac, London, 1896

Yoyotte, Jean, *Le Bassin de Djârouka, Kêmi*, vol. 15, Geuthner, Paris, 1959

INDEX